Jennifer Stone

STONE'S THROW

SELECTED ESSAYS BY
Jennifer Stone

North Atlantic Books, Berkeley, California

Stone's Throw: Selected Essays

ISBN 1-55643-031-0 paperback
ISBN 1-55643-032-9 cloth

Published by North Atlantic Books
            2800 Woolsey Street
            Berkeley, California 94705

Cover and book design by Paula Morrison
Typeset by Campaigne and Somit Typography

This project is partially supported by a grant from the National Endowment
for the Arts in Washington, D.C., a Federal Agency.

Stone's Throw: Selected Essays is sponsored by the Society for the Study of Native
Arts and Sciences, a nonprofit educational corporation whose goals are to develop
an ecological and crosscultural perspective linking various scientific, social, and
artistic fields; to nurture a holistic view of arts, sciences, humanities, and healing;
and to publish and distribute literature on the relationship of mind, body, and
nature.

Library of Congress Cataloging-in-Publication Data

Stone, Jennifer, 1933–
      Stone's throw: selected essays/Jennifer Stone.
      p. cm.
      Includes index.
      ISBN 1-556-43032-9: $25.00. ISBN 1-556-43031-0 (pbk.): $12.95
      I. Title.
PS3569, T64128S76 1988   88-23608
      813'.54—dc19   CIP

dedicated to the men who love

CONTENTS

Finding the Father 1
   Robert Bly and the Warrior/Wimp Syndrome

That Patriarch Patrick 9
   or, Sally Sleepwell Sings the Blues

In Search of Manhood 13

Life in a Phallocracy 19
   *The Reign of the Phallus: Sexual Politics
   in Ancient Athens* by Eva C. Keuls

Steel Magnolia Tells All 25
   First Lady From Plains by Rosalynn Carter

Bitch Is Beautiful 29
   Five on Feminism:
   Black Man, Watch Your Step! 31
   Feminists Have No Sense of Humor? 36
   These Are the Hollow Men 39
   Things Were More Fun in the Old Days 42
   Sins of the Fathers 45

Emerging Women 49
   Alta: Shameless Hussy 51
   A Conversation with Jean Shelton 59

Gertrude Stein in Circles 65
   Genius is What Happens When You Are
      Looking for a Way Out 67
   Each One As She May 74
   Your Little Dog Knows 76

Shakespeare's Sister 83
    Virginia Woolf, Incest Survivor

Oppenheimer: Faust or Fraud? 93

Eros: The Imperative of Intimacy 97
    Alicia Suskin Ostriker's *Stealing the Language,*
    The Emergence of Women's Poetry in America

Notes on the Brontes 111

The Revisionist Imperative 135
    or, Don't Rock the Boat—Sink It!

Homage to James Baldwin 175

Index 183

All I have is a voice
To undo the folded lie,
The romantic lie in the brain...
                    W. H. Auden
                    from *September 1, 1939*

INTRODUCTION

The late James Baldwin once said that if we really believed what we said we believed, we would not be doing what we are doing. When I had nearly completed this collection of essays, I gave them to a friend to read. He sighed, shook his head, and asked why did I want to spit in the wind. He told me that humankind needs the political lie. No use to wave a feminist fist in the air, he said, smiling. When you do that dear, he said, it just makes men stronger — it affirms their power and reinforces their prejudices.

I thought he might be right so I changed the subject. He liked best my essays on literature although he didn't see the Brontes as feminists. We talked about James Baldwin's recent death. I said Jimmy's rage had shown me the way and before I'd be a slave I'd be buried in my grave.... He reminded me that Baldwin had often asked himself what would happen when the day came there was no white man to blame. What will happen to you my dear, he asked, when there is no longer a male threat. We sat in silence for awhile. Then he laughed and hugged me and said that well, maybe mine *was* the last revolution.

About the style of these familiar essays. Writers don't know much and most of the time they don't even write that. I have tried to collect my thoughts and wring out my mind. Patriarchal phrases often strangle my meaning. We cannot mean what we say unless we can say what we mean. As a woman I am anxious to be heard as a serious scholar, yet I want always to be open to what Toni Morrison has called "eruptions of funk." I have tried to be honest rather than sincere. The sincerity of our age is making us sick. Honesty is the work of a lifetime.

FINDING THE FATHER

If I am death to man
I have to know it
His mind is too simple
        I cannot go on
Sharing his nightmares
My own are becoming clearer
        They open into prehistory
Which looks like a village lit with blood
Where all the fathers are crying:
        'My son is mine!'

Adrienne Rich

...Now don't get me wrong. I want to like what Bly's saying, because we all know men are more fun when they're wild. What worries me is the element of woman-blaming in his rap.

Bly tells the story of a friend: this man's father and mother split when he was twelve, and, after ten years of living with his mother in another state, this man took a train to Seattle to find his father. He told his father, "I don't accept any more my mother's view of you." His father burst into tears and said, "Now I can die." Bly says you can't expect a clear picture of your father from your mother.

As the kind of mother who raised her sons to question her view of

(Published in the August 1986 issue of *Poetry Flash*, Berkeley, CA.)

Notes written after hearing an edited tape of Robert Bly's *The Search for the Father*, which aired several times during 1986 on KPFA Pacifica Public Radio, FM 94. Bly speaks of "male modes of feeling," of finding the "wildman" within, and the forming of male friendships "grounded in downward shadow."

everything, I have to say this story hurt my feelings. Now, I'm aware that Bly doesn't endorse witch burning, or even the kinds of plays and rituals done by the old boys' network at Bohemian Grove, but he makes me think of a scene in the movie *Ben Hur*: remember when Charleton Heston greets his male buddy, the Roman soldier, and they clash spears and cry: "Down Venus, up Mars!"

Of course, there's no doubt Bly is onto something. Most of the men I know certainly need more men in their lives. It cheers them up. But Bly doesn't talk about what his all-male groups do to celebrate, I mean the singing and the shouting that I assume he's into. (I could be wrong, it certainly wouldn't be the first time.)

I wish he'd talk about the male malaise and what he's doing to make men feel good about themselves. Personally, I'm not into celebrating stuff we can't help, like maleness or femaleness or whiteness or blackness, but when people get depressed sometimes they need to do that stuff, even if it's a bit pompous. I figure, well, if men do lots of war dances then maybe they'll be too tired to go to war. (See, I'm getting angry already.)

No, seriously, my father always came home from hunting as cheerful as hell, and he brought us presents, and things went swell for days. Everyone knows about the Tarzan/Jane thing, and the cosmic complement, and the yin and the yang of it all.

Virginia Woolf used to say the trick is to be man-womanly or woman-manly. I had a hard time getting that concept across to adolescents when I was a high school teacher. I couldn't get across the difference between an androgyne and a hermaphrodite. Many people seem to think there's only so much room in the soul, as if the battle of the sexes were a battle for possession of the adult self.

In my classes, I used Emily Bronte's *Wuthering Heights* to show what happens when masculine and feminine archetypes are too rigid. Like Greek gods, Cathy and Heathcliff are too much themselves, and so they self-destruct. The problem is, adolescents really get off on swooning females and phallic males. I certainly did. I tried to tell my students that Cathy was suicidal and Heathcliff homicidal and that they were riding for a fall. Blind *hubris*, etc.

"Pray, don't imagine that he (Heathcliff) conceals depths of benevolence and affection beneath a stern exterior! He's not a rough diamond—a pearl-containing oyster of a rustic: he's a fierce, pitiless, wolfish man."

Cathy, on the other hand, is a depressive masochist, the sort of female who's felled by her first bleeding. The menarche transforms her from a free-spirited androgynous adolescent into a dependent, consumptive invalid—the quintessence of Victorian femininity. In the second half of the book Emily Bronte tries (with less success but more courage) to paint portraits of the children of Cathy and Heathcliff, characters who are woman-manly and man-womanly.

There has always been room in literature for androgynous, transcendent characters—Shaw's Joan of Arc, Shakespeare's intellectual clowns, Ibsen's idealists—as well as for women and men characters who are not defined by their sexuality. I'm worried that Bly's campaign against wimpdom presages a return to the simplistic images of Mom as monster. These images shattered my self-esteem as a young mother, and they still haunt my psyche. Phillip Wylie stained the culture for years. The identity crisis apparent in a lot of today's male poets and writers seems to be a backlash to the women's movement. I only hope we do not create a warrior/wimp syndrome the way we created a madonna/whore schism.

Bly says the industrial revolution removed the father from the home. Then he says women took over the home, and men got power in the public sphere and that, because of women's powerlessness (?), they used their power on their sons. Well, you get the picture.

Bly states: "Night is when you see what really happened in your family." Yes, night is when I remember. I remember my beloved father who took his shotgun and shot the tigers who pursued me in my nightmares. In the morning he took me out on the desert and showed me the spot where he buried those tigers. We put some big rocks on their graves, so the dogs wouldn't dig them up. He knew what fathers were for. He had a tiger by the tail, and before he was through, it killed him.

*   *   *

Daddy?
That's another kind of prison.
It's not the prince at all,
but my father
drunkenly bent over my bed,
circling the abyss like a shark,
my father thick upon me
like some sleeping jellyfish.

Anne Sexton
"Briar Rose" (Sleeping Beauty)
from *Transformations*

Listening to Bob Bly. Bob was my father's name. My father. That Blarney Stone. Tense and tired in the morning, getting ready to do surgery at six, slapping his face with cold water, scrubbing his nails with a wire brush, laughing every time he had to face death, and facing it over and over every morning at six. And if he couldn't take it sometimes and got blind drunk, well, so do I.

Bly says the son whose father is absent from the home gets a hole in his psyche, and into that hole rush demons. The demon in my father's psyche was some Mother Machree I never knew. His grandmother raised him. Perhaps she was the demon. Perhaps it was my mother. When I was thirteen I was on a train on the way to my mother's funeral. In the hole in my head, the lacuna of loneliness, I imagined my father sober and wearing an aura of tragic dignity. When I arrived, he was slumped over the kitchen table in his bathrobe, drunk, with his eyes wild and red, sobbing my name.

> I am at times under a strange illusion. I think of myself as the mother, rather than the daughter, of my father.
>
> George Sand
> (Lines deleted from her manu-
> script, *Histoire de Ma Vie*)

In my dreams, I'm still trying to get him to wait for the ambulance so I can get him to the hospital. He clings to me as his soul leaves his body through these terrified wildboy eyes, and he's back in my womb, and I can't bear him. And when he did die, in September of 1961, I miscarried (a biological, not a metaphorical pregnancy). Because of the bleeding and my unmanly cowardice, I didn't get to the gravesite. I haven't got there yet.

I got as far as the funeral parlor. It stood on the corner of Shattuck and Cedar in Berkeley. My husband said how still it was, there in the same room with Bob and no sound of his Irish bombast. Blathers, I called it. And the blathers coming into *my* mouth then, whenever I wanted it and even when I didn't.

In time, my kid brother began to say, you sound like Bob all right, meaning to put me down for being overbearing. I'd take it as a compliment, and then he'd renege and say I hadn't Bob's charm. Then my kid brother left his wife and three sons and went to Vietnam and tried to be a man, and the hole in his psyche filled with demons, and now he's a quadriplegic and a drunk, and his wife raised their sons alone without a dime, and her sons loathe her for being such a man.

I can't remember my kid brother at Bob's funeral. I do remember he came to mother's because at mother's I got hysterical and screamed and wouldn't get out of the car and go into that blue hole in my head, that room where mother lies buried in blue lights and gardenias. But I knew it was unmanly to cry, so I told everyone it was my brother who screamed and acted so childish. I *believed* it too. I remembered it that way until I was thirty-seven years old. Demons rushed into my psyche and filled the blue-black hole with a lie of manliness. I had to be a better man than my father. There he was at her funeral, drunk, upstaging her the way he'd always done, waving his German pistol and threatening to shoot himself at her grave. So I lied. In my psyche I was what mother would have wanted. A manly presence. A dignified mourner. A myth.

The myth of the father. The world has never been the same since God died. Or has it? Who was it said, "The world won't be the same without Big Daddy, or else, perhaps, it will"?

And when he did die (of a brain hemorrhage the day after a fight in a bar), there I was, hysterical again. This time with laughter. I was twenty-seven. I was bleeding, as I said. I beat a hasty retreat, swooning. Couldn't stand the weeping women, what was left of the lovers and five wives and assorted Mother Machrees. I had to go home and lie down. I had to lie. I had to laugh. There he was, quite chopfallen. And then came the wake. Zen slap.

> I would give you some violets, but they withered all when my father died....
>
> Ophelia, *Hamlet*
> Act IV, scene 5

*　　　*　　　*

Part II

But let us bury those old bones — it's blood under the bridge after all. (But the ache is in the bones now, more than the blood.) Let us move on to today and the sons of today and their father. Tall, and acted the man ... of course there is no such thing, but we don't know that when we're twenty. We don't know there is no Father, no Mother, no Man, Woman, Son, Lover, no archetype at all. No parent, no god, no myth, no one but us. Only Bob and Gretchen or Scott and Zelda. Only their sorrow and their silence. But back then, in the fatuous fifties, what did I know? I knew I didn't want a wildman who got into drunken brawls. I wanted a man who kept his mouth shut and his pants on. Guess what.

Raised in a passion play, all I'd known of love was suffering. It sometimes happens that those of us raised to suffer go right out and marry emptiness, believing happiness to be merely the absence of pain. Any guy who could drive within the speed limit looked good to me. (What was it my father used to say? "You'll miss me when I'm dead and gone—you'll see.")

But then came the '60s. And the world woke up for a few years. And the personal became political. And I ran away from home. Well, I moved from suburbia back to Berkeley where I could imagine I was a real person.

I had two little sons by then and they were three and five. And they had a father. And *his* mother said all problems stem from divorce. (*And into this hole rush demons.*) She hadn't rushed into divorce. She waited until her son was grown-up. Her son lived with his father and theirs was a cold war. And the hole in his head filled up with cold.

I asked his mother: where were you when his father hurt him? (And where was Sarah when Abraham took Isaac to sacrifice the child to Yahweh, the biggest Big Daddy yet?) And Bly says the hole in the psyche fills up with fearful images of the older male. But he tells us the images come from woman, from mothers. He doesn't say anything about *his* mother, only about mothers. I wonder if she's dead. I mean enough to bury. And did he love her?

> And even my father came with his white bone
> but I was tired of the gender of things . . .
> Anne Sexton

And then one day ten years ago my younger son noticed that the Rapid Transit trains ran right over to his father's door in Oakland. He was thirteen. He hopped right on a train and went on over without being asked, but his father *had guests.*

About this time I noticed my sons beginning to blame their father's wife for his neglect. I don't know her story. I do know some of his. I'd ask him to take the boys backpacking, but he'd say it wasn't up to him, meaning it was up to his wife. And into this hole rush demons.

Bly states: "The father loses his son in this country five minutes after birth." I tried to give my first baby to his father just for a few minutes on the way home from the hospital so I could run in the store. He demurred. When I finally understood that he was not going to give the babies any physical affection, I asked him why. He said he couldn't relate to them until they reached the Age of Reason.

So he want Right and I went Left and the boys grew up, and all of us still trying to find a father to fill that hole in our psyche. Could I be the father, I asked? I got drunk and sang Irish songs but they didn't buy it.

So what it comes down to is this. It's love and the capacity for love that distinguishes one human being from another. And some men love women, even their mothers. And some men hate women, even their mothers (i.e. Henry Miller, who once wrote: "An old cunt is a dead loss."). But all men love their fathers and women love them too.

Bly says he "couldn't take it" at home, that the spiritual young male flees, goes to India, anything to get away. "Get away from what?" asks my son Peter, a Zen master with a difference.

On the radio, Bly goes on to say that men help men get close to their bodies and this contradicts what he was told about women being the ones who would help him get close to his body. Who was it said, oh yes, F. Scott Fitzgerald, that the test of a first rate intelligence is the capacity to hold two conflicting ideas in the mind at the same time and continue to function. Yes.

Of course the conflict here is an illusion. Bodies (all sorts) help us get close to our bodies. The Revolution of Touch. The way to get beyond this gender-bender is to make love, not have sex. (Djuna Barnes: "I'm not a lesbian, I just loved Thelma.")

The psycho-sexual holes in our psyches are nothing but loneliness. If we don't get love, we get neurotic. Since we're not born adult, we're vulnerable. And Mother has to be to blame. A mother who didn't love us is the very devil: the God that failed. How can She who gave us life be so unjust as not to make it bearable? If Bob Bly's mother loved him, I think he should say so. If not, not. I think he should say the name of the pain. And there are only two kinds of pain: too much love or too little. I got too much.

Looking at the picture of my father on my desk: Bob in high hat and cape standing in road with can of beer in hand. And the picture of my mother, in soft focus and furs. Terminal romantics. He gave me guns and horses and a *crossbow* for crissake. She gave me the arts and those wretched silk dresses with puffed sleeves and *bloomer* gym shorts—ohmygod, she thought they were so damn quaint! And it took both of them to make a hole in my psyche, a schism in my soul. I loved them more than all the gods and devils in all the books and plays. They *are* all the gods and devils in all the books and plays.

I grow old, I grow old, the centre will not fold. In youth I had hardening

of the categories and looked for the father and the mother in every lover.
Then I cracked. Then I fragmented. Then the old man in my soul found the
god in herself, not in some Jungian fairy tale but in the flesh that fell from
the bones and the words that came into my mouth when the look went out
of their eyes.

My father was Irish. My mother was Dutch. They were both born in
1902. I hope to live till 1999. When I get to the River Styx and the ferryboat
comes across through the mist on the dark water, my mother, Gretchen, will
be there in the boat with wine and grapes in the basket on her lap. She will
look into the marfire that glows from the deeps and she'll tell me for
goddessake to sit down and not to rock the damned boat! White and foam
soft, she'll laugh when my father puts down his oar and says: "There, you
see Jenny, I told you you'd be me when I was dead and gone."

17 March 1986
Saint Patrick's Day

THAT PATRIARCH PATRICK:
OR, SALLY SLEEPWELL SINGS THE BLUES

> An Irish lady can say that today is every day.
> Gertrude Stein

My Irish pal, the poet Sally Sleepwell, came by for a sip of whiskey last week, it being Saint Patrick's Day and all. Sally doesn't know whether to be a poet or a realist. Of course, in Ireland, they're the same thing, but in America there's a schism.

Now Sleepwell is only half Irish (and the worst half at that: her dad's from County Kerry). She's afraid she may be only half a poet and half a realist (and the worst half of both?). I console her by telling her she's more an artist than an American. That way she can drink to the Old Country with a whole heart.

Sal's never been to the Isle of Ire, the land of wrath, the land where the ancient Celts westered to a halt, staring out across the slate Atlantic. "What were they running away from?" I asked her. "Who drove the Celts to the

---

Sally Sleepwell was a Berkeley poet I knew during the early '70s. She moved away and I lost track of her. I found I missed her enough to keep her persona alive in a series of pieces I wrote for the Bolinas Hearsay News in 1984–85. I cannot say that the original is much like *my* gal Sal, who is probably my own alter-ego. Still, I like to think Sally would find her amusing. The piece that is included here appeared first in the Bolinas paper and had two resurrections on subsequent Saint Patrick's Days, first in *Grassroots* and then in *Mama Bears News and Notes*.

sea?"

Sally sighed. "They say it was this or that Indo-European group of neo-barbarians, but of course it was the Goddess. They were fleeing from the old religion, the Great Mother. You remember the Great Queen, The Morgan?"

Sally had another little sip of Irish whiskey and held forth: "That fifth-century saint, that patriarch Patrick, he's the one that drove the snakes from the Garden once more."

"And across the sea to New York," I muttered. Sally ignored me, proclaiming forcefully: "He's the one that drove out the serpent of knowledge, the wisdom of woman and her knowledge of life and death in the ancient world. In woman times, there were no illegitimate babies, no fallen women. In the pre-Christian world of kith and kin, whole families married each other."

"There was a low fertility rate, so it made sense," I told her. She snorted and concluded: "In a communal, sacred world, any kid is legit and so is her mom."

I filled Sally's glass and stopped trying to get her to listen to me. The Irish hear everything, but they wouldn't be caught dead *listening*. I asked why the Irish admire Saint Patrick if he was such a male chauvinist prig.

"That's just why!" she shouted. "Patrick didn't go for the old magic. He was into rational order. Today we've still got rational order and it's full of shit because it's based on greed. Here in America in the 1980s the greed that glitters gluts our lives. (Sal is fond of excessive alliteration.) Of course, the Irish are and always have been so poor, they never did get very rational after all. They went right on worshipping women. They didn't even burn witches during all those centuries when Europe roasted nine million. Oh, not that that translated into social or political power! The Great Goddess became the Virgin Mary, and not even Jesus gave *her* any power. He didn't even hang out with her. He stuck with the fellas."

Sally reached for the nearly empty bottle and waved aside the ice. "Women are such fools," she weeps. (Sleepwell is a regular *Deirdre of the Sorrows* when she's in her cups. This time of the year she's always grousing.) "The pagan priestess became a whore in her own temple. Gave away her Mother Right. Profaned the rites of life. There she was, the creatrix and the matrix. She gave birth to man, looked at her creation and found him fair. She fell in love with her own creation, gave him the keys to the car and that, as they say, was that. He became the measure of all things and she became his madonna or his whore."

Sally's right about that last part. Just recently I had a talk with two young Irishmen —only been in the U.S. two weeks —and one of them told me there were two sorts of American women, the mothers and the feminists. The second one told me please not to use coarse language around his wife. They were both charming.

Sleepwell stares into the bottom of her glass and begins to blubber about the old days. She goes on and on about the loss of mystery and women who let go of myth and nature for civilization and reason. They let slip the sacred for the profane, she cries, "All because they were in love with those motherfuckers!"

I do try to get Sally to eat something when she gets like this. The hangover will be no joke. She demands another drink to toast eternal returns. Her imagination proliferates in a Celtic twilight.

"Here's to the resurrection of sacred souls!" she cries, "to the day when spiritual and sexual prowess will once again be the same. To the sacred time coming when we no longer hang upon the modern cross of mind/-body despair!"

At this stage, Sleepwell became impossible to follow. She let go of linear thought, the thought that leads to death. She spun off into the mouth of the gods, drunk with Celtic schemes of cyclical rebirth and regeneration—the transmigration of truth.

Myself, I'm not sure I like to watch a woman get so sloshed. I mean, even when it's Herself is doing it, it's altogether too masculine, if you ask me.

IN SEARCH OF MANHOOD

> All women become like their mothers. That is their tragedy.
> No man does. That's his.
>
> Oscar Wilde

A decade ago I led a weekly workshop for women writers in my living room. We talked a lot about personal pain. "If there were no suffering, it would be necessary for you to invent it," laughed my younger son.

"Well, just as long as you're having a nice time with your women friends," consoled my older son.

One of the women in the workshop took a look at my boys' bedrooms and concluded: "Male chauvinist piglets!" I laughed with the group and quoted Erma Bombeck: "It is better to burn one boy's bedroom than to curse the darkness." Privately I was furious. She was talking about my Apollo, my Dionysus! Fortunately for our forum, both boys were at home the night this same woman locked her keys inside her car. As my boys handed her the retrieved key ring, I couldn't help saying, "So streetwise, my studlets."

At the risk of being unfashionable, I have to confess that children are my *raison d'etre* and for the very simple reason that they're us. It's just ego. As Shakespeare said, "If thou wouldst be immortal, beget children." Of course, like any Irish mother, I am scar tissue to the bone. My sons were born in 1960 and '62. I have been a single mother since 1966. I had a hell of a time with both pregnancies and it still seems a miracle to me that both boys are alive and walking around in the world. To this day I care more

---

This essay appeared in shorter form under another title in *The Berkeley Monthly* in April, 1987.

about their personal happiness than their political correctness. (Oh, they *might* carry a sign or wear a button demanding the right to get pregnant if I really nagged them, but I doubt if that would make my day.)

I hope they'll be structured anarchists, the sort of thinkers who shoulder full responsibility for their own lives and for the society they live in. At this point, Apollo reminds me of John Kenneth Galbraith and Dionysus is a bit like Bob Dylan. Both are pragmatic, perhaps because their mother is prone to ideological excess. If there's one thing their generation has learned, it's that Romanticism kills!

At the Great Peace March in San Francisco in 1969, Dionysus was quick to point out to me he didn't see how we could put a stop to the Vietnam War, even though there were thousands of us marching. He'd looked carefully and he could see we had no guns. He knew about guns. He had carefully shown me the difference between toy guns or "let's pretend" objects, and the real thing. At the age of four he was concerned because I didn't seem to grasp metaphor. He told me over and over that toy guns didn't work. He understood the principle of play.

A few years later he played a Vietnamese peasant during a street demonstration. The skit mimed a mock bombing of Vietnam and it was performed outside the Oakland Induction Center where we were protesting the draft. It was very dramatic and Joan Baez and her mother were arrested. Actually, what the boys had their eye on was a large papier-maché airplane used for the mock bombing. They got to take it home and it hung in their bedroom for a year.

The agony of their adolescent years was not the sort I had been led to expect. The boys themselves were much less upsetting than my male lovers, many of whom felt duty-bound to tell me what I was doing wrong. (I was born in 1933, and most of my male contemporaries belong to the phallocentric set. It's not altogether their fault, any more than my addiction to romanticism is altogether my responsibility. We are all victims of historical inevitability.)

Once, a visiting swain, an ex-Marine, barged into the kitchen while I was trying to fix dinner, demanding to know if I was aware that my boys were taking a shower together. I said they did that every night. He went on to tell me how they might develop "bad habits." "Oh," I said, "they already have those. They get water all over the bathroom floor and drop towels. That's why I tell them to shower at the same time, so there will only be one mess to clean up."

"It'll be your fault," said my gentleman caller, "if they turn queer."

Colette used to call men her "dear enemies." In recent years I've come around to that view. I mean, let's face it, men and women don't worship the same gods. Women prefer love to power. Men confuse the two. Men distinguish lust from love. Women confuse the two. (All of us distinguish the sensual from the spiritual, the classic error of western civilization.) Gender relations are like all human relations: tribal, national, etc. They depend upon finding common ground. Commies too, have babies and breakfasts and want a better world. Men and women both want love. This does not mean that they must give up independence or selfhood. Equal does not mean the same. Mutuality need not be based on similarity. I mean, I worry about the integrity of the image cluster, and Apollo worries about the mobility of the quarterback. What we have in common is worry. It's enough.

One of our biggest problems is language itself. What I call, sex-mantics. Define power. In general women call it "capacity" and men call it "clout." There's a lot of linguistic cement in the cerebral cortex these days and this leads to hardening of the categories. Words like "warrior" and "wimp" don't mean much if you apply them to Attila the Hun and Jesus Christ. In recent years the study of women and men and their respective gods and tribal ways and ceremonial customs has become the new cultural anthropology. You know: men learned from the animals and women learned from the plants, which is why women sit down and men stand up.

The truth is that in the beginning I was more afraid my sons would grow up to be unmanly (sissies!) than I later feared their macho moments would offend my feminist friends. The fact is that in patriarchy, real danger comes from other men. It is males who castrate other males. Any male who doesn't learn to compete (read: defeat) with his brothers is likely to be cut up by them.

When I talk about the primate hierarchy in these terms, expressing my primitive fears, some of my male friends call it a gender bender, and some of my women friends label it counterrevolutionary. I suppose they're both right. But in the long run, blood is thicker than backlash, and while I want my sons to be great souls, I also want them to survive.

I believe men are equal to women in many things, but certainly not in the area of nonviolence, a skill almost exclusive to women since history began. It has something to do with hormone levels. We are all biological units programmed to devour other biological units and much of the devouring is done by males suffering from testosterone overdose. (Of course the responsibility goes right back to Mother Nature when you get right down to it, so the feminine principle is behind everything!)

Not that women can't kill. Most of them eat as much per pound as their brothers. It's just that they need a *reason* to slaughter things. Food for the baby, that sort of thing. Sport eludes them. Only a handful of women go hunting, compared to the incredible numbers of males who stalk the woods and shoot for the fun of it. It's true that women murder from time to time, usually in self-defense. Still, eighty-five percent of the time, homicides are male affairs. Wars are almost exclusively a male privilege. Macho can kill you. Lack of macho can do the same. Seems that men, too, are damned if they do, damned if they don't.

The damned-if-they-do set includes those patriarchal big-daddy types who try to escape pain and death by identifying with an all-powerful immortal father-god who will save them from decay and the inevitable return to mother earth. These are the men with structured belief systems. They believe they can control life and death. They believe in law and order and a black boot. They believe, in effect, that they can play God.

The damned-if-they-don't set includes those men who are victims of big daddy, men used as cannon fodder to promote the primate grandiosity of "patriotic" scoundrels; gone to graveyards since wars began, they too believe in a god/hero principle of sorts, they too are looking for the love of an abstract father. I think of the male children in the Middle East, wearing symbolic keys to heaven around their necks in case they die in battle. Think of the neo-Nazi men who want to join their fathers in Valhalla. Each culture has a warrior heaven and it's strictly a men's club. The poet Robert Bly believes men want to break out of the "force field of women" and return to the stout arms of their fathers. Freud felt this was the reason why God became a guy at some point in human history. That is, the infinite became a father figure in the hope of *immortality*. Men reach out to their father who art in heaven to escape their mother who brought them forth and is sure to remind them that they must suffer dissolution.

What's behind all this? What are these guys doing to each other and why? The psychologist Phyllis Chesler in her book *About Men* writes: "Even now, when fathers kill their sons — at home, at war — the psychologists say, 'Oh, but the father really meant to kill his own father, the child's grandfather. It was only a case of mistaken Oedipal identity.' Young soldiers lie dead, sent there by commanding father-figures. How proud, how sad their fathers are: their fathers who never meant them any harm."

What this says to me is that it's no good looking for gods at all, especially when we discover that they turn out to be our parents. Religion is

all metaphor, after all; at its best, a poetic longing for transcendence and at
its worst an excuse to murder "non-believers." Our gods are projections of
our desires and needs. A good psych course teaches us that the Titans are
just the big people who scared us when we were in our cribs. If we can
outgrow our parents, we can outgrow gods and devils and even structured
belief systems. If we can overcome our fear of individuality and embrace
loneliness, perhaps we can learn to be at home here on the ground where
the truth can be found in the soil and the sea.

My younger son is not into gods, but he does dig the god in man. He
quotes Jello Biafra, lead singer for the Dead Kennedys: "We are all of us
Boat People." We need all the help we can get.

I quote Gertrude Stein who wrote: "What is the use of being a boy if
you are going to grow up to be a man?" What is the use, finally, of being a
lover, an Adonis, a poet, if the only way you can survive as a man is to kill
other men, whether in the military or the marketplace?

In mythology, most men overcome or kill their fathers only in order to
become like them. Myths haven't changed much. Neither have we. In
mythology and reality, most men deny their mothers to prove their
strength. Hugh Drummond, M.D., writes (*Mother Jones*, December
1981): "Any adult male who goes so far as to acknowledge the existence of
a mother invites the contempt of his fellows, just as such actions did in
adolescence."

Simone de Beauvoir asked the question, "Do women exist, really?" I
ask myself, do mothers exist, *really*? My father thought so. He worshipped
women. He was Irish. He believed in women. As many as possible. They
were his source, his audience, his home.

Not too long ago, I asked a young Irishman along to watch my son win
the Berkeley softball championship. (Apollo plays with a team called Free
Base.) I imagined a Celt fresh from the old sod would appreciate my smug
satisfaction in the talents of my "darlin boy. . . ." Halfway through the game
during one of my enthusiastic descriptions of Apollo's better moves, this
same Irishman solemnly explained to me how it is that a man must reject
his mother, and that if he doesn't, it will impede his manhood.

I spilt my coffee just where I hoped it might impede his manhood and
that was the last I saw of him. I exist all right. It's only that sometimes I get
the feeling it's not even as a "dear enemy" but as a dread enemy. I
considered whether I needed to reject my father, whether he impeded my
womanhood. Freud felt the Electra complex was a sensible sort of thing.
Prepared women for marriage in the sense that wives, at least in Freud's

day, were pretty much daughters anyway.

I gave up thinking and watched the game. I wondered if my presence throws off my son's concentration. (It doesn't. When I was in school plays, my father's presence made me a self-conscious wreck.) I wondered if it embarrasses him when I tag along. Unlike the vast majority of men, both my sons treat me, and other women as well, as if we were *their fellow men*. After the game, one of the players came over and thanked me for coming. He sounded really grateful. A fellow man.

Manhood is a curious concept. I believe that manhood is mostly made of courage. The kind of courage that can make peace. The trouble today is that there are too many one-eyed cats among us. You know, cats who see with an ideological Left eye or an ideological Right eye, or a masculinist/feminist dialectic or a good/evil cross. The trouble is such vision is always flat, two-dimensional, lacking the depth of vision we get when we use both eyes. My left eye sees my son the Mahatma and my right sees my son the Machismo, when in fact there is only a man. A man is someone who can love. A man is a male or a female who can laugh and who can make peace—not the kind of peace that has to do with quiet, but the peace that is the moral equivalent of war; the kind of peace that exhausts most males and many females who are sick to death of talking and of the endless process of problem-solving and who long for the peace and quiet that comes out of the barrel of an Uzi submachine gun.

My son is dancing out the door with his frisbee in his briefcase, singing: "Automatic weapons are not the answer. Pizza is the answer." Of course, I want sausage and he likes only pepperoni and his younger brother is into dietary purity and. . . .

LIFE IN A PHALLOCRACY

The Reign of the Phallus: Sexual Politics in Ancient Athens by Eva C. Keuls

Was the castration caper perpetrated in Athens in the summer of 415 B.C. the work of feminist vandals? If women *did* mutilate the public statues — and it seems rather likely that they did — no one ever found out. The so-called "Mutilation of the Herms," was an act of subversion so scandalous that the phallocracy or male supremacist power structure was simply blind to the most obvious suspects.

Only that spring, Athenians had seen Euripides' play *The Trojan Women*, perhaps still the definitive anti-war tragedy. (Aristophanes' *Lysistrata* was produced four years later in 411 B.C. and is still the definitive anti-war comedy.) A year earlier in 416 B.C. the Athenian army had

---

In the summer of 1985, I reviewed a Harper & Row book for the *San Francisco Chronicle*; it was titled *The Reign of the Phallus; Sexual Politics in Ancient Athens* and written by Eva C. Keuls, a classics professor at the University of Minnesota. Because of the scholarly nature of this work the editors at the *Chronicle* felt I needed to rewrite my review which was irreverent and perhaps a bit flippant. After all, the book is a study of the Age of Pericles, that famous era in classical Athens that lasted from about 480 until 415 B.C. In calling this period *The Reign of the Phallus*, the author is referring to the rule of male supremacists and the socio-political oppression of women. Well, I still like my original take on this book and I include it here because the book has been pretty much neglected since it first came out and I think it has more popular appeal than the usual text dealing with the revisionist feminist imperative of our age. So here is my first draft, my impressionistic take on this remarkable study of what was really going on back at the Parthenon.

slaughtered the entire adult male population of the city of Melos, and the women and children of that island, like the ancient Trojans, had been enslaved. In midsummer 415 B.C., the imperialist playboy Alcibiades was mounting a large expedition into Sicily with much hoopla. The Peloponnesian war with Sparta was in full swing, although the Athenians eventually lost that one. What was coming was the turning point, the transition from megalomacho militarist expansionism to anti-war feminist liberalism.

Is it any wonder that Athenians awoke one morning to find that a band of vandals had knocked off the handles (penises) of literally hundreds of stele statues of the god Hermes Lest anyone gasp in horror at the thought that the vandals were not art lovers, the fact is that these statues were not much more than pillars. The author writes: "Herms consisted of busts of the bearded Hermes, set upon smooth stone pillars out of which protruded, at groin level, more or less realistic and erect genitalia." One thinks of what we now call "the pillars of society." (When I was going to school at U.C. Berkeley, there were Greek lads in full erection carved upon the Sather Gate at the entrance to the campus, just over the inscription which remains to this day, "Erected by Jane Sather." Fortunately for new generations of students, these lads have gone back to the classics department.)

By a not-so-curious coincidence, the above mentioned vandalism occurred just at the time of year when the Athenian women celebrated the counter-culture festival of Adonia. The exotic god Adonis was an embodiment or expression of the gentle son/lover so adored for his ability to give women orgasms rather than babies. Adonis is a sort of Romeo, antithetical to the phallic rapists so dominant in the mythology of the age: jockocrats like Theseus and Heracles, to say nothing of that Big Daddy rapist, Zeus himself.

During the festival of Adonia, it was the custom for the women to be released from their homes, at least as far as their rooftops. Could the wine and song have started the first "make love, not war" movement? Did the women of ancient Athens stage an anti-war protest, vaguely reminiscent of the sixties?

The author uses a vast array of illustrations to challenge many of the assumptions of earlier scholars. There are 346 halftone illustrations in the text which back up her conclusions. She concludes that the story of phallic rule is at the root of Western civilization, yet has been suppressed not only because of prudery and censorship but because until recently all historical research has been male turf. Since males, like the rest of us, tend to see what they look for, it's reasonable they should "see" a culture (both ancient and modern) in which the male was the measure of all things and the female, according to Aristotle, was merely a "maimed animal." Here Aristotle anticipates Freud, whose penis-envy theory is far from ancient history.

The author refers to Aristotle as a "visceral misogynist" who believed that women have fewer teeth than men. She also reports that Bertrand Russell's opinion was that, if Aristotle had allowed his wife to open her mouth once in awhile, he might have known better.

Plato, on the other hand, had no wife and was a practicing homosexual which, Keuls says, may account for his feminist sentiments. Among the later misogynists who expounded upon Athenian culture was Nietzsche, who wrote that he found it "inevitable that an advanced and creative culture should reduce its women to the status of vegetables."

Until very recent years, history has told us more about historians than about the past. Art historians are no exception. The suppression of pornographic Greek vase paintings has probably been more general than the suppression of, say, the comedies of Aristophanes, although there's no proving it. In her search for the truth about sexual politics in ancient Athens, the author looks past literature and toward the imagery of the age. This is necessary because she has found no scrap of fifth-century writing that can be attributed to a woman and no records were kept of Athenian women citizens. She says women's names are found on their gravestones only if they died in childbirth (analogous to men who died in battle).

Historians and lovers of Greek culture will be either irritated or intrigued by this update on the ancients, depending upon their own perceptions of Attic angst. The author sees gynophobia, the fear of women, in direct proportion to the degree of their repression. She finds ample evidence of the battering and humiliation of older women prostitutes on countless vase paintings. She concludes this practice helped banish the mother image from men's souls. Scenes depicting symposia (symposia meant literally "drinking together") indicate that a liberal education for Athenian male citizens included the demeaning of slave prostitutes. Sound familiar? A stag party?

The often romanticized hetaerai or courtesans were seldom well-to-do. As in the case of the modern call girl, the imagined prosperity of such women was a sop for male guilt. The famous Aspasia, Socrates' teacher and Pericles' mistress, does seem to have prospered by her wits, one of those exceptions who prove the rule. The rule was slavery and prostitution. There was a brisk trade in girl babies. The marriage age was fourteen for female Athenian citizens (eighteen in the more egalitarian city state of Sparta), followed by a lifetime of segregation at the back of the house where even the food was inferior to that served in the men's dining room.

Male pursuits were public, conducted out of doors in the open air where the architecture was sublime. Female chores were private and confined to the dark boxes called women's quarters. The author finds no pictorial evidence of what we would consider Lesbian erotica. What she does find is bondage motifs and an iconography of aggression and glorified violence on a scale with our own. Omnipresent always was the image of a wounded or dying Amazon, her breast pierced with the Greek warrior's symbolically phallic sword.

Was this art or propaganda, or the best of both? The image makers, the potters and painters, were exclusively male, just as today's pornographers are all, if not actually male, at least working for a male market. They banish the feminine principle and exalt the masculine. The overwhelming prevalence of male dominance and female submission revealed in the imagery of the age was more than just male fantasy. All brothels were male-owned, and it was unheard of for a woman to have economic independence. Today there are token females in the flesh markets, but the real entrepreneurs are still men.

What Keuls does not emphasize is the homoerotic subtext of much of Greek visual art. She takes it for granted that the reader is aware that the Greeks had a word for it. I can't help but think of my own classics professors back in the 1950s. They were for the most part randy enthusiasts who were, consciously or unconsciously, drawn to the homoerotic. It delighted and titillated them. Vase paintings showing group sex were for them symbolic of pagan orgies and a release from their own prudish Victorian heritage. Even Keuls refers to the dying words of Socrates, "We owe a cock to Asclepius," as a "salacious phallic allusion." Could be. She notes that there is no extant Greek tragedy about homoerotic love, although comedies abound. She concludes that the homoerotic was "only half-heartedly condoned."

Most of my professors thought that Greek "friendships" were ideal, that they expressed an intellectual and egalitarian love ethic. In historical fact, sex between males in Athenian culture usually involved older men with boys, reducing it to the dominance/submission pattern so familiar in all phallocratic societies. So-called Platonic love, so dear to the hearts of apologists, is a misnomer invented by male chauvinist prigs who equate higher (intellectual or spiritual) relationships with sexlessness. It's a disability that crippled the Christians. Plato himself was in fact both a feminist and an active homosexual. He did not suffer the mind/body split so familiar in later philosophers. He states in his *Republic* (so popular with

Roman matrons in later years) that women should be educated insofar as possible in order that their talents not be wasted. He advocated the abolition of the nuclear family on the premise that children should be cared for in common. Of course Plato neither married nor was he known to have had any sexual relations with women, so his speculations as to their uses were always made at a safe philosophical distance. (I do recall once reading the name Archeanassa in connection with Plato's, although theirs may have been only a "Platonic" affair.)

As mentioned above, Plato's pupil Aristotle had had more hands-on experience with women and he was distinctly not user-friendly. He passed on his contempt for the sex to his infamous pupil, Alexander, the Macedonian madman, still referred to as "the Great" in many modern textbooks.

What I discovered in this account of the birth of Western civilization is further proof that the less room there is for women in the world of reality, the more they invade and occupy the imaginations of men. Images of women are everywhere in Greece, just as they are in America today. Male fantasy is perhaps one of the hardest realities women have to deal with. It seems the Greek psyche had a split which mirrors our own, a schism between the sacred and the profane, between the ancient religion of the Mother Goddess and the new religion of phallocracy, what has been called the conflict between nature and reason. (Medea and Jason are often cited as embodiments of nature and reason, of primal power and intellectual power, that sort of thing.)

The popular art of ancient vase painting was as full of profanity as today's girlie magazines. The denigration of women was matched only by the iconography of weaponry. Phallic residuals are everywhere in our own culture and today's monolithic evidence of phallocentrism can be found on every billboard and military base. For every image shown in this book, I could wish scholars would find the matching photo taken from our centerfolds or *Hustler* grotesques.

I think Eva C. Keuls has provided us a valuable piece of research. Although she touches only lightly on Greek drama, it is there that I think we find the psychiatric key to the age. Sophists point to the satyr plays (the ones which satirize) which, like the vase paintings, leave no sacred stone unturned. But this was only one aspect. In reality, the Greek plays are monuments to the depths of the human psyche, to the magnitude of human tragedy. They are, in a word, humane. Keuls writes: "Men's feelings about their mothers, wives and daughters that, for the purposes of everyday life they had banished from their consciousness, gushed forth on the tragic stage of Athens."

It is a great irony that the ruling-class males who wrote these paeans to justice never allowed a woman to act on stage. (Whether women attended performances is still debated.) Greek drama contains all the human archetypes, the extremes of passion, id and ego and superego let loose, Titanic forces in society, even the *dea ex machina* who can save us. *Até*, *Hubris* and *Nemesis* (sometimes called Fate, Destiny, and Retribution) are the dramatic goddesses who hold the threads of life. *Até* is blind impulse or passion, *Hubris* is arrogance or overweaning pride, and *Nemesis* is justice—the goddess who knows enough is enough. A play like *Antigone* taught me, once for all, that art and justice are the same thing.

Those of us who studied and acted in these plays have no doubt in our minds that Clytemnestra is somebody's mother, Andromache is the wife some guy never had, and Antigone is the sister every man wants. I sometimes find myself wondering what sorts of creatures women would create in fiction and poetry if the men in their lives ceased to be authentic and became only projections. I think of Heathcliff, the most masculine hero of romantic literature, created by a woman who never once deigned to look at a man. Perhaps we should be grateful there were no real men in the life of Emily Jane Bronte. Perhaps not.

The chorus in the Greek play is often made up of women. They represent the oppressed, the underdog, the people who will suffer if the rulers make a mess of things. Women are not just metaphors for the underclass, they *are* the underclass. They are the first ones to suffer from the results of militarism or the power trip of some king or general. The Greek chorus is often found outside the palace on the steps staging a demonstration. (Any of this ring a bell?) In *The Trojan Women*, the conquered women of Troy cry out amidst the flames of their burning city. They ask their conquerors to stop and reflect, to acknowledge a tragic flaw (*Hubris*, an emotional blind spot, often an oppressor's failure to see himself as others see him). Their role is basically that of street protesters, representing all those who are outside the system trying to change it by appealing to the ruler's and the public's conscience.

The goddess of justice, *Nemesis*, was a woman. It is woman who gives us our comeuppance. Something's got to give. The Greeks had a word for it: moderation—the Middle Way. I think that when Euripides wrote his plays he wrote not just out of male guilt and fear at having denied the feminine in reality (although we all do that), but out of deep conviction and from an androgynous heart which sought the peace that follows war, which knew what his mother knew—that what goes up, must come down. . . .

STEEL MAGNOLIA
TELLS ALL

First Lady From Plains by Rosalynn Carter

Rosalynn Carter is too much the politician to spill the beans. She holds us with the personal stuff while avoiding some of the bloodier issues. She confesses that Jimmy kissed her on the first date. She was seventeen and he was twenty. As a girl in Plains, Georgia, she churned butter and helped her mother take in sewing. The privy was outdoors. In the White House, she wore long underwear during the energy crisis when the heat was turned down. On Inauguration Day, she worried about her hair.

The wealth of detail makes this autobiography a good read while at the same time whetting the appetite for more backstage stories of the political pressures of the time. Rosalynn writes that the Lincoln bed in the White House is too hard, while the mattress on the queen's bed is too soft. She didn't change them; she thought they might make people think.

Born Eleanor Rosalynn Smith in 1927, she's not precisely a rollback to *the* Eleanor (Roosevelt), although she certainly gives it her best shot. Both women had great difficulty becoming public speakers, yet they are the only First Ladies on record to testify before Congress, Mrs. Roosevelt on behalf of the coal miners and Mrs. Carter on behalf of the mentally ill. Both learned to travel and campaign on their own. Rosalynn writes, "If I go with Jimmy, I just sit there."

Although Eleanor Roosevelt was born to old-money privilege and

---

Well, hardly *all*. *First Lady From Plains: Eleanor Rosalynn Smith Carter: Her Story* was published by Houghton Mifflin in 1984 and I reviewed it for the San Francisco Chronicle (5-13-84) but the editors deleted some of the political projections of Rosalynn so I think it's worth including here in its entirety.

Rosalynn Carter came from farmers in Plains (she says her first memory is the red dust of Georgia), they share that Christian conscience once thought to be the spine of public servants, and certainly fashionable in the wake of Watergate. Today, when we have such a servant problem (the Reagans seem both bored and irritated by the concept of a "public" which they are duty-bound to serve in the American tradition—they take a *nouveau riche* approach to power, behaving like the parvenu who thinks the role which power or money has given him is a sort of toy or present to be used for his own pleasure), it is refreshing to read the views of a woman who seems to take her civics lessons seriously.

It is interesting to compare the histories of Eleanor Roosevelt and Rosalynn Carter. Both suffered early loss. Eleanor adored her alcoholic father who died young and under a cloud. Rosalynn blamed her own "bad thoughts" (at age fourteen!) for her father's early death. Her subsequent struggle to "do the right thing" all her life, has given her a public image which, like Mrs. Roosevelt's, is perhaps too virtuous for some tastes. Nancy Reagan's greed and vulgarity (what was it *Time* said? "The rich are always with her.") seem more in keeping with the 1980s, although there are some signs the mass of people are sick of hypocrisy and the downright unkindness which seem to characterize so many of our public servants.

Rosalynn herself expresses a little irritation at Jimmy's "rather be right than President" approach to the 1980 election. Still, she accepts his view of the situation in the end. Readers may smile at her pluck as she gathers courage to visit Cambodian refugee camps, or struggles with her tears as she tries to help the mentally retarded. Her efforts were not always popular. The press told her that mental illness was "not a sexy issue." Obviously "no booze in the White House" was. Rosalynn writes that in fact, the wine-only policy was an attempt to restore thrift, not Prohibition.

The section of the book that stays with me over time is the portrait of Lillian Carter, Jimmy's mother. Miss Lillian cared for Rosalynn's father all through his last illness. As a nurse, she stepped across racial barriers in an era when that involved risk. During Carter's term in office, Miss Lillian went to India with the Peace Corps where she lost a good deal of weight. When she returned she had a lot of trouble getting back into the habit of eating. I have listened to Jimmy Carter speak of his mother over the years and following her death. She seems not only authentic but humorous. What was it I said, honesty is the work of a lifetime?

Reading between the lines, one catches a hint that Rosalynn found Lillian Carter a bit overwhelming. It's as if she were speaking of a public monument. In most other areas, her pragmatism is a triumph. She con-fesses she wishes they had never let the Shah of Iran come to the U.S. She is the first to proclaim her bitterness when the 1980 election went to Ronald Reagan: "Jimmy could have blown up Tehran and been re-elected."

As an envoy to Latin America, Mrs. Carter believed that her husband's Human Rights policies had recaptured the youth. She writes: "As a south-ern woman, I have seen the beneficial transformation of our lives that came with the end of the discrimination and oppression of black citizens in our region. The flaming desires of the 1950s and 1960s in our nation are now mirrored in other countries of the world, and nowhere more vividly than in Central and South America. I learned on my trip to Latin America that *Derechos Humanos!* is a cry that cannot be stilled. For our own government to stand silent and even to align itself with torturers and murderers such as those in El Salvador is a disgrace to us all and a shameful violation of the principles espoused by the American heroes who have offered their lives for the cause of freedom and human rights."

Mrs. Carter states that of all the projects with which she was involved during her husband's term in office, her greatest disappointment came with the defeat of the Equal Rights Amendment. She quotes Erma Bombeck's description of that proposal: "the most misunderstood 24 words since 'one size fits all.'" Jimmy's efforts on behalf of women are impressive if not whole-hearted. (The Bella Abzug episode is not exam-ined.) The list of his political appointments of women is quite long. Perhaps most significant in this area is Rosalynn's own full partnership with her husband. There is a touch of grace in the large-looming of Lillian, Jimmy Carter's heroic mother, and this is mirrored in his acceptance of Rosalynn as autonomous and independent. Jimmy also had a very close relationship with his sister, Ruth, and Rosalynn states there was much jealousy on Ruth's part in the early days and only Miss Lillian came to her aid. It would seem the Carters' marriage is a Christian competition to see who can contribute the most. Not a bad basis for a relationship.

Autobiographers cannot always tell the truth, not the whole truth. Rosalynn says as much. She also is concerned about hurting people's feelings. Politeness is an occupational hazard for politicians' wives, whose *raison d'etre* is often their facility in preventing the feces from hitting the fan. (For another slant on the Carter years, try *Three Press Secretaries on the President: Jody Powell, George Reedy, and Jerry Horst*, also published in 1984.)

I like Rosalynn's book because it is so personal, and because it is an inside look at the working life of a grassroots politician. Rosalynn went

door-to-door to campaign for Jimmy. They are obviously a righteous team
and too good for the political mire of our age. Rosalynn even includes in
her book her response to the press after that infamous interview in which
Jimmy Carter confessed that he "lusted in his heart" after other women.
Rosalynn said, "Jimmy talks too much."

BITCH IS BEAUTIFUL
FIVE ON FEMINISM

During the years I wrote for the Berkeley newspaper *Grassroots* (see page 135), I also wrote a dozen columns for a San Francisco paper, *Appeal to Reason*. Editor and publisher John Bryan is a veteran of radical rags and the *Appeal* was no exception. This brazen underground paper gave me a chance to literally swagger, to shake my feminist fist in the air. At first I called my column "Bitch is Beautiful" but I got so many letters telling me that such a title indicated the depths of my internalized oppression, etc. that I gave up and dropped it. For my *Grassroots* column, "Bread and Roses," I tried to be sincere, to remember I was somebody's mother. My tone was hopeful most of the time. Perhaps because it was a Berkeley paper, I permitted myself the occasional reference to my own life, to my children, to my friends. For the *Appeal*, I let myself get rowdy. I made up dialogues between hypothetical women and men. Sometimes the result was didactic, but it was feisty and did the job better than an essay might. On the theory that one parable is worth a thousand polemics, I laid it on a bit. I have decided to include a few examples here because they have a freedom, a thumb-to-nose air which has gone completely out of fashion and which I miss like anything. These pieces were written in the early '80s. Like Virginia Woolf, I was trying not to be shrill, I was trying to be ferocious.

'BLACK MAN, WATCH YOUR STEP! ETHIOPIA'S QUEENS WILL REIGN!'

> Mr. Black Man, watch your step! Ethiopia's queens will reign again, and her Amazons protect her shores and people. Strengthen your shaking knees and move forward, or we will displace you and lead on to victory and glory.
>
> Mrs. Amy Jacques Garvey (widow of Marcus Garvey) in an editorial in *Negro World* published October 21, 1925.

(Our scene is set in a coffee house where She and He are studying. Today they are Afro-Americans. She is reading Michele Wallace's *Black Macho and the Myth of the Superwoman*. He is reading the May/June 1979 issue of *The Black Scholar*, an issue devoted to a "Black Sexism Debate." He also refers to the March/April 1979 issue containing an essay by Robert Staples, "The Myth of Black Macho: A Response to Angry Black Feminists.")

She: Did I tell you my mom has been promoted? She's the first black woman to head a department in her college.

He: Affirmative action?

She: Damn right!

He: You know that means your mother is what they call a "two-fer"—by promoting her, they get two affirmative action points, one for promoting a black, and one for promoting a woman—two for the price of one wage.

She: Who cares? After twenty-seven years busting her ass, she deserves it.

He: That's not the issue. The real issue is what happens to the black man who lost out on that job. Robert Staples says, "There are over 84,000 more black women enrolled in college than black men. There is every reason to believe that by the turn of the century, black women will exceed black men in terms of occupation and income."

She: I've read that guy. He's a male supremacist. Look where he writes that black women "*threaten* to overtake black men by the next century." (Italics mine.) Some threat. Black women are still the poorest people in America.

He: My dad always said the only free people in America were white men and black women.

She: If black women are "free" then so is an ox. You're talking about procedural freedom, not substantive freedom. Freedom from want is a substantive freedom, one that most black women have never had.

He: Maybe that's why they're so bitter against black men.

She: Oh, give me a break. All the women in my family *love* black men, love 'em so much they give 'em everything they got. I think they should quit all that. Make the men grow up. See what Audre Lorde (the poet) says. (She thumbs through the May/June issue of *The Black Scholar* until she finds Lorde's article on "Feminism and Black Liberation: The Great American Disease.") Listen to this: "Staples pleads his cause by saying capitalism has left the black man only his penis for fulfillment and a 'curious rage.' Is this rage any more legitimate than the rage of black women? And why are black women supposed to absorb that male rage in silence? Why isn't that male rage turned upon our oppressors? Staples sees in Shange's play (Ntozake Shange's *For Colored Girls Who Have Considered Suicide When the Rainbow is Enuf*) a 'collective appetite for black male blood.' But my female children and my black sisters lie bleeding all around me, victims of the appetites of their brothers. . . .

"It is for black men to speak up and tell us why their manhood is so threatened, and by what, that we should be the prime targets of their justifiable rage. What correct analysis of this rotten capitalist dragon within which we live will legitimize the wholesale rape of black women by black men that goes on within every city in this land?"

He: That's the kind of shit white people want to hear. Gloria Steinem eats it up. She called that mess you're reading (Michele Wallace) the "book of the '80s." (He takes the book from the table and leafs through it, handling it as if it were soiled.) Listen to this bitch — "The black man (in 1966) had two pressing tasks before him: a white woman in every bed, and a black woman under every heel." Hell, she even says Richard Wright was "more concerned with making a lasting impression on whites than he was with self-revelation or self-exploration."

She: There's some truth in that you know. None of us can escape the age in which we were born. Wright was born in 1908 and he wanted to make it in the literary world of that time. Remember his book *Black Power*, the one he wrote in the '50s after his trip to Africa? He thought black people were backward, uncivilized. He *was* an anglophile in his way. He wrote that African women knew he was westernized, that they instinctively covered their breasts when he looked at them. They knew he saw with white eyes. (Richard Wright was African, Scottish, Irish, and Other. However, as his white grandmother told him, in America it is color, not race which distinguishes us. In America, she told him, you will be called a "colored man.") History is an ass, honey, but there is no escaping it.

He: Black history is nothing but colonialism. You know that's what all this is all about don't you? And what we're doing is only second stage colonialism. Attacking each other makes *them* strong. White male rule depends upon all this tension and fear. It's Machiavelli's trick: divide and conquer. Set people at each other's throats and then it's easy to exploit them from the top. What we're doing is ghetto behavior: like crabs in a barrel we turn on each other. Women have to understand what's happening, how they're being used by the system to destroy us from within.

She: That's the old capitalist cop-out. You can't go on blaming the system for your lousy behavior. The pecking order sucks. I know what happened to all the women who stepped aside in the '60s so the men could be the boss. I won't be the slave of a slave just so he can be on top *someplace*! Shit, we're all victims. And if a male rapes me or beats me, what do I do with my rage? Pass it on? Beat my kid? I know black men got it tough. Lots of 'em dead or in jail. No one knows what you suffer better than a black woman, but *she can't help by soaking up black male rage*. Time to put your rage to work where the real repression is. Seize some power and take care of business!

He: Well, I've got to graduate first. Did you mean what you said about typing the rest of my paper tonight?

She: I'll do it, I'll do it. I only have one book left to review and I got it read last night. It's real tough. Have you read it yet? (She digs Alice Walker's

The Color Purple out of her backpack.)

He: I've heard about her. She's another writer who scapegoats the black man, labels him a rapist.

She: You wouldn't say that if you'd *read* her! She *loves* black men. So does Ntozake Shange. So do I, come to think of it. Sometimes I even love you. If I didn't there'd be no problem. I'd just take a walk. But I can't take all your defensiveness. My gain is not your loss. Can't you see that? Our little don't make your big. Women can't go on being mirrors to magnify men. It doesn't work anyway.

He: Alice Walker doesn't love men. What she really writes about is women loving women.

She: Well, somebody has to. Women got to love each other or die. Got to love the men too, best we can. Which ain't easy, these days.

He: Damn white of you.

She: You know what I mean. Women are hurting. 1980 Census says black women head-of-households went from 31 percent in 1970 to 45 percent in 1980.

He: It's all economic. Monopoly capitalism exploits us all. All our personal man/woman conflicts have a socio-political origin. It's all in my paper. You'll see when you type it.

She: It's not just capitalism. Socialist countries are sexist too. Women are a *class*. The niggers of the world. You won't stop messing with us until we stop letting you. We got to put a stop to exploitation for your sake too. It's not good for your soul. The black man should know, if any man does, how absolutely power corrupts. We got to save you from your bad selves. Sweeten your karma cause we *love* you, and you are just too pretty to go on this way.

He: Let's go to my place. I'll let you prove it.

She I'm a woman, sweets. Don't got to prove a thing.

(This dialogue continues in other articles, and She and He try to discover why women prefer love to power and how this may lead to their destruction at last. In the final dialogue, she gives up on him for the duration, telling him to go out and find himself. She uses a line from an old song as she departs to go her own way for awhile: "Bye, Pharaoh, honey." An additional reference for this series of dialogues is the November/December 1981 issue of *The Black Scholar*, an issue devoted to "The Black Woman." In the work of Robert Staples, referred to above, I noticed a series of cruel contradictions in his treatment of the sufferings of both black men and black women. Staples writes: "Many of these (black) men are acting out because, of all groups in this society, they have no basis for any sense of self-actualization, or *somebodiness*." But then Staples goes on to *blame* black women for their sense of *nobodiness*, saying that their aloneness (his statistics indicate that 54 percent of black women never marry) is a factor in the anger of black women towards black men. Thus he uses the same argument with which to *accuse* one sex and *excuse* the other.)

FEMINISTS HAVE NO SENSE OF HUMOR?

What the Left needs is a few laughs. I hear that everywhere. The feminist Left isn't laughing. On the other hand, it is a *source* of humor. Throughout history, women's fight for freedom has provided the world with many of its lighter moments. Read Aristophanes.

Back in the nineteenth century one of the larger laughs was Amelia Jenks Bloomer (1818–1894). Bloomer wrote and published *Lily* (1848), the first U.S. newspaper founded by and addressed to women. The joke, of course, was Amelia's "bloomers" and the "bloomer girls" who followed her example by wearing the early pantaloons which allowed them to do scandalous things like ride bicycles.

In fact, Amelia was no joke. She was stuffy and rather sensible. In a letter to a friend, dated June 3, 1857, she wrote: "The costume of woman should be suited to her wants and necessities. It should conduce at once to her health, comfort and usefulness; and, while it should not fail also to conduce to her personal adornment, it should make that end of secondary importance."

As you see, this was not a woman adept at comic turns of phrase, but you know how easy it is to amuse men — they'll laugh at anything in pants.

In the twentieth century, we have learned that laughter does not always indicate a sense of humor. Humor is that deep sense of the absurd which leads at last to the well of tragic irony. Laughter can be many things. It can express contempt and derision and is often used to belittle those one wishes to gain power over. Women themselves can be afraid of humor. As Djuna Barnes writes in her novel *Nightwood*: "Any woman with a sense of humor is a lost woman."

Sigmund Freud defined humor as rebellion: "It signifies the triumph not only of the ego, but also of the pleasure principle, which is strong enough to assert itself here in the face of the adverse real circumstance." Humor is courage. Courage to face adverse real circumstances like the defeat of the Equal Rights Amendment.

The Equal Rights Amendment reads simply: "Equality of rights under the law shall not be denied or abridged by the United States or by any State on account of sex." That's all it says. But obviously it's not funny. As Cato the Elder observed in 195 B.C.: "Suffer women once to arrive at an equality with you, and they will from that moment become your superiors." Sharp old dude.

The subordination of women and the control of sexual need is the first duty of any authoritarian state. Laughter is one of the tools used to keep women in their place. Women laughed when Flo Kennedy said, "A woman without a man is like a fish without a bicycle," and "If men could get pregnant, abortion would be a sacrament." The men did not laugh. They put together punitive legislation and called it "Family Protection Act" and "Human Life Amendment." Woman-hatred or plain old misogyny became more subtle. Feminists and in particular lesbian feminists became the subject of derisive laughter. Men assured the "real" women that they were still in the club. It's the old divide-and-conquer game. Once it was the whores who were "other." Today it's feminists. The male-identified women, the ladies, stand by their men.

Exhibit A is our First Lady. (It takes a gentleman to make a lady, a bitch makes it on her own?) Nancy Reagan should by rights, provide us with a source of laughter. What is depressing is that the masses seem to be taken in. She's fixed up the White House to look like Elizabeth Arden's and no one seems to notice how vulgar it is

Nancy behaves like a socialite, not a statesperson. As some wag once said: "The rich are always with her." She and Ronnie are like aged Ken and Barbie dolls. She says he never worries, sleeps like a baby. He calls her "Mommy" and basks in what journalists have called "The Gaze," that glazed look she turns on him in public. She provides the essential service of the professional wife: she's a flak-catcher. He's the one with the bomb. She's the one who tells him what to do with it? This iron mannequin is always cold, turning the heat up to 85° or 87°, according to some reports. Nancy represents the triumphant return of the total woman (totalled, that is), the flip side of the male jock. Men can dismiss her as an airhead. Or detest her for interfering. She and her husband make a perfect team. Together they are Mr. and Mrs. America grown old, gone senile, living in a film noir like a couple on a crumbling wedding cake, gone stale, dinosaurs in human drag.

Any of this funny? Afraid not. Remember what Dorothy Parker told us: "I heard someone say, and so I said it too, that ridicule is the most effective weapon. Well, now I know. I know that there are things that never have been funny, and never will be. And I know that ridicule may be a shield, but it is not a weapon."

What kind of weapon is needed? Moral outrage? Denise Levertov has said that there comes a time when only anger is love. What do women do with their anger? They hold meetings to discuss such things. Last time I went to such a meeting, I said to a young woman who wept and asked us what we thought she should do with her anger — "Have you looked into international terrorism?" She thought I was being facetious. Actually, she finally admitted she just wanted to meet men who were different.

I gave her a copy of *The Bitch Manifesto*, written by Joreen in 1970. Essential to being a Bitch is not only having an irrepressible sense of humor, it is the quality of being always a subject, never an object. Joreen writes that Bitches "may have a relationship with a person or organization, but they never *marry* anyone or anything: man, mansion, or movement. . . . Like the term nigger, bitch serves the social function of isolating and discrediting a class of people who do not conform to the socially accepted patterns of behavior. . . . To the extent to which they (men) relate to her (the bitch) as a human being, they refuse to relate to her as a sexual being. Thus she is not a 'true woman.' Our society made women into slaves and then condemned them for acting like slaves. Those who refuse to act like slaves they disparage for not being true women."

Bitches are the women who know what hit them. Bitches are the ones who are in on the joke. Once a woman figures out what is really going on, she can never go home again.

When love is tyranny, revolution is order.

THESE ARE THE HOLLOW MEN

A fallen god is not a man: he is a fraud. . . . They (males) would
not seem to be dwarfs if they had not been asked to be giants.
Simone de Beauvoir
The Second Sex (1949)

I was talking with some young men in the coffeehouse one day. They were young enough to be my kids. Well, they were under thirty. One said he was having all kinds of trouble getting girls. The guy he was with apologized for him and explained to me that what his friend meant was that he had trouble *meeting women*. This second young man was fully aware that women tend to react strongly to what they *hear*. Men respond almost entirely to what they *see*. Most women want to know that the men they relate to aren't idiots. Thus the smart fellow watches what he says, taking care not to give himself away (literally). Oscar Wilde once said that to be articulate is to be found out. Often men maintain silence and withhold themselves as a way of dominating women. This masculine imperturbability devastates some women who do not understand that it is in part a defensive tactic. Many women suffer from a culturally induced sense of inferiority and they are conditioned to try to please. When men feel inferior, they often withdraw. It is curious that the rare male who exposes himself emotionally, who expresses his feelings lavishly and freely, is more often than not taken for a fool. The man who loses himself in love is often a turn-off and the woman involved may become disenchanted and flee. After all, all-for-love is *her* role.

The first young man at my table in the coffeehouse sighs and complains about his last date. He insists he did all the politically correct things—he even *let* her pay her own way. The second young man straightens him out and recommends some research. Then he defers to my opinion. I suggest Simone de Beauvoir's book *The Second Sex* for starters. Simone asks the existential question of all time: "Are there women really?" Published in France in 1949 and in the U.S. in 1953, this book is especially useful for male beginners because it is distanced, charming, and French. First of all, it appeals to men because de Beauvoir's subscript is masculine.

Her sympathies are with men intellectually because she is basically bored with her own sex. Not with herself, only with women in general. She hung out with Jean Paul Sartre most of his life.

She has the trick, so particular to French women, of combining intellect with sensuality without the seams showing. She is also dead wrong some of the time. This stimulates the young to make corrections and bring her up-to-date. Of course, it's not her fault that recent research into prehistory has altered much of her data. Her intentions are good and most of what she says holds up today. She has little compassion for lesbians: "They act like men in a world without men." Yet, she sees clearly that they are free to get their work done as often as not and that there is a sort of practicality in such relationships. She saves her wrath for the heterosexual woman in love: "Every woman in love is more or less paranoiac." Most important, she studies in great depth, as did her lover Jean Paul, the monumental issue of Bad Faith between lovers.

For Simone, bad faith means (1) setting oneself up as the sole essential for another; (2) respect for women's lies, even those touchingly awkward and comic behaviors which result from women's dependent condition (if she's going to wear those silly shoes, let her break her neck). She writes that the courtesan's inner life is a monument to bad faith. Such a woman's whole life is a show without spontaneity or real emotion. Such women are performers, masks. By extension we see this can be true of the lives of many modern wives. In turn, the bad faith of their lovers/husbands is evidenced by a need to demand from women that which is missing in themselves. Finally, bad faith is the imposition of one's ideals and expectations on another. The dream of a lost parent found again in a lover, or the desire to have one's significant other act out one's own myth, perform in one's own play—these are the expressions of bad faith which both sexes indulge in.

Both the young men at my table agreed with this assessment of the situation. They said they weren't about to put on an act for any woman. No, indeed. I thought for a while of my parents and a time that seems now quite archaic, a time when there were even more illusions than we have today. My mother thought that masculine meant strength and feminine meant refinement. She read a lot and she knew that for most people, gender was more habit than style. For the ordinary men and women of my youth, there was none of the self-consciousness of Simone and Jean Paul. In the conventional world, men grow up to be stuffy and women grow up to be sweet.

Simone feels that many women do not have authentic being because they are not the authors of their own existence. She is particularly hard on women writers. She accuses them of being seductive. "Writing or smiling is all one to them." She states that *Wuthering Heights*, in spite of its grandeur, does not have the sweep of *The Brothers Karamazov*. Again she falls into the error of measuring rather than thinking. If man is the measure of all things, then woman can never been his equal because she can never be the same.

At this juncture, we were joined by a New Woman. She put her hiking boots up on the table, Hemingway style, and appraised both men with a bright eye.

"Either one of you guys want to come over tonight? I'm having a party to celebrate moving into my new loft." Both the young men demurred, although the second fellow said he hoped he'd see her around again some time real soon (so *he* could make the first move next time?). Both men swallowed their coffee and split. She looked after them with an expression of mixed regret and relief. We quickly spread our work out across the table and went over some copy as both of us were facing deadlines the next day. We scribbled in silence for more than an hour. When it was time to get up and go home, I asked her if she was really having a party to celebrate her new loft.

"Actually, I moved in six months ago," she said, "but you know how it is, a forward pass gives me all the space I need every time out."

THINGS WERE MORE FUN IN THE OLD DAYS

> The history of men's opposition to women's emancipation is
> more interesting perhaps than the story of that emancipation itself.
> Virginia Woolf
> *A Room of One's Own*

Today the battle of the sexes is being waged with much nostalgia by a pair of old Lefties in their fifties. They sip their cappucinos at the *Med*, Berkeley's *Caffe Mediterraneum*.

She: (Watching the parade of Telegraph Avenue types as they pass by the picture window.) Didn't this place used to be called the *Forum*?

He: No, that was another coffeehouse, across the street somewhere. Back in the '50s.

She: I've been reading Linda Simon's biography of Alice B. Toklas. Simon says some of Alice's old San Francisco pals hung out in the *Forum* during the '50s. A sculptress, Annette Rosenshine, had an entourage there. Alice didn't much care for her sculpture. When Rosenshine visited Alice and Gertrude in Paris, Alice set the sculptures in a far-off corner of a large room and turned the lights down so low Gertrude didn't have to look at them.

He: Sounds catty to me.

She: Or kind.

He: What I liked best about Telegraph Avenue in those days was Pauline Kael's Cinema Guild. It was my first chance to see foreign films. I could always get a date for an Ingmar Bergman movie.

She: Not with me. I'll take Hollywood any day. Last night I was watching that old Howard Hawks' movie, *I Was A Male War Bride* (1949) with Cary Grant. Now *that's* a feminist film.

He: Howard Hawks once did a television interview with Dick Cavett. I remember Dick Cavett accused him of portraying women sympathetically and they got to talking about women's lib.

She: *Liberation* dear heart. Four syllables inspire respect. *Lib* is some land where the whores play basketball with the lesbians — strictly a male fantasy.

He: Well, whatever. Anyhow Hawks said the libbers were right and all that, but they were no fun.

She: Neither were the abolitionists! It's hard to sink the boat when everybody's having such a good time. Somebody has to get wet.

He: That isn't what Hawks meant. I know how he feels. He's saying that today's feminists are unattractive. They have no joy or charm.

She: To me they are the most romantic women around. What you're saying is that they don't appeal to male vanity. They don't court male approval. If I remember correctly, the Black Panthers weren't very attractive to white people when they got those automatic weapons and strutted around the Sacramento legislature back in the '60s.

He: Well, that was done for theater, to make a political point. It was sure as hell dramatic.

She: You mean they scared people. Male rage is legitimate. You guys all respect prick power. Pussy power is simply *not power*. It's a contradiction in terms.

He: Women's power is not overt. It's intrinsic. It comes from just *being* women, having the innate power to create life. You don't have to display your power the way men do. You don't have to prove anything.

She: I never said I did. I don't want to push. I've told you again and again, I only want *not to be pushed around*. I want my life. I want my kid's life. And I could use a little help from you once in a while. Men have got to do some of the washing up in the world.

He: It's nice to be righteous but I don't think you're going to alter human nature much. It seems to me that if women want men to nurture the world, which means they just want men to love *them*, if they want some serious husbandry, well they just have to make themselves lovable. How else are they gonna motivate men?

She: Or move mountains. Still the same old poop. You and my second husband both. Why is it you always argue that you have to be *won*? Is it my job to make you act like a real man? I'll tell you what. If you'll have the babies, then you can *be* the boss and I'll devote all my time to helping you raise your family and save the world. If you'll just have the kids, then you can call all the shots. I'll be your wife, secretary, nurse, handmaiden, breadwinner, you name it.

He: You were a lot more fun in the old days.

She: Back when I needed you to approve of me? Back when I was scared to death of losing my looks?

He: "For me, dear friend, you never can be old. . . ." And I'll never forget how you looked in that blue sunsuit.

She: And when my hair too, is blue?

He: *Age cannot wither her, nor custom stale her infinite* veracity. . . .

She: God how I needed men to give me confidence.

He: You needed the approval. You were rebelling against your father, just to get his approval. It's the naughty daughter neurosis. He expected it of you when you were a kid and after he died you just went right on making scenes. Do you remember what you were doing when I met you?

She: Vaguely. I joined WITCH. (Women's International Terrorist Conspiracy from Hell.)

He: And SCUM (Society for Cutting Up Men). And now you're acting with that group from the Plutonium Players.

She: Ladies Against Women. It's satire. See my button: "Save the Males." We try to get to the events where Phyllis Schlafly and her crowd hang out. We wear pillbox hats and white gloves and say a lot of silly submissive things. It's consciousness-raising.

He: Robin Tyler is the only feminist comic I've seen. I don't think she's very funny.

She: Not to you dear. She says that by the time a woman is strong enough to live with a man, she's the kind of woman no man wants to live with. I think that just about sums up our situation don't you?

He: Who said anything about living together.

She: Want to go to the movies?

He: What's playing?

She: How about *The Big Sleep*?

He: Sure. I'll even fix breakfast.

SINS OF THE FATHERS

Even now, when fathers kill their sons—at home, at war—the psychologists say, 'Oh, but the father really meant to kill his own father, the child's grandfather. It was only a case of mistaken Oedipal identity.' Young soldiers lie dead, sent there by commanding father-figures. How proud, how sad their fathers are: their fathers who never meant them any harm....

... Only yesterday, I asked a male psychiatrist to tell me about the male fear of male violence. He said that *that* wasn't the problem at all. No, what really frightened him were the gangs of teenage girls who took up the whole sidewalk! No, he said, lighting his pipe, it is *women* that men fear most of all.

Phyllis Chesler, M.D.
About Men (1978)

(Once more we are in the coffeehouse. He and She are ending their affair, with a touch of angst for the memory. They are also finishing a course in political theory. He is reading a letter from his father. She is skimming through Gabriel Garcia Marquez's *The Autumn of the Patriarch* (1975).

He: I thought you said you were only going to read women's books for this course.
She: Only?
He: You know what I mean.
She: Yes, I'm afraid I do.
He: Oh, for crissake, it's not my fault I was born anatomically other. (He carefully puts the letter he has been reading into his backpack.)
She: Maybe. (She looks closely at him.) Your father still at it?
He: (Ignores this.) Is that the book about the fall of the phallic state? (Note: In Kate Millett's *Sexual Politics* she mentions the psychoanalytic term for the generalized adolescent tone of men's house culture—"phallic state." The phallic state is a citadel of virility, which reinforces the most saliently power-oriented characteristics of patriarchy.)

She: It's about the death-principle. Kind of a cult thing. You know, totalitarianism, nuclear technology, the world we live in. It's a real inside view of a total dictator. Read it when you get a chance.

He: You really think a guy's eye view of power can ever be objective?

She: No, but that doesn't mean it isn't true.

He: Cute. You really think the male power trip is congenital don't you? Pregenital more likely, some kind of caveman script, a sort of testosterone overdose.

She: Did you know testis is literally "witness"—The dictionary reads "witness (to virility)" as if somebody had to prove it.

He: You *are* a bitch, you know that.

She: Why must you take every damn thing so *personally*. You're so emotional. It's your burnt-child reflex.

He: It *feels* personal. Especially when you keep saying it's males who want to blow up the world.

She: Well, not all of them. But a few will do. You've got to work on your perspective. You're too touchy. Listen, when I was involved in the Civil Rights Movement, I didn't get all hung up when I ran into black people who rejected whites. I mean, I figured they had their reasons. Why can't you feel that way about feminists?

He: You can't generalize that way.

She: Like hell I can't. I know what I see. I've seen two black males rape me and I don't get them mixed up with *the race*. I don't go around hating black men. Just rapists. You act as if women are out to get you just because that little snit Peggy turned you down again last weekend and her mother sneered at you on the phone. When you're hurt, you sulk and you react subjectively to everything around you and you don't even know it. Gracious Goddess, *think*! Just because one woman cuts you up, doesn't mean you can condemn the sex. You're supposed to be a scholar. You've written papers on the historical oppression of women.

He: Women have their compensations.

She: So do farmworkers!

He: I'm going to tell you something. I hope you won't say anything to anyone. Peggy's mother told the campus police I should be watched. Can you tell me why?

She: If I were Peggy's mother, I might have done the same thing. I can't imagine what I'd do if I had an eighteen year old daughter to worry about.

He: (A rather long pause. He lights a cigarette.) Do you honestly believe that I am a danger to any woman? Do you really think I'd *hurt* a woman?

She: You've hurt me, off and on, for three years.

He: That's only true if you want to believe it. You've always done exactly what you wanted.

She: What are we talking about? Let's just once talk about what we're talking about.

He: I've never forced myself on you. I've never hung around when you didn't want me.

She: What are we talking about?

He: You tell me.

She: I've got a book for you.

He: I'm not interested in any more angry feminists. They just depress me.

She: This book is about fathers and sons. It's Phyllis Chesler's *About Men*.

He: A woman is going to tell me about men?

She: Chesler's a psychiatrist. She wrote *Women and Madness* in 1972. That was the book that blew the whistle on the psychiatric professionals who oppress women. In *About Men* she examines males from four points of view: mytho-poetic, visual, autobiographical, and traditional psychological. She says that fear of their fathers breaks men's lives. Mostly it's unconscious and the fallout from this relationship is one of the things which breaks women's hearts.

He: Women's hearts never break. You're made of iron. What's that line you always use: the woman with an iron whim. Is it a whim to give birth to these sons-of-bitches? You're the source you know. Talk about aggressivity! What is more violent than procreation?

She: We're more than half the problem, that's for sure and certain. Listen to what Chesler says: "The color of the sky over Hiroshima, over Nagasaki — a color I never saw, a color that has shaped my generation's mood. The strange red of that sky. The red color of black children's blood in Birmingham; the red-stained color of My Lai; and the bloodless color of Auschwitz smoke; gray, black, wordless; of Dauchau smoke: gray, black, worldless, across the European sky. All, all these colors have been painted by fathers and sons, by 'bonded' and by womb-less men. ... How shall I speak of woman's involvement? Woman's complicity in man's battle against herself? Woman's profit from, indifference to, phobic fear of the public or 'male' arena, which alone determines the quality of the air her children breathe,

the quality of the food her children eat, whether her children will live or die, and certainly the quality of her own and other women's survival. Ah, but this is not a book about women."

He: Maybe I'll read some of it this weekend.

She: Anyway, read the section about Chesler's marriage to an Iranian in 1961. It isn't her young husband who destroys the marriage, it's her husband's father, an old patriarch who acts like someone in the *Old Testament*. Chesler is almost in love with him by the time she pulls herself together and splits back to the U.S.

He: (After a pause.) My father has always been decent to the women I know.

She: How many does he know?

He: Well, he met my wife the first year we were married. And once after the divorce. He took us out to dinner both times. (Pause.) Well, he did what he thought was right. (Grim laugh.) He has this structured belief system he got from his father. He still wants me to "make something of myself." (Lights another cigarette.) Shit, he doesn't feel a thing when he writes me these crappy letters about the grandiose nature of my failure to live up to expectations. (His voice breaks.) Shit, wait till he hears the cops have me on their list of those most likely to molest young girls.

She: (Puts her hand over his.) Jesus. I really am sorry. Honestly.

He: (Stung, he snatches his hand away.) Oh, fuck off. (He exits abruptly, brushing against the couple entering the coffeehouse.)

She: (Puts out his cigarette and moves his cup to the next table. Then she reads to herself from Chesler's book.) "And slowly I began to understand that father-wounded sons never recover, never confess, never remember; slowly, I began to understand why women can never satisfy the longing of boys who are love-starved for their fathers; women can never exorcise the grief of men, lured by their fathers into wanting the impossible . . . a magic male amulet, a son's shield against the rising hot shame of childhood vulnerability." (She gets up and orders another cappucino.) The poor son-of-a-bastard.

EMERGING WOMEN

During the mid '70s I wrote for a magazine called *City Miner,* the brainchild of Mike Helm, who is today a Bay Area book publisher. I have included two representative articles from 1976 and '77. Both are interviews done with what was then called 'emerging women,' that is, women who work for themselves. In the interview with the poet Alta, I asked her where she sees herself ten years hence. She says she never sees herself in ten years but now I do and she is flourishing and has become a great pal. She is selling Shameless Hussy Press, one of the first feminist publishing houses to make it in the '70s. She has other fish to fry. Jean Shelton's Acting School was in Berkeley when I did the interview with her in 1977. Today, in 1988, she has moved to a glamorous location in San Francisco. She and I have both quit smoking.

ALTA: SHAMELESS HUSSY

Winter, 1976

I'm meeting Alta for dinner at the Tora-Ya restaurant in Berkeley. I try to remember how I felt about her work the first time I read it. I want to tell her it was a liberating experience. I want to say that she gave me courage when I needed it, that I was a closet scribbler and her poems and short stories seemed to give me the right to write in my own language. In her work was the beginning of my understanding of women's shared experience. I know there is a core of fear in women. Nearly every woman I know wears a mask to hide fear and pain. Alta seemed to burn away the mask (while the more decadent burned their bras?). I found her books by instinct. I think she was more read than talked about at first. At least by me. I was shocked. Lines like

> don't bother coming over,
> my box is zipped tight
> front to back

stunned me with their toughness. It is impossible to romanticize Alta, something I have always done with women poets. She said things I felt, but without touch-ups, without being pretty while she was doing it. It was Picasso or Gertrude Stein who said the first time a thing is done it will seem ugly. The others will come along and do the same thing but the shock will be gone and so they can make it beautiful. I put Alta's poems on tapes with Sappho's, Edna St. Vincent Millay's, and Christina Rossetti's, and I listened to them all for a long time. Discovering Alta through such books as *Letters to Women, No Visible Means of Support, Song of the Wife, Song of the Mistress*, was discovering that there was a woman going through what I was going through and admitting it, yelling it. She wrote directly from personal experience (or made me believe she did) without transmutation or changing the names to protect the guilty. She writes what she knows. (Most poets don't know much and they won't even tell the truth about *that*.) Reading these books from Alta's own press (Shameless Hussy) brought the shock of recognition. I got the same shock reading Christina Rossetti for the first time. This recognition had nothing to do with style or subject. It had to do with human integrity. It had to do with expressing the deepest feelings the writer is capable of. That's what I need to hear when a poet speaks.

> *come honest to the bone.*
> *peel away the lies*
> *(i'm afraid)*
> *—be yr stone self & i will always like you. . . .*

One night I was counting the pills and downing the bourbon and feeling sorry for myself because some man had let me down. I came across these lines:

> *there is a down*
> *that doesnt get back up every time*
> *if you get there &*
> *dont see anybody else you*
> *forget the way out if you*
> *let go the string & the maze*
> *is all around you, you can*
> *let yourself die of it.*
> *we must all be very careful*
> *not to destroy ourselves. . .*

When we met for dinner, I thought I might thank Alta for using her pain to educate me. Then I considered that might be too personal an observation for an interview. So we ate. We talked about children and money and women and men and the meaning of it all. I was comforted to find that Alta agrees with me that dinner at one of Berkeley's favorite Japanese restaurants has a lot to do with the meaning of it all. The katsu curry is swell.

Jennifer Stone: Here we are eating ourselves into oblivion in a Japanese restaurant. Today is August 6th, 1975. Thirty-one years ago today we (the U.S. military, Harry Truman, somebody in Washington) dropped the first atom bomb in history on the city of Hiroshima. Do you think we've been forgiven?

Alta: According to my Japanese friends, no. They haven't forgiven us for the camps, either. But neither have many Americans forgiven Japan or Germany. Those things take more than one generation to heal.

JS: Are you a feminist?

Alta: There's only one way to answer that: yes.

JS: What, for you, is feminism?

Alta: Feminism is not being ashamed of being a woman and not using woman as a swear word. It also means not hating women you don't approve of simply because you don't approve of them. Finally, I think it means turning to women for comfort and when you have comfort to give, sharing it with women.

JS: Why do feminists fight among themselves? Is this a bad thing?

Alta: Ghetto behavior: hit those who won't hit back. Sure it's bad.

JS: How do you feel about competition among women writers? Does it hurt our work? Does it hurt our friendships?

Alta: Women are usually supportive of each other's work. We were taught to compete and be jealous, but luckily it usually didn't take.

(Picking tofu out of the bottom of my soup bowl, I ask Alta for a biography, the events or the history of her life.)

Alta: I was raised in Reno, Nevada. My mother and father owned a piano shop. We had to move to California when I was twelve because my brother is blind and there were no schools for him in Nevada. We came to live here so he could go to the California School for the Blind in Berkeley, which is how I ended up in the Bay Area.

JS: Were you happy here?

Alta: I was very happy in high school. I went to U.C. about 1960. They tried to flunk me out. They had to flunk out forty percent of their freshmen (freshpersons?) in order to hang onto their funds. I talked back in class. I was a working-class kid. I didn't feel at home until I joined a student co-op where I met some of the people who have become lifetime friends, like Susan Griffin, Sarita Waite, Sue Bender.

I quit school to go teach in the South in Prince Edward County, Virginia. Segregation had closed the public schools; whites set up private schools and so I went to try to set up schools for blacks. Obviously they didn't need some white chick from California. I found out my job was to fight racism in my own community among whites. It was good to learn, but I was embarrassed and sorry I hadn't known it off the top.

JS: It was a lesson a lot of us had to learn in the '60s. What did you do after your missionary period?

> she and i each got married
> it was the only job we could find

Alta: My first marriage.

JS: Let's have another cup of tea.

Alta: I was amazed that I got suckered in so completely. The suburbs, monogamy, constant housework; you can become a frigin' yoga alone like that.

> *for a minute, i thot my neighbor was*
> *coming over.*
> *but it's ok, she was just walking to her edge*
> *of the grass.*

I vacuumed the whole house every day. I washed the windows every two weeks.

JS: I know. I used a Q-Tip to clean the aluminum edges of my windows. What made you, what made both of us, do it?

Alta: I didn't know I had a choice. School stunk. If I got a job I was immediately fired. Marriage was better than working for a living. One good thing though. I was happy with my daughter. We had more time together than we've ever had since. I miss that.

JS: So how long did this go on?

Alta: Five years, until 1967.

JS: What happened?

Alta: My husband left me.

JS: Were you glad to be free? Of marriage? Of him?

Alta: Up to that time, it was the worst experience of my life. I'd thrown myself into marriage. I'd given up other men, writing, music almost entirely, the integrity of my body — I was always on a diet, I bleached my hair. It was like studying for a test, answering every question correctly and getting an F.

JS: You didn't want to escape the marriage then?

Alta: I suppose I'd still be there if he hadn't left me. Maybe not.

JS: You moved to Berkeley and then back to the suburbs. Why did that happen?

Alta: Well, John (Simon) and I were living together and he couldn't stand the anti-Semitism of the suburbs, not to mention the anti-everything else. When I lived in Berkeley, I helped form a women's commune as a refuge for women who were coming out of bad marriages. It was there that I began Shameless Hussy Press. Certain women in the house threatened me. After they kicked me out, four of them told me that if I didn't give them money, they would destroy my press.

i stepped into the ring
cause i thot poet of the people,
responsibility of the voice to listen
to the mind.
very revolutionary i thot.
they beat me up.
don't know what i expected.

JS: How did you survive after being kicked out of the commune?
Alta: Actually I lived on the street. I whored for three months.
JS: Do you want me to write that?
Alta: Oh, sure.

At this point we left the restaurant and moved on to a coffeehouse on Berkeley's Northside. We sat down with cappucinos. Alta, as she had done in the Japanese restaurant, sat up against the wall, this time in a corner. She rubbed her wooden bracelet and began filling in the pages I had with me. Pages about writers she admired, writers she was reading. Dorothy Parker, Hemingway, and film books by Lillian Gish, Anita Loos and David Niven.

JS: If you could make a recommended reading list, who would be on top?
Alta: All the hussies: Susan Griffin, Ntozake Shange, Jerry Ratch, Mitzuye Yamada, George Sand, Calamity Jane, Paul Mariah, etc.
JS: Who taught you the most?
Alta: My children. And of course my parents.
JS: Why aren't your children living with you now?
Alta: They say life in the suburbs is the pits. They live with their father during the week. It is very painful for me to see them only on weekends. I feel powerless to stop the damage I can see being done to them by others. My younger daughter's laugh was so free. People tell her, don't laugh so loud. My father and my aunt always gave me permission to laugh, to be myself. I want to give that to my daughters.
JS: Do you have any gods? Any people or beliefs or principles which are sacred to you?
Alta: Let's pick a field so I can limit it. I'm so pantheistic we have to limit it somehow. All the old staples like truth and love and work and family and cappucino in a white cup. All people are sacred, although I don't like everybody equally. I wish no one any harm. (People only hurt each other when they're in a state of misery. Like everyone, when I fall out of grace I am

harmful. I need love everyday, just to maintain.)

JS: For many writers (particularly women), economic survival is a lifetime struggle. How do you pay your bills?

Alta: Except for short periods, I've always lived my adult life with a man who has a job. I am unemployable so I don't have a choice of jobs.

JS: In an interview in the last (July) issue of *City Miner*, Lawrence Ferlinghetti stated he felt poets should live in such a way as not to need government grants. Do you agree with him?

Alta: I assume I wouldn't get money if I asked. I did ask twice. The first time they told me I was nobody and they didn't give nobody grants. The second time (a year later) they told me I was too established.

JS: You're in your mid-thirties now. Where do you see yourself in ten years?

Alta: I never see myself in ten years.

JS: That was a dumb question. Who loved you most of all?

Alta: The people I felt loved by were not necessarily the ones who loved me. And different people have loved different sections of me. But so far my children have loved the total person that I am more than any adult ever has.

JS: Who hurt you most in your life?

Alta: The people I let into my heart. Especially the women at the commune [in Berkeley following her second divorce] who kicked me out. And my husbands.

JS: I want to take some random shots. I want to know if you like what I like. How do you feel about Gertrude Stein? Anais Nin?

Alta: Stein is brilliant but classist and sexist. Anais Nin has compassion as great as her talent.

JS: Do you think men are equal to women and if so in which ways?

Alta: Physical strength. I have never met a non-emotionally crippled man. The world will not change until fathers can love their sons. I think it's inhuman to ask a woman oppressed by her husband to love and raise a boy child.

JS: I have male children and I agree with you. The best I can do is raise them by myself. They still have to take a lot of anger from me that should be directed at adult males who oppress me. How would you want things to be for your daughters in, say, ten years?

Alta: I hope they won't have to relate to the type of men who exist now.

JS: How could they? Everything will be different.

Alta: Will it?

JS: What are your priorities? Day by day. What about the children?

Alta: How do I put together mothering and writing? Sporadically. I have just about given up hope of having a normal life.

JS: Do you really want one?

Alta: Yes. I wish my children could be with me whenever we wanted; I wish I were employable, so that not having a job would have been a choice rather than an inescapable situation. I wish the lovers I've had had not punished me for every success and I wish people didn't hate me on sight.

My main priority is to get through the day feeling good. It seems to be an almost impossible demand. My pal Reba says, "If the world would just stop stopping us, we could be innocent and pure, instead of all this wasted energy and grief."

JS: Is there any way you can describe your creative process, how it has changed or developed? What was most important in the beginning? What is most important now?

Alta: I can't remember the beginning. I've been creating all my life. The most important things are space, time, and people who care. My aunt, who was my piano teacher, was very encouraging. She was one of those who loved me most. I was praised all my life, especially by my family, until I got married.

> *take me to the woods sometime instead of*
> *your girlfriend/see how you like it.*
> *what is this role WIFE that turns women bitter.*
> *mrs. dan bosserman. mrs. john simon.*
> *does anybody know my name?*

JS: Tell about Shameless Hussy Press.

Alta: There are some things simpler in the world than publishing a book but not many. Even so, there are only four nationwide women's presses in the U.S. when there should be at least three dozen. There are not enough support systems for women.

JS: You plan for the press to continue without you: Why do you want to drop out of Shameless Hussy Press?

Alta: I want to make a movie. I've made five videotapes and one of those has been made into a film. The next one will be feature length. It's an adventure story called *Pauline and the Mysterious Pervert.* It's about a woman who fights back almost all the time.

JS: Why would you want to make movies and videotapes instead of more books?

Alta: You can play with the knobs.

JS: What about the ultimate taboo? What about death?

Alta: Well, the latest news is that it's not as bad as we've been taught. My latest information is that once dead your fellow spirits cannot mess with you the way people can when you're alive. That is, the state you achieve by the time you die will stay with you.

> printing alone nitetime in the garage
> with a moth for company
> suicidally banging herself against the light.

JS: Alta, you say a moth came to you when your father was dying and told you death is no tragedy but dying is hard. I can't believe that death is anything but a great void of non-being and dying is hard because everyone struggles to hang onto consciousness no matter how great the pain.

Alta: One of my students who's a nurse told me about a patient at Alta Bates who died on the operating table and was revived. The patient was very angry. She said, "How dare you, I could almost see the light at the end of the tunnel!" So the next time Becky had to save a life, she patted the lady on the shoulder first, "Excuse me, but it's my job," and gave her mouth-to-mouth resuscitation.

JS: Do you feel the woman writer of today has a special responsibility, either to feminism or to anything else? Say to the abolition of nationalism?

Alta: If a writer is not willing to recreate, to create something new, then there is no point. If she's going to write like Norman Mailer, why bother?

JS: Gertrude Stein says, "If a thing can be done why do it." What kind of vision do you think women might have?

Alta: A vision of what *can* be. A world where everybody cares about everybody else and no one is done in by violence of any kind.

JS: I've heard people say there is too much pain in your poetry. How do you feel about that?

Alta:

> You think weeping sounds bad,
> you should hear me laugh.

A CONVERSATION WITH JEAN SHELTON

17 April, 1977

Jean and I sit in Walker's Pie Shop on Solano Avenue. We go through our usual rationalizations about food; she has the diet special and I have pumpkin pie with whipped cream. She tells me she's going to Europe this summer and certainly there is no question that Europe looks better if you're thin.

In case anyone is unfamiliar with the theater scene hereabouts, I should say that Jean Shelton's Acting School is a phenomenon unique in the Bay Area. Jean's classes began at the Berkeley Repertoire Company in 1968. I remember at that time there were a number of actors, including myself, who wanted to work intensively. Jean was asked to teach. We met and worked. The school moved to a church on Prince Street and finally to its present location at 8th and Dwight. When this move was made in 1974, the need was felt to create a Performance Workshop which evolved into The Playhouse Company. The school is lodged in a mammoth warehouse which required a fervor of group effort to shape into a theater. It is now complete with classrooms, work space, storage space, and room to expand.

Sitting across the table from me, Jean reminds me for a moment of an innocent Jeanne Moreau. I've known her for more than ten years now. I just realized we have the same initials. How can I type this interview? Last names.

Ms. Stone: Jean, how did you come to the theater?

Ms. Shelton: When I was 19 and at the end of a marriage, my father left me $2000 and I couldn't decide whether to go to Europe or to go to New York and become an actress. I had never taken any drama in college, never seen any theater. I was trying to write, for some reason.

Stone: Isn't everyone?

Shelton: The theater was fascinating to me so I decided to spring the money on that. I was very naive. Marriage offered little that was exciting.

The theater seemed the opposite of everything I'd known up to that time.

Stone: Is theater a place where women can grow?

Shelton: I suppose it's the search for identity. That's certainly always been my problem. An artist, an actress, struggling with a part is very similar to a woman searching for herself. In acting you begin to search for what you feel and what you want and in essence who you are. It's very strange because a lot of people think, well, actors, they have no identity, playing all those different roles, but it's not true. There's a focus, Jennifer, and I have a number of younger women tell me that going through this process has really changed them. As people they want to be more independent. The introspection required, the self-study, can't help but raise their awareness. Of course, women can be victims in theater as well as anywhere else — victims of their directors, of their fears.

Stone: So you chose the examined life over a trip to Europe. What if you go to Europe this summer and decide you made the wrong choice?

Shelton: Eat your pie.

Stone: Do you feel the success of your school and the theater is related to the growth movement, to the desire of a lot of people to do their own thing?

Shelton: Yes. So many people are frustrated. The world doesn't seem to have that much to offer. Jobs can be grim. Materialism is depressing. Where is the spiritual life going to come from, if not from the arts. Personally, I think the theater saved my life. Husbands come and go, lovers come and go, children grow up and go away. Work is the one constant, the thing that endures.

Stone: "We must go and work in the garden," says Voltaire. Sorry, I'm pontificating . During the '60s a lot of creative artists found themselves on the barricades instead of in the garden. There is a time for artists to express their political views directly and sometimes it's hard to know just when this should come about, as well as when the time is ripe for reflection and turning inward and the private vision. Since there is a lack of overt political expression just now, do you think this may be one reason for the renaissance in all the arts?

Shelton: Yes, we're more creative. When as many people in as tiny a town as Berkeley are working so hard creatively, something's happening. Of course we can't know what the result will be. Do you know there were scores of theaters functioning in the East Bay last year? It's impossible to keep posted on all the work that's going on.

Stone: And a lot of that work got its impetus from your school. So many students have studied with you and then gone out and created their own theaters. I think you have understood that's how things really change. Slowly through people.

Shelton: Communication is so difficult. In any relationship, with children, with a lover, whatever. In art, you're free to say what you feel and you don't have to censor yourself.

Stone: The mask gives you permission?

Shelton: At least it keeps you from getting arrested.

Stone: You have five children. How do you manage to be an entrepreneur? Do you have a housekeeper?

Shelton: If I did I'd have to clean up beforehand. No, I have too much guilt to let someone clean up my mess.

Stone: Isn't that a little socialist for someone from the South? So, after all is said and done, the dishes aren't? What about the children?

Shelton: They resisted when they were young. They wanted me home; everyone else's mother was home. With time they became proud of my work. They come and they criticize. They have their opinions, this or that stinks, you know; but they're proud that I've done the work.

Stone: Someone (Clarence Darrow?) says the first half of our lives is made miserable by our parents and the second half destroyed by our children. You've spent more than half your life raising children. Would you do it again?

Shelton: Let's talk about theater.

Stone: OK. Constantin Stanislavski says, among other things, "An Actor must work all his life, cultivate his mind, train his talents systematically, develop his character; he may never despair and never relinquish this main purpose —to love his art with all his strength and love it unselfishly." How do you imagine young actors reconcile statements like this with the success of Farrah Fawcett Major?

Shelton: I avoid the subject of commodities. The business of entertainment is one thing, the art of acting is another.

Stone: Last night I dug out my ancient college papers on Stanislavski. I got a B– on *The Actor Prepares* and an A on *Building a Character*, but after I read *My Life in Art* the professor told me to cool it. That was in 1952. Lot of blood under the bridge since then. You and I have talked so much about the evolution of the Method. Back in New York in the '50s, I can remember Method actors who were positively dangerous. I guess they began to believe themselves.

Shelton: Of course, putting your life in danger won't necessarily move an audience; and that's what acting is about. I think the Method is the best foundation for actors. The books (the works of Stanislavski) should be read like novels, not like the *Bible*. The Method has been glorified so much that actors have been intimidated. In class I try to demystify the art of acting. Of course if you totally believed you were the character you play on stage, you'd need a doctor. The Method is a technique, a structure, something to use to get you inside a character. An actor must have self-control, a sense of humor, and do the work. As in any art, no amount of inspiration or feeling, no matter how intense, will take the place of work.

Stone: But what about innate talent?

Shelton: Talent is what you know.

Stone: Don't you mean the *expression* of what you know? Or is that technique? I'm getting tangled in my words.

Shelton: I just want it said that art is not something mystic.

Stone: But you said the creative life is spiritual.

Shelton: I think I'll have a coke.

Stone: I agree with you, of course. The theater has always been my religion too. I was a child in the theater. Most of the joy and celebration in my early life centered around a stage. What is this feeling a lot of actors have, that the theater is home?

Shelton: Again, it's the question of identity. Some of us need the ritual, the celebration of the theater. Remember the theater grew out of religious ceremony. Sports grew out of the same experience. The conflict or the drama is the acting out of desires, the recreation of life.

Stone: When I was a kid I always put on plays in the back yard and made my parents and their friends come and watch. Do you think kids today get a chance to express themselves?

Shelton: Well, art is subversive by definition. Freedom of expression is political suicide if carried far enough. Our system depends on repression. Art is a way to get permission, to stand alone, individually, and say what is felt. It may make us feel good to break windows but there are consequences. There is a time to go to the barricades and there is a time to go back to the workshop.

Stone: Do people working in the theater have a responsibility to the audience, to the community?

Shelton: Certainly, I think theater people for the most part have always been very socially responsible. The playwright certainly communes with the public and the theater must serve the play.

Stone: What about your own choices? Actors, plays and so on.

Shelton: Lenny Bruce, Bob Dylan, Marlon Brando of course, Ingmar Bergman as film maker, Eugene O'Neill as playwright. . . .

Stone: The dark ones?

Shelton: Yes, I feel closer to them.

Stone: Can an actress expect to find better parts today than she did ten or twenty years ago?

Shelton: No. The parts are worse and there are fewer of them. There won't be more parts until more women are writing plays and getting them produced.

Stone: What about women as directors? I think actresses have always had some clout in theater, I mean for the last century or two, but I think it has been the power of the courtesan. Even if they had great talent, they charmed their way.

Shelton: A woman who wants to direct has to be brave enough to be the boss. An actor has presence, and certainly power, but it is the director who has the largest choices, the real impact. She creates the whole. Many women hesitate to take the initiative that strongly. They feel guilt, perhaps, or feel a director's role is unbecoming. I feel that women who do direct are just that: direct. They are forthright and specific. I don't mean you have to be a son-of-a-bitch. Women seem able to set aside their own needs for ego gratification and get on with the work.

Stone: How do you feel when you direct a play?

Shelton: It was a problem only in the beginning. Men test you at first. Does she know what she's doing? Now I can be whatever I want. It's the one area in my life where my freedom is absolute. I can be mama if that's what's needed. Actors believe me when I tell them what choices work.

Stone: You don't threaten the men in any way?

Shelton: Maybe it's my accent.

Stone: You know you have no accent.

Shelton: This conversation is getting a little too esoteric.

Stone: Before we go on I want to go back to where you said there are no parts for women. Ibsen had a few.

Shelton: Men don't understand women. It's hard to write about what you don't know. Maybe that's why Tennessee Williams comes closer than most, because he's homosexual.

Stone: You don't have to be gay but it helps?

Shelton: *Anything* helps. Sensitivity, perception, imagination.

Stone: What's in the future? Are you making new plans for the school?

Shelton: Yes. I want to use the Theater Metamorphose which we are renting at the moment. It's in the warehouse. I want to put together a directors' training workshop so we can experiment with new plays. It's all very well to train actors but we need talented directors if the work is to be done.

Stone: What about video tapes?

Shelton: Of course everyone wants to see themselves. I'm not sure how valuable video tape is. It's not so hot as a teaching tool. Perhaps if an actor has a continuing acting problem, a mannerism, the tape may help to point it out.

Stone: Don't you want to preserve a record of performances?

Shelton: I think the magnitude of the theater experience is its very transitory quality. It will happen only once and it will never happen the same way again. In live theater there is all the pain and humor and margin for error there is in life. I think that's why people love the theater. It's imperfect but it's alive. The audience is part of what's happening. When an actor feels an audience respond, her performance changes.

Stone: Sounds like a love affair.

Shelton: Isn't everything?

I went with Jean to her evening class and I talked with her students. They told me Jean's work is done with the utmost simplicity. Wisdom (says a Zen master) is skill in action. One student referred to The Jean Shelton School of Humility. When I asked him to explain, he said he did not mean humiliation but the quality of self-effacement that Jean demands from her actors and personifies in herself. "Ah," I said, "this is doubtless Stanislavski's ideal of one 'who loves the art in herself, not herself in art.'" The student quickly passed me on to someone else who told me her picture of Jean always included a Tab in one hand and a cigarette in the other. I asked her if she felt there was any sexism present here as everywhere, and she said, "Oh, no, the theater is so androgynous I never think of anything like that."

After class Jean and I went to her favorite pub for a denouement. We got a little lurid and talked about men and meaning and she even remembered an electric blanket I gave her once at the end of an affair. We had another sip of brandy and I asked how, with all the emotional ups and downs in her life, she managed to keep working day and night.

"Hell," she said, "just show me where I make my entrance."

GERTRUDE STEIN IN CIRCLES

Three familiar essays, like three roses, and all of them red.

GENIUS IS WHAT HAPPENS WHEN YOU'RE LOOKING FOR A WAY OUT

Civilization, said Gertrude Stein, begins with a rose. If art is civilized magic, then the three roses of Gertrude Stein are the magical mystery of modern poetry.

When Gertrude Stein was lecturing at the University of Chicago a young student in her seminar asked her for the meaning of "rose is a rose is a rose." This was her answer: "Now listen. Can't you see that when the language was new — as it was with Chaucer and Homer — the poet could use the name of a thing and the thing was really there. He could say 'O moon,' 'O sea,' 'O love,' and the moon and the sea and love were really there. And can't you see that after hundreds of years had gone by and thousands of poems had been written, he could call on those words and find that they were just wornout literary words. The excitingness of pure being had withdrawn from them; they were just rather stale literary words. Now the poet has to work in the excitingness of pure being; he has to get back that intensity into the language. We all know that it's hard to write poetry in a late age; and we know that you have to put some strangeness, as something unexpected, into the structure of the sentence in order to bring back vitality to the noun. Now it's not enough to be bizarre; the strangeness in the sentence structure has to come from the poetic gift too. That's why it's doubly hard to be a poet in a late age. Now you all have seen hundreds of poems about roses and you know in your bones that the rose is not there. ... Now I don't want to put too much emphasis on that line because it's just one line in a longer poem. But I notice that you all know it; you make fun of it, but you know it. Now listen! I'm no fool. I know that in daily life we don't go around saying '... is a ... is a. ...' Yes, I'm no fool; but I think that in that line the rose is red for the first time in English poetry for a hundred years." (Quoted by Thornton Wilder in his introduction to *Four in America*.)

Stein goes on in this lecture to explain that the excitingness of pure being is not the same as being excited. An artist, she says, must be exciting, not excited. Like history, this takes time.

One of the most common rebukes directed at Stein during her lifetime and even today is that she is/was precious—that she indulged in art for art's sake. Now I have to come right out and say that this is true, and there was never any question about it. Now listen! I'm not stupid. I know that in daily life today, art for art's sake is *verboten*: especially when there's no money in it.

The phrase is a curious one, if you think about it. In *L'Art pour l'Art*, written in 1834, Theopile Gautier denounced any art that intended to be utilitarian, to draw a moral or to serve any cause. Gautier wrote that anything useful is ugly, because the useful expresses *need*, and the needs of men, he concluded, are disgusting.

Well, I for one don't think Gertrude Stein found human needs disgusting. I imagine she believed artistic expression itself was a human need. She needed to think. She called her process conscious consciousness. At the same time she liked being the very human being that her little dog knew. Art did not dehumanize her. She adored all the bourgeois comforts as well as the bohemian and even the lesbian pleasures of living in Paris early in the century. She was very concerned about meeting all her own human needs, and she did not find them disgusting. She did distinguish between human nature and the human mind. For her, this distinction was not the mind/body cross of modern despair: it was the release from biological definitions, the liberation from sex roles, the freeing of her mind from the prison of her body. Much as she loved Alice Toklas, Gertrude was first and foremost a Steinist, a narcissist in the sense that she was in love with her own reflective soul. She said that human nature is not the human mind because she wished to sort out her thoughts and distinguish them from her feelings. Now as we know, this was probably a good idea at first but today the intellectuals take it too far.

For Stein, thinking was being. If you are a thinker, she wrote, you will change the language. You will not use the words the way the others do. What she did had not been done before and so some resented it and some laughed at it and almost no one would publish it. There was no money in it until she was nearly sixty, and even then it wasn't for what she considered her serious work, it was for a charming pseudo-autobiography of Alice B. Toklas which Gertrude Stein wrote because Alice couldn't find the time. It was published in 1933 and it is a collection of anecdotes and stories about the eccentricities of her many friends in Paris—the painters and poets of the time —and it was humorous and original but as Stein herself has said, "Remarks are not literature."

About that world of Paris expatriots, Sherwood Anderson wrote: "It was a time of a kind of renaissance in the arts, in literature, a Robin's Egg Renaissance.... It had perhaps a pale blue tinge. It fell out of the nest. It may be that we should all have stayed in Chicago." (Quoted by John Malcolm Brinnin in his 1959 biography, *The Third Rose: Gertrude Stein and Her World.*)

After the popular success of *The Autobiography of Alice B. Toklas*, Stein was creatively blocked. She says the money was funny. She felt recognition had come for her personality, not for her real work. She had trouble getting started again and she wrote a kind of detective story, *Blood On the Dining Room Floor*, which is about Alice's cooking more than anything else.

In our pragmatic, materialist, even barbaric world, the practice of any craft which is not done for profit is, by definition, the work of a dilettante. Or a genius. Which was Gertrude? I think the evidence suggests she began writing in order to dig her way out of a Victorian identity crisis, a psychological *cul de sac* brought on by the knowledge that she was a lesbian and a rather insecure one at that. She describes herself as "rather desperate" as a young woman. (See a work called *Things As They Are*, not published until after her death.) It was perhaps her rather desperate inner life which drove her to write. Then the art took over, the "it" she says you are when you are creating something, not the you you are when you are you as your little dog knows you.

Gertrude needed a muse and so she found Alice Babette Toklas, a wife for life. Now a muse who can say yes to your writing and who is also a good cook is enough to turn anyone into a genius.

So at first the work was a way out, and then it was a way in. Finally, for Gertrude Stein, writing was a religion. In her world view, consciousness was a religion. As she said, in the twentieth century, consciousness has replaced the soul. William James, her teacher at Radcliffe, remarked that any final or total attitude toward life could as well be called a religion, and in that sense her work is religious because it is forever concerned with finalities. She always said she wished to be historical. And now she is.

There is the question of meaning. Did she mean it? What she wrote, that is. And did she make sense of it. The meaning of it. Sometimes yes and sometimes no, but really, finally, it does not really make any difference.

Are there too many theres there? Is it there where she is or isn't? Or did she make that up? Sometimes, just as she says, it *does* make sand. Just as with everything else. Where *there* is, is a question. Where *is* there, and where is it not. Not in Oakland, ha ha, but she loved California and space. She said that here on this coast there was more space where people were not than space where they were and that was very lovely.

Things were very lovely or they were very interesting or they weren't. She wasn't into adjectives. She told Hemingway to cut out the adjectives and so he became a very masculine writer. She was his father figure when young. Then she went after the nouns. When she wrote *Tender Buttons* in 1914 she explained: "So in *Tender Buttons* and then on I struggled with the ridding of myself of nouns. I knew that nouns must go in poetry as they had gone in prose if anything that is everything was to go on meaning something." And then on and on about the feeling in the verbs and the meaning in the nouns and the meaning in the morning and the feeling in the evening.

She and Alice both loved vistas and views and Alice said Gertrude loved a view but she loved to sit with her back to it or Gertrude did. With all her love of the open spaces, Gertrude never met Isadora Duncan when they both lived in Oakland, Isadora dancing on the beaches and living right down the street. Stein wrote: "Two things are always the same the dance and war."

When at last Gertrude did meet Isadora and the Duncan menage in Europe, she dismissed them as "carnival people." (She was a Republican, after all.) Stein was not into dance as far as feet go. There is a description of her at a dance gently swaying too and fro and then stepping first on one foot, then on the other. It was in her of course, but it was not in her human nature it was in her human mind and she wanted to dance in her mind. As Virginia Woolf says, the glow comes when we light the light at the base of the spine with good food and wine and the light becomes a language —a beginning again being existing.

In repeating, Stein wrote, is going on being existing. What people love they repeat, she said, and what they repeat, they love. Of course not always. I do get tired sometimes, of her run-ons and ons, but they are like the begats in the Bible, you can skip over them if you like. Still, they are not there just to hypnotize you, they are there to be going on existing and begetting being. They become being.

Sometimes the repeating says something. In the opera *Four Saints in Three Acts* there is a chorus — the wed/dead dead/wed chorus that goes on repeating those two words and yes that says something. And *A Long Gay Book* in which we can count hundreds and hundreds of gays on page after page, and yes that says something about how many gays there are in it. Some say it is Gertrude who gave us the word to mean what it means but others deny it.

And is there a message? (Remember the old theater joke? you want a message? Call Western Union!) In fact, there is. If you want one. Stein's song is about freedom. The structured anarchy at the bottom of things. Repeating, she says, is in everyone. In her big book *The Making of Americans* she tries to get to the bottom nature of everyone who is coming to be someone, to find out all the kinds there are and were of every kind of a one, while she herself was only all in one, one who is not coming to be one who is a kind of a one.

Of course at first she was. She was the usual kind of a one, a lonely one. A woman too. A lonely lesbian woman born in Victorian 1874 and a Jew too with dark dresses and collars up to her ears and overweight always and when she was in love often there was a triangle and that hurt. She looked to learn to live and part of her heart is the black flower *Melanctha*, a story in the 1902 book, *Three Lives*, subtitled *Each One As She May*.

Melanctha is a kind of dramatic monologue. It is the history of the process of a passion. It is about the search of a young black woman to find fulfillment or anyway to get knowledge of being and she looks for this knowledge in other people and so at last she loses herself.

Someone said to me once about that Melanctha girl that well she needed to get into therapy. Yes, I said, psychotherapy is the study of self-deception, but fortunately psychotherapy did not come along until after literature. Today, of course, psychotherapy has damn near done away with literature but never mind, we still have the theater.

In *Everybody's Autobiography* Gertrude Stein writes: "One of the things that happened at the end of the nineteenth century was that nobody knew the difference between a novel and a play and now the movies have helped them not to know but although there is none there really is and that is the reason I write plays and not novels."

Melanctha is a play in its way although Gertrude calls it a story. When asked about this story, Gertrude said: "Well, now this is the beginning of modern American fiction."

In an essay, *Composition As Explanation*, Stein writes: "In beginning writing I wrote a book called *Three Lives*. This was written in 1902. I wrote a negro story called *Melanctha*. In that there was a constant recurring and beginning there was a marked direction of being in the present although naturally I had been accustomed to past present and future, and why, because the composition forming around me was a prolonged present. A composition in the world as it has been these thirty years it was more and more a prolonged present. I created then a prolonged present naturally I knew nothing of a continuous present but it came naturally to me to make one, it was simple and it was clear to me and nobody knew why it was done like that, I did not myself although naturally to me it was natural."

The critic Donald Sutherland tries to explain the difference between a prolonged and a continuous present: "... (difference) may be defined as this, that a prolonged present assumes a situation or theme and dwells on it and develops it or keeps it recurring as in much opera, and Bach, for example. The continuous present would take each successive moment or passage as a completely new thing essentially, as with Mozart or Scarlatti or, later Satie. This Gertrude Stein calls beginning again." (This passage is found in *Gertrude Stein: A Biography of Her Work*, published posthumously in 1951 by the Yale University Press.)

Donald Sutherland also points out that *Melanctha* is a narrative, a tragic love story ending in death from consumption, so that it is available to the traditional literary taste and the educated emotions. Furthermore it is, as Carl Van Vechten said, "perhaps the first American story in which the Negro is regarded as a human being and not as an object for condescending compassion or derision."

Sutherland advises the reader to go slowly. "It has been said that her work means more when one reads it in proof or very slowly, and that is certainly true, the work has to be read word by word, as a succession of single meanings accumulating into a larger meaning, as for example the words in the stanza of a song being sung. Unhappily all our training and most of our reasons for reading are against this."

What seems hardest for the critics to say is that Stein is a poet. I did not know this at first because I did not know what poetry was for. At first I thought poetry was supposed to give me an emotional catharsis, and yes it is supposed to do that and does. But it is also supposed to open up new areas of the mind which have hitherto been unavailable. Stein uses the music of language, the math of language, to do things that remind me of what Albert Einstein used to do. Einstein was another Jew with some funny ideas and together they made a quantum leap into new dimensions of thought.

I had read bits of Stein as a schoolgirl and I knew she was supposed to be avante garde and witty and that she hung out in Paris and had lots of arty friends. I did not feel moved by her work at first although I loved the humor: On Ezra Pound, she commented that he was a village explainer which is all very well if you are a village but if not, not. The first time I *felt* the power of Stein was in the late '50s while staying alone at a friend's house I could find nothing to play on the phonograph (were there stereos in the '50s) but Stein's opera *Four Saints in Three Acts* with music by Virgil Thomson. I can still remember the shock. Strangeness, she calls it. Oh, later I wrote stuff about lines that meant a vision of the holy ghost — "pigeons on the grass alas and a magpie in the sky" — but the meaning is not important. Sometimes it is *exciting*. "It takes weather to make saints, and there was Saint Teresa standing half in and half out of doors." And that wild stuff about whether or not you can kill ten thousand chinamen by pressing a button — 'Saint Teresa not interested." That started me thinking in the late '50s. But mostly it was the stunning power of lines like "when this you see remember me" coming out of Virgil Thomson's thundering score and grabbing me by the throat. This was a sensibility I had never known. It was not romantic yet it felt sensual beyond belief. Why did it give me such chills? During the following years I found my mantras in the works of Stein. I spent my teaching years muttering the lines of Susan B. Anthony in Stein's opera, *The Mother of Us All:* "Do you know because I tell you so or do you know do you know."

PART II
EACH ONE AS SHE MAY

Each One As She May is the subtitle of *Melanctha* which is the second of the stories in Stein's book *Three Lives.* Melanctha's name means "black flower." (When I teach this book, I like to compare it with Toni Morrison's *Sula,* a book written three-quarters of a century later. Sula has a rose tattoo over her eye. She too is a pariah, an outcast, one of those whose mythology is heroic. In both books, each woman seeks knowledge, the fatal fruit of the tree.)

Melanctha is a prose poem. It is also the most penetrating sex book I've ever read. It sets forth parallel conversations between woman and man — talk that runs on and on forever like railroad tracks, endless and never connecting. It is theatrical: whenever I hear actors reading Melanctha and her lover, the conventional doctor Jeff Campbell, I am astonished at how haunting and heartbreaking their words are: no matter how hard they try, *they cannot touch minds.*

Melanctha is split. (Actually it is Ida in another story in *Three Lives* who says: "You, you one of these days you will split in two, you, you.") Melanctha looks like her pale and self-effacing mother, but she feels like her black and breakneck father. Always Melanctha only finds more ways to be in trouble. Hers is the melancholy of the modern soul. Her woman lover, Jane Harden, begins by dominating Melanctha but then their roles are reversed as Jane falls away into liquor and hard living. (Sula, too, has a female counterpart. Not a lover so much as a friend who represents what is best in herself. Is it perhaps the *self* we are looking for, rather than the significant other?)

Melanctha's real love is her friend Rose. Rose Johnson takes Melanctha's love but never really returns it. When Rose sees her husband

---

I had believed that Stein was an intellectual and I had been told that intellectuals do not mess with the emotions. No one had prepared me in any way for the sensual shock I got from Stein's *mind.* When I came to the study of her work as part of an M.A. degree, I began with her most accessible work, *Melanctha.*

Sam turning to Melanctha, she rejects her altogether and this, for Melanctha, is the death blow. Rose is a pragmatic soul:

"Melanctha told Rose one day how a woman whom she knew had killed herself because she was so blue. Melanctha said, sometimes, she thought this was the best thing for her herself to do.

Rose Johnson did not see it the least bit that way.

'I don't see Melanctha why you should talk like you would kill yourself just because you're blue. I'd never kill myself Melanctha just 'cause I was blue. I'd maybe kill somebody else Melanctha 'cause I was blue, but I'd never kill myself. If I ever killed myself Melanctha it'd be by accident, and if I ever killed myself by accident Melanctha, I'd be awful sorry.'"

William Gass, writing in the Introduction to *The Geographical History of America,* a book by Stein published in 1973 by Vintage Books, says of *Melanctha:* "The rhythms, the rhymes, the heavy monosyllabic beat, the skillful rearrangements of normal order, the carefully controlled pace, the running on, the simplicity, exactness, the passion...in the history of language no one had written like this before."

F. Scott Fitzgerald carried a copy of *Three Lives* with him wherever he went. Richard Wright loved it. Some critics said it was written by an effete intellectual so Wright read it to some black construction workers and he said they recognized both the characters and the language and they roared with laughter. Modern critics still say it's racist. Well, so is *Porgy and Bess*—both works include black men who drink and fight with razors. I think it's just that critics look for what they know how to write about.

No one knows how to write about something that is unique. *Melanctha* is a fatherless book. The critics insisted Stein was reading Flaubert when she wrote it. The avante garde whispered that she was looking at Cezanne when she wrote. It's all true of course. And none of it means a thing. *Melanctha* is what Stein said it was, the beginning of modern fiction.

PART III
YOUR LITTLE DOG KNOWS

Simone de Beauvoir once wrote that we are not born women, we become women. What she meant is that we learn subservience. Gertrude Stein was born a man and she stayed one. Of course she was not always happy and full of herself. She had the conventional crisis early in her psychosexual development. She fell in and out of love, as we all do. She suffered from the isolation and confusion that a young woman who was not only a lesbian but a thinker must suffer if she is to create her own world.

She decided that, all things considered, the best plan was to become a genius. This was not in the cards in Baltimore and other places she might have settled. Nor was it likely in the medical profession, which she escaped by virtue of her famed excuse: "You do not know what it is to be bored." So she headed for Paris and the bohemian life. Basically she was a bourgeoise but she found no contradiction between her financially secure background and the Montmartre milieu in which she metriculated so comfortably. She was not as wealthy as some of her detractors assume. She was once asked why she wore sandals and corduroy skirts. She replied that well you could buy clothes or pictures and she preferred the pictures.

All the evidence suggests that Stein's lifelong attachment to Alice B. Toklas was one of the great love affairs of the twentieth century. Alice lived on for many years after Gertrude's death in 1946. She worked until the end of her life in 1967 to promote and protect the literary heritage of the woman she loved. She had the manuscripts stored at the Yale Library and published where and when she could. She kept up an endless correspondence with editors and it is certainly due to her efforts that Gertrude's place in the history of letters is secure.

It is impossible to separate Alice and Gertrude, either in their lives or in their work. I am not one of those who tries. Alice was only a few years younger than Gertrude, born in San Francisco in 1877. She lived on for twenty-one years, planning always for her reunion with Gertrude. She was buried next to Stein with a Catholic service. Gertrude, on the other hand, was once heard to remark that when a Jew dies, he's dead.

Stein often visits me in my dreams. Once, during a rough period in my life, I dreamt she was clumping around out at the back of my house. She was wearing great fishing boots. The water was beating at the back door and the walls were giving way under the rust and the onslaught of the sea.

Why in hell do you go on living here? she demanded. I was so embarrassed. I told her I had nowhere else to go. Then learn to live underwater, she laughed and hugged me and went sloshing through the rooms and rooms of my flooded and barnacle-encrusted Victorian house.

A sculptor once said she had a face like Stonehenge. She has been described as a Buddha, a Roman Emperor, and a Girl Scout leader. F. Scott Fitzgerald called her an old covered wagon. Behind her back of course. For me, she is Liberty, the spirit of the new age. "Why don't they read the way I write?" she asked. That's when I knew she was the one.

"Once upon a time I met myself and ran," she wrote. She ran away from America and homophobia and heterosexual roles for women. She said Paris was the place that suited those that were to create the twentieth century art and literature. She wanted to write her way out of the nineteenth century. The twentieth century, she said, is a time when everything cracks, where everything is destroyed, everything isolates itself. It is a more splendid thing than a period where everything follows itself.

She always said America was her country but Paris was her home town. She said it wasn't what Paris gave you that mattered so much, it was what Paris didn't take away from you that counted.

She wrote her way out of the hierarchy. In *Things As They Are* Stein writes: "Can't she see things as they are not as she would make them if she were strong enough as she plainly isn't. . .now it had come to her to see as dying men are said to see clearly and freely things as they are and not as she wished them to be. . . ."

"Patriarchal poetry makes no mistake," she wrote. She knew that real men don't give themselves away. They hang on to the property and the poetry both. "Feudal days were the days of the fathers," she wrote.

In an essay on *Poetry and Grammar* she explains the principle of patiarchy: "We still have capital and small letters and probably for some time we will go on having them but actually the tendency is always toward diminishing capitals and quite rightly because the feeling that goes with them is less and less of a feeling and so slowly and inevitably just as with horses capitals will have gone away. They will come back from time to time but perhaps never really come back to stay. Perhaps yes perhaps not but really and inevitably really it really does not really make any difference."

In her jazz riffs and two-steps she is telling us that we can live without masters, without phallic symbolism. She is processing anarchy. She took an axe to syntax. She said that stories would have to go, just as representative painting has gone. Once we got photography, painting changed. Now we have video and so as she predicted, narrative is not needed. She destroyed nineteenth century word order just as Walt Whitman destroyed nineteenth century metrics and verse forms.

Stein was an American pioneer, an inventor. She was not interested in what had been done. "If a thing can be done why do it," she wrote.

Gertrude's ego has been much maligned. Her colossal self-confidence was not her birthright. She made it up as she went along. It was partly a put-on which sprang from her comedic spirit. As we all know, those outside the heterosexual world must brazen it out, must deflect criticism and derision and disbelief. Like Oscar Wilde before her, Getrude had to create a persona for herself in a world which did not acknowledge a gay humanity or even a lesbian lifestyle. When Oscar Wilde arrived in New York for his famous American lecture tour in 1882, he said he had nothing to declare but his genius. When Gertrude Stein arrived for her lecture tour in 1934, she said much the same thing. As she once told a friend, besides me and Shakespeare, who do you see?

Gertrude said her older brother, Leo, thought he was to be the genius in the family and when it turned out Gertrude was to be the genius, well, he went sour. Leo was dogmatic. Gertrude was charismatic. Gertrude wrote that Leo, "said it was not it it was I. If no one knew me then the things I did would not be what they were."

Leo, it seems to me, was in some way Gertrude's cast-off self. He was a sort of sketch for what she became. They were very much alike in the beginning. In childhood there was an attachment, even a symbiosis, although Gertrude said they never shared their inner lives.

I think Leo represents, in his own way, what Gertrude was up against. That is, the patriarchal assumption that genius is a masculine quality. There were five Stein children. Daniel and Amelia Stein were German Jews who planned to have five children. Well, they had five but two died and so there was room. Gertrude once said that it was curious to consider that she and Leo might never have been born. This may have been a bond in the beginning in the days when they were the two youngest and most pampered of the family. They outgrew each other in time and yet there was still a resemblance in old age. Mabel Dodge said Leo was "an old ram," and

Gertrude, she added, "had a laugh like a beefsteak."

Leo and Gertrude were not sorry to go their separate ways. There is a letter from Leo written to his friend Howard Gans dated 8 July 1946. The letter is all about himself and his ingrown neurotic themes and his identity crisis (at age 74) and about having written *the* book of the future on a 1915 Corona typewriter. This book is apparently all about what religion is not. Most curious is the postscript: "P.S. I just saw in *Newsweek* that Gertrude was dead of cancer. It surprised me, for she seemed of late to be exceedingly alive. I can't say it touches me. I had lost not only all regard, but all respect, for her."

That letter I found in a book called *Journey into the Self,* Letters of Leo Stein (1872–1947) edited by Edmund Fuller and published in 1950. Leo Stein died the year after Gertrude. There is a foreword to this book written by Mabel Weeks in which she states that she thinks that Leo's work — articles for *New Republic* and the book *Appreciation* — will endure long after Gertrude's work is forgotten. "Leo may appear as the more significant of the two when the time has weakened the impress of Gertrude's remarkable personality."

By the time Leo moved out of their home in Paris, Gertrude had found Alice B. Toklas. Leo had become a third wheel. Leo found lovers and he married Nina Auzias, but he seemed never able to reconcile his misogyny with his pose as a free thinker. Before their marriage, he writes to Nina: "Since you can't do anything else, have love affairs. These will be your education and experience. For you the possibility of action is in love affairs." He goes on to say to his wife-to-be: "I answered [a friend] with a letter full of very wise reflections. I shall not repeat them because they are very profound and you, poor dear, you would not understand them."

I have only read fragments of Leo's last book. In some ways his theme is similar to Gertrude's in that he is searching for complete consciousness. He writes: "The most serious of all confusions is that between one's real and one's assumed self." This difference presented no problem for Gertrude, as she *was* her assumed self. Sooner or later. There is a story about the Picasso painting of Gertrude in which someone keeps insisting to Picasso that the painting does not look like Gertrude. He answers, don't worry it will.

Gertrude's identity crisis turned her into an artist. Leo's caused him to suffer a lifelong crippling neurosis. He was a disciple of Freud. He grew crabby and deaf with age and "shriveled into a complaint." (Who said "shriveled into a complaint." Ezra Pound? T. S. Eliot? Phrasemakers!) Gertrude's phrases got her through the wall of self, through an identity crisis during which she recognized herself in her work and which allowed her to live in the firm conviction that her own mind was worth her undivided attention. "In my generation I am the only one. I had a family. They can be a nuisance in identity but there is no doubt no shadow of doubt that that identity the family identity we can do without."

It is true that Gertrude was what today we would call a media event. She was a star. People kept asking her why she didn't write the way she talked. She explained that though she loved to talk and though she talked most of the time, talking has nothing to do with creation. She explained that you're not the you your little dog knows when you are creating anything.

She lectured about the problem of the subject of things, saying that everyone already knows all about the subject of say, *Hamlet,* and about the psychology of it. She insists that any woman in any village can tell you all about psychology. No, psychology does not make masterpieces. Stein ends this lecture ("What Are Masterpieces and Why Are There So Few of Them," written in 1936 and delivered at Oxford and Cambridge) by saying:

"If there was no identity no one could be governed. But everyone is governed by everybody and that is why they make no master-pieces and also why governing has nothing to do with master-pieces and that is why governing is occupying but not interesting. Governments are occupying but not interesting because master-pieces is exactly what they are not."

Finally, it is Stein's style that makes the masterpiece. It is not what she says, the subject of the thing. If form *is* content, if the manner *is* the matter, then Stein's song will endure. If writing is about words, as painting is about paint, then she is an artist for the ages.

Stein does not imagine that the self, in and of itself, is of much interest. She knows that identity kills it. Of course, it is of interest to one's little dog but it is of no interest to the world. *Unless it has style.* The style *is* the substance. Alfred North Whitehead (one of the three geniuses Alice Toklas mentions in the *Autobiography* in the passage in which she describes hearing a bell ring three times in her life, once for each of the geniuses she met) once remarked that style is the ultimate morality. This is a hard concept to illustrate. Gertrude Stein does not write about life's letdowns as any other writer might do. Instead she writes:

"Disillusionment in living is the finding out nobody agrees with you not those that are and were fighting with you. Disillusionment in living is the finding out nobody agrees with you not those that are fighting for you. Complete disillusionment is when you realize that no one can for they can't change. The amount they agree is important to you until the amount they do not agree with you is completely realized by you. Then you say you will write for yourself and strangers, you will be for yourself and strangers and this then makes an old man or an old woman of you."

Now if you study that passage you might say, however reductively, that she is complaining. Why then, is this such an uplifting and cheerful paragraph? She does not write, as Leo does, that the world doesn't understand her or that she is too bright to hang out with ordinary mortals. She writes a poem which acknowledges the loss that wisdom brings.

For me, Gertrude Stein will always be the first woman in space. The one who, more than any other, wrote it her way. For Stein, a sentence is a part of speech. Question marks are for branding horses. "What is poetry and if you know what poetry is what is prose." I know Stein is poetry and prose is no problem.

> *I am Rose my eyes are blue*
> *I am Rose and who are you*
> *I am Rose and when I sing*
> *I am Rose like anything*

For Gertrude Stein, the rose of the world was woman. In her case, the woman was Alice B. Toklas who wore black dresses and long earrings like a Spanish gypsy. Gertrude needed someone to say yes to her writing and Alice said yes and so the writing continued.

The three roses are the trinity, the original trinity. They are the triple goddess, the ancient godhead of maiden, mother, crone, the mother of us all. They are the budding pink rose of youth, the full blown red rose of womanhood, and the winter thorns on the rose of rebirth.

SHAKESPEARE'S SISTER

> It is useless to go to the great men writers for help, however much
> one may go to them for pleasure.
>
> Virginia Woolf
> *A Room of One's Own*
> 1928

Who's afraid of Virginia Woolf? Virginia herself. "I know that I must go on doing this dance on hot bricks till I die," she wrote. Virginia knew that she was dancing with the devil, a daimon who drove her to create as well as into periods of psychotic withdrawal. It is important to remember that Woolf was not just neurotic or high-strung, she had bouts of psychotic madness during which she had to be subdued, nursed, and cared for in isolation.

Virginia's mother died when she was thirteen years old, evidently worn out by the demands of Virginia's father, the autocratic Leslie Stephen. Near the end of her life, Virginia writes that her father was one of those insiders (she considered herself an outsider) turned out by the University machine, the sort whose colorless English prose she says she respects but does not love, does not savor. These thoughts are found in her diary from the years 1936 until her death in 1941. Her early years were scarcely as objective. She apparently tried to kill herself for the first time just after her mother's death. She suffered what is believed to be her first psychotic episode at that time.

During her childhood, Virginia was the victim of continued sexual abuse. In a letter to Ethel Smyth, written on 12 January 1941, she writes: "I still shiver with shame at the memory of my half-brother, standing me on a ledge, aged about six or so, exploring my private parts." The half-brother, George Duckworth, was Virginia's mother's son by an earlier marriage and he would have been in his twenties at the time. Virginia's nephew and biographer, Quentin Bell (son of Vanessa, Virginia's full sister and closest to her in sympathy and age) writes that his aunt "felt that George had spoilt her life before it had fairly begun. Naturally shy in sexual matters, she was from this time (the time of the abuse) terrified back into a posture of frozen and defensive panic."

Quentin Bell has the limitations of his sex and era, and his interpretations of Virginia's psycho-sexual life are simplistic. He quotes a letter in his biography and comments: "Virginia alludes to her frigidity." Here is the letter, written to a woman friend shortly after her marriage to Leonard Woolf:

"Why do you think people make such a fuss about marriage and copulation? Why do some of our friends change upon losing chastity? Possibly my great age makes it less of a catastrophe: but certainly I find the climax immensely exaggerated. Except for a sustained good humour (Leonard shan't see this) due to the fact that every twinge of anger is at once visited upon my husband, I might still be Miss S."

The "great age" she alludes to is thirty. When I first came across this reference I filed it next to a letter written by Charlotte Bronte, a woman who married in her late thirties, and who had apparently the same sort of "what's all the fuss" reaction to marital bliss. Is this frigidity or simply lack of fulfillment. What's the difference anyway?

Virginia's sister Vanessa also suffered from the prurient attentions of George Duckworth. She went on to a life of sexual fulfillment, that is, orgasms, as well as children and lovers and so on. Yet she did not manage to have a contented and happy marriage which by all accounts Leonard and Virginia did sustain during the more than a quarter of a century they were together.

Vanessa writes of the period following Virginia's honeymoon: "They seemed very happy, but are evidently both a little exercised in their minds on the subject of the Goat's coldness. I think I perhaps annoyed her but may have consoled him by saying that I thought she never had understood or sympathized with sexual passion in men. Apparently she still gets no pleasure at all from the act, which I think is curious. They were very anxious to know when I first had an orgasm. I couldn't remember. Do you? But no doubt I sympathized with such things if I didn't have them from the time I was two."

I find this letter written by Vanessa to be very revealing. It struck me as one of the more blatant forms of denial, one which I, myself, choose at one period in my life. It is a choice whereby one *joins* the oppressor (if you can't beat 'em, join 'em?) and becomes a partner in the game. In this way, the woman is not a victim but a participant, a comrade in erotic achievement. Unfortunately, this role is not always authentic although it gives women the illusion of choice, as well as a part to play in men's lives. Vanessa is a fascinating woman, and by some standards her life may have been richer than her sister's. By identifying her own desires with those of the men around her, she was able to bury herself in womanliness, literally. Like her mother Julia, and her older half-sister Stella (who died at age twenty-eight) she devoted herself to serving a male mystique, although there is ample evidence that she enjoyed it. Lovers and children possessed her.

Virginia was not like that. Vita Sackville West, perhaps the woman closest to Virginia after Vanessa, wrote that Virginia "dislikes the possessiveness and love of domination in men. In fact she dislikes the quality of masculinity." Perhaps the tyranny she suffered, both from the sexual abuse (which continued over a period of many years) and the psychic abuse of men like her father and Vanessa's husband Clive Bell (one of Virginia's "cock-a-doodle-dum" tormentors) sensitized her to a deeper need—the need to keep her soul her own.

And she loved Leonard Woolf. She writes that after twenty-five years they can't bear to be separate, that it is an enormous pleasure to be wanted, to be a wife. She writes about how complete their marriage is, how they walk about the square love making, share in the garden work, and about how much it means to show him her work. Yet she physically assaulted Leonard during psychotic episodes.

In the beginning, Virginia seems to have had some notion that Leonard could awaken her sexually. Perhaps because he was a Jew, she imagined he was more erotic than the Bloomsbury blokes she hung out with, blokes like Lytton Strachey (gay) to whom Virginia was once engaged for the better part of a day. Perhaps what Virginia calls Leonard's "passionate nature" is just English for someone who cares. It seems he loved her. In any case, he developed a real capacity to nurture her genius, a willingness to love her *as she was*. She writes that she loves to be loved. Yet she has a physical aversion to her husband. Hot bricks indeed.

In 1939, the Woolfs received a visit from Sigmund Freud. Freud gave Virginia a narcissus. When I first read of this incident, I supposed he meant to chide or insult her. Then I thought about it. Today most people use the word narcissistic to mean self-obsessed or even selfish. But in some mythologies, the god Narcissus also represents the reflective soul. [I think of the moment Virginia Woolf describes in the opening section of her essay, *A Room of One's Own* in which she is gazing down into the water of a pond and trying to grasp her own thought. She is interrupted by a fussy male authority figure who tells her that women aren't allowed on the grass and she must go somewhere else. When I was a college student (luckily for me, in a woman's college) this passage made a deep and lasting impression on me. The right to be alone with my thoughts and not to be interrupted by some officious man became not just a right but a duty.] Of course, it is still true, even today, that if Freud or any other man gives a woman a narcissus, he is probably accusing her of being less than outgoing. At the end of the visit, Virginia wrote that he struck her as an alert, "screwed-up, shrunk, very old man." He'd asked her what the English were going to do about Hitler.

Well, what Virginia was going to do was kill herself. She and Leonard had discussed suicide if Hitler invaded England. In fact, it seems that her own fear of another mental breakdown, always a recurring nightmare in her life, was what really drove her to her death. She was fifty-eight in 1941 and she suffered from auditory hallucinations. She wrote in her suicide note that she heard the voices again. She had tried to drown herself once before. She succeeded on 28 March 1941. She had to put large stones in her pockets to drown in the River Ouse, "the one experience," as she had said to Vita, "I shall never describe."

Woolf's experience is of value to us, not just because of the skill with which she wrote and thought. I value her life because for me it is prophetic. In the beginning, she was a woman of her time, in spite of what she writes about going against the current and working with her back braced against the wall. In the 1920s she wrote the brilliant feminist primer, *A Room of One's Own,* in which she insisted that we must avoid bias and that the cause of women can only be served by those who have no axe to grind. She cautioned women against being *shrill.* By the time she came to write *Three Guineas,* published in June of 1938, she seems to have realized that it's a little late for justice. By then, she had put two and two together and she realized that fascism begins in the home, that the personal and political are one.

Woolf was what is today called an ecofeminist. She looked at Hitler and she looked at her father and she had an ah hah! experience. She was an out-and-out pacificist, unlike Leonard. She believed that the "beastly masculine" reaction was the source for the dark days descending on them. *Three Guineas* is genuine protest literature and it denounces oppression and real evils in such a way that it was sure to turn off the male intellectuals. Biographer Bell says his own reaction at the time of publication was to feel that an attempt to involve a discussion of women's rights with the far more agonizing and immediate question of what we were to do in order to meet the ever-growing menace of Fascism and war was to attempt a connection between two questions most tenuous—he also adds that Virginia's positive suggestions are wholly inadequate. Even Vita did not like the book. Maynard Keynes said the argument was silly and hastened to add that in addition it was not very well written.

Even today, attempts to connect the war on women with the war on humanity in general, meet with resistance. I can't help reflecting that just recently I was sitting with a young woman and talking about the problem of date rape on her college campus. Her father entered the room and the conversation became awkward and both the young woman and I found we had switched to oppression in Central America in order to assure the father that our real concerns were for larger issues.

When I read Woolf's essay *Three Guineas*, I can't help but recall Emily Bronte's schoolgirl essay *The Butterfly*, a cruel and poetic sketch in which Emily sees the world as a vast destructive machine, a hierarchical and violent place in which all life exists to devour other life. Of course, Emily is didactic for the purposes of Victorian prose, and she does state that order can be forged from chaos and transmutation can occur. Woolf is a modern and it is her conviction that things fall apart.

When I take Virginia Woolf into the classroom, I usually begin with her novel, *To the Lighthouse*. For younger readers, it seems best to go right to the family, the heart of the matter. The subject of Woolf's politics must begin where everything begins, at home. *To the Lighthouse* is, of course, about the maternal mythos of Virginia's mother. It is about the monumental Victorian illusion of the sacred nature of home. Letting go of that grand illusion is perhaps the hardest thing any modern has had to do.

To the Lighthouse is a story about a family and how it is held together by the mother and her illusions. It is a portrait of certain aspects of Woolf's youth. Woolf's mother, Julia, died in her late 40s and Stella two years later and then Vanessa and Virginia were pressed into service by Leslie Stephen. Julia was the woman Woolf has described as the "angel in the house."

In *To the Lighthouse,* the mother, the house angel, is the center of gravity, the inner sanctum, the force which is holding everything, everyone, together. Perhaps, if she were removed—and she is—things could fall apart. Did Woolf believe that the mother provides the support system upon which all patriarchal assumptions rest?

In her own life, Virginia rejected the role of angel in the house. She is neither sacred cow nor maternal monster, she is only an artist. As an artist, she claimed the right to be let alone, to abdicate the feminine responsibilities of her day. She writes that she uses her friends, and depends on Leonard. Their light, she says, widens her landscape. Just as she has no desire to play the role of ministering angel, so too, she has no use for those who make demands, who wish to dominate, either personally or politically. She believed that patriarchal families and patriarchal governments, even British ones, maintained the same sexual and class divisions, the same militarism, male aggression and hierarchical oppression. She saw war as the desire to annex personal property. In *Three Guineas* she declares: "As a woman, I have no country." Before the Woman's Property Act in the 1880's, women in Britain could not own property of any kind. Virginia herself writes that she would rather have money than the vote. She got money, enough to have a room of her own, on 7 April 1909 when her Aunt Caroline Emelia Stephen died and left her a legacy of 2,500 pounds. It was this shred of security which allowed her to compete with Shakespeare.

In *A Room of One's Own,* Virginia Woolf paints a grim picture of a woman she calls Shakespeare's sister. Seems Judith Shakespeare, like William, came up to London to seek her fortune. Of course, she was knocked up and knocked down in record time. By Virginia's day she was a real possibility. And yet. Woolf writes again and again of the need to put aside the personal in order to be a great writer. Over and over she speaks of Shakespeare and Jane Austen as writers who put all of themselves into the writing but never reveal themselves, never talk about themselves. She even chides Charlotte Bronte for putting some of her own resentments and frustrations into *Jane Eyre,* saying that Emily Bronte never made that mistake with *Wuthering Heights.* Why was Virginia so hard on herself? Surely she knew that aesthetic distance is just one more patriarchal plot, just one more way the malestream literary establishment has contrived to drive women out of the academy. Well, of course she *knew.* It was just that she wanted to go the men one better. To reach for a new aesthetic. Poetry should have a mother as well as a father, she wrote. And the way to be one of the mothers of literature is not to fall in with the fathers, not to do things their way. Woolf wrote:

"All the older forms of literature were hardened and set by the time *she* became a writer. The novel alone was young enough to be soft in her hands. . .who shall say that even this most pliable of all forms is rightly shaped for her use? No doubt we shall find her knocking that into shape for herself when she has the free use of her limbs; and providing some new vehicle, not necessarily in verse, for the poetry in her for it is the poetry that is still denied outlet."

Equal does mean the same. Women no longer wish to write as men do. I think of Alice Walker's book *The Color Purple* which many English teachers fuss about, asking is it a novel or no. I think of all the editors who write to me saying well, it's not a novel, whatever it is. Saying it's poetic and has a riff on each page (this from a *kind* editor) but how to market it? Well, as Woolf writes, each succeeding generation of women carries the torch and today women are even using their pens to write about the love of woman for woman, a thing that Virginia said stopped the pen in her time.

Virginia has a great deal to say about the measurements of the Headmasters, about the giving of approval and what she calls receiving of highly ornamental pots. She states: "To submit to the decrees of the measurers [is] the most servile of attitudes. So long as you write what you wish to write, that is all that matters; and whether it matters for ages or only for hours, nobody can say. But to sacrifice a hair of the head of your vision, a shade of its color, in deference to some Headmaster with a silver pot in his hand or to some professor with a measuring-rod up his sleeve, is the most abject treachery, and the sacrifice of wealth and chastity which used to be said to be the greatest of human disasters, a mere flea-bite in comparison."

Did Woolf live up to her own standards or *was* she afraid? She writes: "I thought of all the women's novels that lie scattered, like small pock-marked apples in an orchard, about the secondhand book shops in London. It was the flaw in the center that had rotted them. She [the woman writer] had altered her values in deference to the opinion of others."

Well, Virginia, were you altering your opinion or only being charming when you wrote such things as "pessimism about the other sex is always delightful and invigorating. . . . " Perhaps both. Virginia knew that men do not read "shrill" women. But she had to get her anger out. Just like Shakespeare. When Shakespeare did it, it was called *King Lear*.

Shakespeare wasn't afraid to be "shrill." In *King Lear* "shrill" translates to rage, a masculine emotion which I find as hard to bear in men as many men find the quality of "shrillness" unbearable in women. It's all simply anger, and neither sex wants to hear the other's wrath. Now Will Shakespeare, the man, did not like his daughters. He had such contempt for them, and perhaps for the sex in general, that he *did not teach them to read*. Not that it was common practice to do so in England in the Elizabethan age, it just lets us know that the Bard's love for the word did not extend to his hearth and home. Of course, he may just have been trying to avoid trouble.

Now what Shakespeare was doing was giving full vent to his rage and exasperation with his daughters. Woolf's father comes in for a few subtle jabs in *To the Lighthouse*, although she is never shrill. I remember how my own father loved to quote from *Lear*. "More bitter than a serpent's tooth it is to have a thankless child." Here is male subjectivity at its most passionate. Shakespeare did what poets do, he laid it on a bit. He made Lear's daughters out to be wicked beyond belief in order to find relief for his own feelings. Then he indulged himself by imagining an angelic daughter, the idealized Cordelia, the sort of child he really wanted. (Now, all's fair in the theater and I go along with this stuff. It's just important to look at what goes on backstage, in the writer's mind, just so we understand what archetypes are up to.)

Today we know that male fantasy can be a serious threat to women. (Snuff films, etc.) Still, I believe poets should have a little license. I mean Shakespeare was writing about himself. Just the way I do. Just the way Virginia Woolf tried to do. (Through a glass darkly?) Shakespeare wrote about an old man whose daughters made his life a living hell. Of course, if you look at the play from a woman's point of view, he does tend to be a difficult old guy, King Lear. (It's a play about parenting?) He never goes anywhere without a bunch of rowdies he calls his entourage and when he visits his daughters they create a regular bruhaha. Now some of us know what it's like to clean up after a hundred guys who've been partying. But all that aside, Shakespeare is an artist and he sees to it that Lear wises up and gets in touch with his feelings. Lear realizes he's been a lousy parent. "Thou shouldst' ne'er been old, till thou hadst been wise. ..."

It's true that from a certain feminist point of view, Cordelia is a lie about women. However, she is certainly not a lie about Shakespeare. She is his dream child: "Her voice was ever soft gentle, and low; an excellent thing in woman." Again I remember my father's facetious delight in quoting this line over and over as my voice grew louder and stronger with the years. Of course, the message coming from his subscript *was* teaching me to seize power, to become not Cordelia, but something more.

In *Women and Writing*, editor Michele Barrett quotes Woolf: "It is becoming daily more evident that Lady Macbeth, Cordelia, Ophelia, Clarissa, Dora, Diana, Helen and the rest are by no means what they pretend to be. Some are plainly men in disguise; others represent what men would like to be, or are conscious of not being; or again they embody that dissatisfaction and despair which afflict most people when they reflect upon the sorry condition of the human race. To cast out and incorporate in a person of the opposite sex all that we miss in ourselves and desire in the universe and detest in humanity is a deep and universal instinct on the part both of men and of women. But though it affords relief, it does not lead to understanding. Rochester (in *Jane Eyre*) is as great a travesty of the truth about men as Cordelia (in *King Lear*) is of the truth about women."

It is obvious that Charlotte Bronte's romanticism is anathema to Virginia Woolf. Woolf's quest on earth did not lead to Bronte's "stout embrace in the arms of a lord of creation" because Woolf was not susceptible to that particular mental illness — romanticism, that is. She wrote that the truth is, we go alone. That only when we realize that there is no arm to lean on will we arrive at the shores of reality, the place from which we can perceive the new world, the world in which the manly woman is just as valid as the womanly man. Judith Shakespeare is alive and well. She always was. And today, for the first time, the masses are reading her.

OPPENHEIMER: FAUST OR FRAUD?

In my novel, *The Man Who Would be God* (1959), I told the story, with many of the circumstances changed, and with characters wholly invented or greatly disguised, of an atomic scientist destroyed by his invention ... It achieved what I wanted to achieve, which was to show that the dropping of the atomic bombs on Hiroshima and Nagasaki was a tragic error which has plagued the world ever since, and that the human instrument through which this was accomplished was one of the most gifted, brilliant, selfless and dedicated of men, imbued with a love of humanity that made him almost saintly, who was used by the Powers for ther own purposes, and eventually destroyed. I wanted to show that the whole venture of the making of the bomb was poisoned from the start, that it was a venture in which good men were committed to doing the wrong thing for the right reason, and that it was doomed to create untold havoc.

Haakon Chevalier
*Oppenheimer: The
Story of a Friendship*
(1966)

The story of J. Robert Oppenheimer has all the ingredients of a Greek tragedy. Pride goeth before a fall. So do arrogance ambition, romanticism, narcissism, and the American Dream.

The *American Playhouse* six-hour production of J. R. Oppenheimer's follies aired on PBS in the spring of 1982. Sam Waterston and Jana Shelden played Oppy and Kitty. In spite of criticism about its veracity, the show was

---

This article appeared in almost identical form in the August 1982 issue of *Plexus* under the title, "The Oppenheimer Legacy."

an artistic triumph and a coming of age for a world soaking in post-atomic angst. (This is a *play*, and not to be confused with the pertinent documentary, *The Day After Trinity*, which makes a valuable double-bill.)

The man who headed the wartime research project at Los Alamos, the "father of the atom bomb," was essentially a sweet, brilliant guy. His fall from grace was, if not Faustian, at least American. What the script glosses over is that in 1943, in order to get a security clearance, Oppenheimer lied through his teeth and sold out his friends on the Left. (The friend he betrayed, Haakon Chevalier, says he was insecure. Born in 1904, Oppenheimer belonged to a precarious Jewish elite, and Chevalier believes he acted out of fear.) In the end, Oppy, as his friends called him, didn't so much go to the Devil as to that oblivion reserved for the terminally naive. As his alcoholic wife, Kitty, indicates in the play—his is the saint's script. He courts crucifixion.

Oppenheimer's tragic flaw was his inability to imagine fully the long-range consequences of his actions. (Of course, he must have known he wasn't inventing penicillin.) Like Oedipus Rex, he was blinded by ambition and desire. Like Oedipus, when his eyes were opened, he put out his own light. His drama is the result of wrong choices made during a time when the furious fight against Fascism obsessed the nation.

As a college student in 1954, I saw a film documentary of Oppenheimer. It was not required study. It was brought in by Arch Lauterer, then the head of the drama department at Mills College. He seemed sad that there was such a small and disinterested audience. Perhaps a dozen students. Lauterer tried to make us grasp the level of apathy in which we existed. He told us Oppenheimer was a broken-hearted man trying to reach people and make them understand the enormity of the tragedy brought into the world by the megabomb.

The film is one I have never seen since. I have no knowledge of where it is available or if it has even been preserved. My few requests for information about its existence have been futile. It shows Oppenheimer speaking directly into the camera for perhaps forty minutes. His despair is genuine. He weeps. His suffering is apparent on several levels. Physically, he is a wraith. His depth of expression is still with me after all these years. Toward the end of the film, through his tears, he made a plea for what he termed, "affection between governments." He was a living ghost and this was thirteen years before his death.

Chevalier writes of him: "He had a peculiarly haunting look, impossible to describe, but which one associates with a person who has been through a searing ordeal, or who has pulled up stakes and gone over 'to the other side' and then come back. When I later learned about the *shaman*, I at once realized that this was what he evoked."

My first glimpse of Oppenheimer when I was a student was offset by what I learned of him later. I do not argue but that he had Christ consciousness, or whatever we are calling it this year. He had the awareness of the heroic figure of mythology who descends to the underworld and embraces his darker self. But Oppenheimer's tragedy is scarcely his own. He took us with him.

From a more jaded point of view, Oppenheimer was to the saint what Willie Loman was to the salesman. (See Arthur Miller's play, *Death of a Salesman*, written in the 1950s.) Willie was "liked, but not well liked." Oppenheimer was a brilliant theoretical physicist, but he was no Einstein. He was not a creative genius, simply a high-tech scientist who had to settle for being a star.

In the June 1982 issue of *Mother Jones*, Hugh Drummond, M.D., writes: "(Oppenheimer's) narcissism had a strange and protean quality. At Los Alamos, running his hand along the brim of his porkpie hat like John Wayne, he commanded the greatest single collection of advanced scientists the world had ever known. ... Later, like someone out of Dickens he pronounced, 'We physicists have known sin.' And still later, when persecuted by Joe McCarthy and stripped of his security clearance, he looked for all the world like Jesus Christ on the cross. ... What I found evil about Oppenheimer was not his Faustian genius. And it was not just his narcissism. It was that his narcissism was a stranger to him."

My friend, the late Mathilde Moore of Berkeley, an activist and a leftist, remembers inviting Oppy to dinner in 1938. She told me, "He was such an attractive man. He liked a woman I knew, a waitress who was out on strike. He brought her roses and an algebra book. He loved mathematics." Over dinner one night, she spoke to him of her concern over his involvement with the Left. An activist then as she was when I knew her in the 1970s, she was afraid he might mislead the workers. He finished her sentences for her, saying that yes, intellectuals sell out the workers. According to Chevalier, Oppenheimer was always finishing other people's sentences.

Oppenheimer has become a legend of sorts. Since his death in 1967, there have been a number of efforts to evaluate his life. In fact, his life is the least interesting aspect of his existence. Whom the gods would destroy, they give what they want? Oppenheimer was grandiose and he wanted power. He was not an infantile Rambo or a tyrant or a torturer. He used his mind. Part of it.

Sam Waterston's Emmy award winning peformance in this production of *Oppenheimer* does much to suggest Oppy's surface veneer, his superficiality, and his frailty. Still, it's hard to swallow. This is a fallen angel, a death angel, a man who definitely believed he was one of the better known Hebrew prophets, a latter-day voice crying in the wilderness. Trouble was, it was *his* wilderness — handmade.

Oppenheimer *was* the American Dream. A nightmare of unprincipled achievement from a poetic guy who attended Ethical Culture School from the age of six to sixteen. Doubtless he studied the classics and the Greek concept of *hubris*.

In the play, when he witnesses the bomb blast which follows the Trinity test (this is still a *test* remember, not the subsequent bombing of Hiroshima and Nagasaki in which he took part at the planning stage — so much for not knowing what the damn thing was really capable of), he quotes from the *Bhagavad-Gita*: "I am become Death, the destroyer of worlds." Accurate, but smacks of the God complex which all the moderns who are in love with the bomb seem to evidence when brought into its holy presence. Yahweh, the thunder god, an Old Testament myth of fire and brimstone — the wheel has come full circle, here we are. The worship of death began in the caves. Oppy's remark is the most vainglorious statement recorded by any man in my lifetime. For my money, I'll take his companion's remark which follows in the script: "Now we're all sons-a-bitches."

EROS: THE IMPERATIVE OF INTIMACY

Alicia Suskin Ostriker's *Stealing the Language, The Emergence of Women's Poetry in America*

In male mythology, Eros and Thanatos are both guys. Love and death, both personified as males. Figures. Today, the feminists are trying to get into the act and naturally they insist they are on the side of the angels, that is, on the side of Eros, the good guy, on the side of love as opposed to death. Of course, enlightened women who have awakened to the Zen end of things are perfectly well aware that there is a flip side to everything.

Personally, I'm not often in favor of either love or death, but that won't make them go away. What I want to examine is the existence of women and whether or not their influence on the culture at large might make things a bit more loving and a lot less deadly. There is growing evidence that women want to get away from Thanatos (our death culture) and get back to Eros. Well, some women poets want to. The men seem split between their subversive longing for the feminine (the uncontrolled world in which mystery is the only reality) and their need to please their fathers (the aspect of their fathers which says men can control their world, can be God, in fact). The wisest of the poets have always tried to convince us that the feminine can be fun, that Eros is eternal youth, and "love in the open hand," as Edna St. Vincent Millay calls it, can be had for the asking if we are willing to let go of ourselves.

This essay had its genesis in a KPFA Pacifica Public Radio show, which aired on December 2, 1986. A short excerpt was published in different form in *Mama Bears News and Notes* March, 1987.

Stealing the Language, The Emergence of Women's Poetry in America, was published by Beacon Press in 1986. It's written by an old friend of mine, Alicia Suskin Ostriker. Alicia is the kind of poet/scholar who is never without a notebook in one hand and a bottle of wine in the other. We met in the early '70s at the Berkeley Poets Workshop and Alicia's patience and concern with individual poets was my introduction into a new world. When I was growing up, the artists and poets competed and criticized each other, not for the sake of the work itself, but more often to crush confidence, to say to each other that no, that is not the way.

I do not mean to imply that Alicia suffered fools gladly. She was unfailingly kind but she always said what had to be said. When we talked about my work, she did not say to leave wringing of my hands and get on with it. Instead she smiled enigmatically over my nihilism and despair and sighed, ah, Jennifer, who needs another *Wasteland*?

Chapter Five of Alicia's book is called "The Imperative of Intimacy: Female Erotics, Female Poetics." It begins with a quote from the poet Alta:

> i felt the joy of being a body,
> of being inside a body, of
> another body being inside my
> body; the unbearable joy

Now things get touchy when we talk/write about sex. Gender benders abound when men say they love this or that and a loose curl at her neck. And then, years ago, along comes Leonore Kandel and says she loves to fuck. Most of the men I knew thought that was pretty aggressive although I still remember two men who could handle a woman like that.

Words mean different things to men and women. It takes a lifetime to sort this out. (A course in Sexmantics?) Gertrude Stein's lover Alice B. Toklas is "the rose of the world." A rose by any other name would not smell so sweet. When Henry Miller writes, "An old cunt is a dead loss," his "cunt" is not mine. Or perhaps it is. It is almost exclusively a male word. I wonder why I can't use it in my own work? It is *not* that women are more refined than men. That is a nonsense invented by male prudes. It is a difference in perception which sees cunt as the entrance to heaven (Eros) or hell (Thanatos). Try explaining to a man that the words "beloved pussy" are a contradiction. I believe that many women mistake lust for love. They have to. I say they mistake, because loving lust is not a concept which is easy for us in today's world. In a man's world, lust is dangerous, even violent. D. H. Lawrence once wrote that he found Charlotte Bronte's novel *Jane Eyre* verging on the pornographic. He writes of the suppressed smoldering sexuality of Jane as a bit indecent, unhealthy even. Truly, sublimation into soap opera is one of the masochistic routes that female Eros takes, just as repressed Eros in males often erupts into violence.

About the words themselves. I think of letters I have received from male and even female editors. I'm still confused by a woman editor who told me how much she liked my work but that the editorial board — all women — felt there was too much "male imagery." I looked over the material and all I could find was a broken beer bottle. Often, when I imagined I was writing sensual poetry, male editors would complain. If they didn't like a poem, they would use words which I use to describe female sexuality. Words like: free associative, abstract, diffuse, fragmented, loose, repetitious, tangential, muted, subjective, circular, dreamlike, and intangible. (Remember D. H. Lawrence saying that only that which is utterly intangible matters? Come to think of it, only *matter* matters, David Herbert. Why don't you read what you write and try to be less subjective!)

The most irritating editors, most of them male, are the ones who try to help. I have a file of letters from men who exhibit what I can only call a phallocentric focus. They want me to: follow the main thrust, stick to the point, tighten it up, strengthen the climax, simplify the action, and keep the lights on, *literally*.

None of this can be helped I suppose. We are all of us biological units. I am always reminding beginners that the women learned from the plants and the men learned from the animals and that is why women sit down and men stand up. Women look around and tend to have what is called field-relevant vision; that is, they can see these little circles or life cycles out of the corner of their eye. Most men prefer to look straight ahead. This laser look is very powerful and sometimes women think it means the man loves them when in reality the force of the look is meant to subdue them. Or perhaps, from a male perspective, that's what love means?

Now I do not wish to strain this metaphor or to go on writing about things which are straight and things which are curved. After all, everything which exists has a tendency to be one or the other. What I wish to understand is the nature of poetic perception in women. Does the brain have breasts? Perhaps it does.

The pen, in spite of Sigmund Freud, is not a phallus. And perception is the great mystery of life. Perception, for a poet, is a passion. You can't make poetry out of thought. Poetry is passion. As Virginia Woolf told us, poetry must have a mother as well as a father, and while a mother's passions may be less likely to *hit the nail on the head*, so to speak, they are just as likely to kiss the joy as it flies.

In her chapter on intimacy, Alicia quotes Freud as he struggles with Eros and Thanatos, with the impulse to live and the impulse to die.

> The fateful question of the human species seems to me to be whether and to what extent the cultural process developed in it will succeed in mastering the derangements of communal life caused by the human instinct of aggression and self-destruction. In this connection, perhaps the phase through which we are at this moment passing deserves special interest. Men have brought their powers of subduing the forces of nature to such a pitch that by using them they could now very easily exterminate one another to the last man. They know this—hence arises a great part of their current unrest, their dejection, their mood of apprehension. And now it may be expected that the other of the two 'heavenly forces,' eternal Eros, will put forth his strength so as to maintain himself alongside of his equally immortal adversary.
>
> from: *Civilization and*
> *Its Discontents*

Now what if—what if Eros is a woman? At least half the time. There is plenty of death or Thanatos connected with women and women's poetry. So why not admit there is love as well. Alicia comments: "If the release of anger is a major element in women's poetry, so too is the release of a contrary passion which in part explains the vehemence of women's rage. What do women want? was a question ancient before Freud asked it. A provisional answer, were we to trust women's revenge poetry, would be that they want man's phallus, or what the phallus represents—the power to conquer and punish."

My own term for penis envy is "socio-cultural underprivilege" but it's not nearly so catchy as Freud's. Castration fantasy is a taboo for women. Rage must not be acted out. I remember back in 1972 I did a performance piece in which a woman confesses to castration and murder. She describes her life surrealistically. She is at the end of her existential rope and to relieve her feelings she recalls the night she cut her lover's throat and left bits of him all over the Boston Common—pontificating, pretentious old prick that he was. She mails the tools of his love to his mother in a coffee can with three black silk roses. Why three black silk roses? Why not. Now this little play or monologue was a fantasy and what it is really describing is the woman's revenge on the man who killed her "baby." Her baby is her bush soul, her true self. The male mystique has robbed her of the part of herself that wants to be a poet and a pantheist and a priestess. I was trying to express a woman's anguish over the loss of her authentic being. Her revenge is only an afterthought, a shrug which suggests the depths of her bitterness toward the linear Eurocentric masculine world which has no place for her beliefs. She admits cheerfully to killing her tormentor. Well, she says, someone had to.

Now I mention this because what was interesting was that after a performance of this play at the San Francisco Intersection Coffeehouse (as it was then), two men in their thirties, white and apparently middle class, took the time to threaten me. Very obliquely and very cryptically, but very carefully. I left off performing the play for more than ten years. I did an excerpt at Wolfgang's Nightclub in 1986 and was curious to find that times have changed or anyway the audience has. One young man in particular seemed overwhelmed when I assured him I was just a tired mom with two sons his age. He kept asking how I could live with so much depression. I explained that the cure for depression is expression and that that's what I was doing.

Alicia writes: "Another answer, if we judge by the poetry of feminine desperation, is what the sibyl said to the boys in Petronius' *Satyricon*, which T. S. Eliot quotes as the epigraph to the *Wasteland*: 'I want to die.' The violent desires arising from the contemplation of powerlessness are suggestively interchangeable, and those women who express them most dramatically and thrillingly make clear at the same time that the wish to kill/die confirms a dualized world and a dualized sexuality."

I date the demise of my own death wish from the menopause. Somewhere around my mid-forties I ceased to want to kill/die. As I said, we are all of us biological units. There is less love to lose after a certain age. I believe I was a masculinist romantic much of the time until I was forty-four. Both my mother and sister died at about that age. As my younger son suggested to me on several occasions, the time had come to burn out or rewire.

Oh, I exaggerate of course. I still have romantic twinges from time to time. But the point is that if women can break away from the death culture, from the desire to kill/die, either by expressing and thus dissipating that desire or by simply outliving it, then they can come back to Eros. Alicia writes: "We have now to look at a quite different form of female desire and to delineate an alternative portrait of female pleasure. For it is not only women's aggressive impulses which have been thwarted and made taboo in her past life and literature. Her eroticism has suffered equally.... Where female aggression has been twisted into manipulativeness, female ardor has been chained to submissiveness. To love, for a woman, has meant to yield, to give herself.' As we have known since Karen Horney and Simone de Beauvoir, the addiction to love relationships in which the woman is powerless and suppliant—what Rachel Blau De Plessis calls 'romantic thraldom'—is woman's peculiar curse."

I can't help thinking of a day in 1987 when I ran into Maxine Howard (the blues singer) at the movies and she pressed on me her copy of *Women Who Love Too Much*. Oh no, I thought, not you too. Seems every woman in Berkeley is clutching that book. So much for our new age awareness. Romantic thraldom is a good term for it. I used to call it sexual slavery. As an actress I could handle some of that stuff but as a writer it began to take a toll. An actress can immerse herself in a role and take pleasure in her ability to get what she wants by becoming something she's not. I did it often, and it gave me imaginative skills I still use. But sometime in my late thirties I was hit hard by a strange version of the Eros and Psyche myth. I began to turn on the light and look at my lovers. Of course thought breaks the heart and things fall apart. What I did learn was that romance is unsatisfactory as a religion. It is no use looking for the infinite in the eyes of another.

Alicia does a fascinating job of exposing Freud's definition of religion as a definition of Freud. She writes: "At the opening of *Civilization and Its Discontents* Freud quotes a letter from Romain Rolland describing a 'sensation of eternity,' a feeling as of something limitless, unbounded, something 'oceanic,' which he defines as the core of religion. Freud does three things with this. First he insists that he cannot 'discover this oceanic feeling in myself' and therefore concludes that it is an illusion. Second he traces this 'feeling of indissoluble connection, of belonging inseparately to the external world as a whole,' to the feelings of the infant at the breast whose 'ego includes everything.' 'Normally,' says Freud, 'there is nothing we are more certain of than the feeling of our self, our own ego. It seems to us an independent unitary thing, sharply outlined against everything else,' except, he significantly adds, when love 'threatens to obliterate the boundaries between ego and object.'"

Looking at my copy of Alicia's book I find the above passage marked with purple pen. Herr Freud seemed to believe, not only that man was the measure of all things, but that Freud was. He worries that love threatens to obliterate the boundaries between the ego and the object. He's afraid of losing himself.

Now it's common knowledge that women in general have blurred ego boundaries. This can be called compassion or it can be called confusion. Some women just don't seem to know where they end and someone else begins. Several serious modern thinkers have suggested that this may be the case because women have other people growing out of them from time to time, and indeed sharing their cosmic space for nine months at a time. Personally I think that is just so much metaphysical speculation and has yet to be proved on paper.

Alicia believes that Freud was trying to get away from it all, that is to get away from connectedness (mom, the earth, etc.) and reach out for our father who art in heaven etc. She writes that Freud: "Having assumed that what 'we' are certain of is non-delusory, Freud goes on to point out that the independent ego forms itself as a result of deprivation of the mother and concerns itself ever after with the will to control others who may be sources of pleasure or pain. Thus the sense of intimate connectedness is associated by Freud with 'infantile helplessness,' 'limitless narcissism,' and illusion, while the reality principle brings us the autonomous ego, the 'primary mutual hostility of human beings,' and the aggressiveness underlying all relationships."

Freud saw human beings in an adversarial relationship to their environment. He saw the world in terms of us and them. Whatever makes for separation among humans — alienation, tribalism, nationalism, racism, sexism, etc. — is perceived as reality. Now there is certainly some justification for his beliefs and it is useless to deny the reality of what is still called a man's world. Alicia goes on: "As to religion, Freud derives it, of course, not from the psychic residue of mother love and the sense of 'indissoluble connection' but from separation and fear. He says: 'The derivation of the need for religion from the child's feeling of helplessness and the longing it evokes for a father seem to me incontrovertible, especially since this feeling is kept alive perpetually by the fear of what the superior power of fate will bring.'

Over against this Freudian formulation we may consider the developing consensus of women writers who propose alternative female structures in the areas of psychology, morality, religion, and literature based on connection rather than separation and modeled on the powerful continuity of the mother-daughter bond."

To speak elliptically for a moment, consider that the poet Alta has said that things won't change for men until fathers love their sons. Fathers must affirm their sons and refuse to kill them in wars and the metaphors for wars men call the marketplace and the monetary system. So too, women must affirm themselves and their daughters and seek to create alternative structures and beliefs.

Recent books by Barbara Walker give us multi-layered information about prepatriarchal thought and religion. *Women's Encyclopedia of Myths and Secrets*, as well as *The Crone: Woman of Age, Wisdom and Power* present a panoramic vision of an earlier age and a time in which human beings seem to have been in balance. Not that they were good, or even wise, only in balance. Eden was not a paradise. Dialecticism or the setting up of measured evils is one of those advanced developments associated with patriarchy. The original image of God, logically enough, was the image of an old woman, a crone. When I saw this image on the cover of Walker's book, I refused to touch it for months. Like all patriarchal people, I fear and loathe age and all that goes with it. Walker's premise is that mankind or humankind has always acted more out of fear than out of love. Perhaps it is time to fear the old woman again. Perhaps Yahweh knew what he was doing with all that thunder. The image of God as a woman, while a less fearful image for many of us, is still a threat. Kali is the mother of destruction and she will throw us all back into a cosmic cauldron in the end. She stirs the cauldron of blood until it boils over. Perhaps we need to look into her dark eyes and understand what really governs the universe. Then we might change our self-destructive behavior. What would happen if a young woman today truly spoke to her mother as if her mother were holy. Truly, that is. Who can imagine such a thing? Even to take a mother's advice is not common. No, in a patriarchy, young women as well as young men must reject and deny the words of their mothers. It is for this reason that women poets must speak/shriek.

Alicia Ostriker's book looks carefully into the work of women psychologists and their findings on mother-daughter bonding, female psyches in general, and ego boundaries and body boundaries. Mostly she explores how women poets have expressed these things.

First of all, women poets tend to have a more hands-on approach to sexuality and sensuality than male poets have. So much for male 'objectivity.'

Alicia writes: "Need, want, look, touch, and joy are key terms in the poetics of intimacy. June Jordan's early exploration of the intersection between sexism and racism puts it in upper case: WHO LOOK AT ME? WHO SEE,' as does Diane Di Prima's *The Party*: 'I NEED TO BE LOOKED AT/be seen/& not twice a week/I'm not a Brancusi bird.' Another of Kathleen

Fraser's poems, *What You Need*, concludes, 'You are brave. But you need to be touched.' Nikki Giovanni complains, 'I want to touch you and be touched. ... But you think I'm grabbing and I think you're shirking,' and elsewhere asserts that touch is 'the true revolution.' Anne Sexton, who grew up among 'people who seldom touched—though touch is all,' not only insists upon the absolute human value of openness, trust, and vulnerability throughout her work, but asserts that human intimacy accomplishes, if only briefly, what religion promises."

As I read these lines I thought of the times in years past when I had tried to explain to some man that he was my religion. Well, I was never quite *that* foolish, but still I remember the awe that intimacy inspired in me and the male withdrawal that sometimes occurs when love becomes too reverential. For many men, raunchy intimacy is most comfortable. It's a question of style. The madonna/whore syndrome suggests that since males have had to reject genital sex with their mothers, they associate it with lesser beings and prefer to label the act with anglo-saxon expletives. The more a woman takes on the aura of wisdom (crone-mother), the more she loses her sexual appeal for males conditioned in a patriarchal culture. Even friendship can be a turn-off because it implies equality and comradeship, and patriarchal man cannot violate his "fellow man." Luckily for some of us, all this is a subject for farce, not tragedy. But in western culture, the tragedy persists.

The revolution of touch will indeed be the last revolution. To touch with tenderness and love is Eros. To touch with violence and hate is Thanatos. Alicia goes on to write of Anne Sexton: "Touch for Sexton is 'the kingdom/and the kingdom come,' or 'Zing! a resurrection.' At the advent of any lovemaking, 'Logos appears milking a star.' Elsewhere in Sexton, even more boldly, the conventional concept of God as love translates to 'When they fuck they are God. ... When they break away they are God. ... In the morning they butter their toast./ They don't say much./ They are still God.' Sharing the same faith, Marge Piercy begins *Meditation in My Favorite Position* with the greeting 'Peace, we have arrived ... know you and be known,/ please you and be pleased.' This is St. Paul's rapsody of love, but inverted: instead of seeking through a glass darkly on earth and expecting 'to know, even as I am known' only when released from the flesh, we find that flesh alone makes knowledge possible. For these and other women, where Eros exits, Thanatos enters."

Sexuality as a resurrection has been celebrated in song and story since language began. As the poet Diane Di Prima says, "the flesh knows better than the spirit, what the soul has eyes for." Even the male poet D. H. Lawrence tried to write of the mystery of the flesh. In *The Man Who Died* Lawrence resurrects Christ himself as a man who needs a woman. Lawrence's Christ finds his mate in a priestess of the old religion. Their union gives a whole new connotation to the line, "I am risen." After the priestess conceives his child, Christ leaves her in the temple and continues his quest for whatever. I used to ask students to compare this story to the Arthurian legend of the search for the holy grail.

Alicia's research makes the disturbing point that for many male poets and scholars, it is the absence of flesh that makes love transcendent or perfectly beautiful. D. H. Lawrence celebrated the flesh and this is perhaps one of the reasons why he appeals to women. (Anais Nin wrote her first published work on Lawrence.) But Lawrence was a male supremacist even in bed and he insisted that woman's role is the worship of the phallus, even to the point of transcending her own orgasm — that is to say, *she must not have one* because she is lifted beyond animal pleasure when she is in the presence of a man-god. The fact is, the flesh instructs the spirit. The spirit has no other teacher. Lawrence speaks always of blood knowledge, as if our blood were separate from our brain. It is the curse of western man, always to have a mind/body split and to imagine that sensuality is in opposition to spirituality. Alicia quotes Diane Wakoski:

> If the heart is caught in a trap
> you can't gnaw it off and run away:
> to cut out the heart
> is to —
> this is obvious —
> cut out life.

When I glance over my shelves of books written by women the word I always hear is *longing*. A longing for intimacy and an end to loneliness underlies every word that women write. I remember once an interviewer asked Simone de Beauvoir why she began writing and she answered that well, she just wanted to talk. To be lifted out of the self and to reach another, this is the thing. This is the longing so many women express in their work. I think of a letter written by a friend of Charlotte Bronte's in which the friend expresses the view that Charlotte was only reaching out for friendship and society. By the time Bronte had written her heart out and gained an entrance into the literary world, she was too nervous and frail to enjoy the society of those she had so longed to be with.

Alicia examines the poem *Sanctuary* by Jean Valentine in which the poet criticizes the self as a prison-sanctuary which prevents us from entering another's mind to know 'what it is like for you there.' The poet asks herself what she most dreads, answering: "Not listening. Now. Not watching. Safe inside my own skin./ To die, not having listened."

Alicia studies the empathy inherent in women's erotics. She writes: "In women's love poetry the imperative of intimacy means goodbye to the hero, goodbye to the strong silent type. 'It was never the crude pestle, the blind/ramrod we were after,' says Adrienne Rich. 'Merely a fellow-creature/with natural resources equal to our own.' 'I like my men/talky and/tender,' explains Carol Bergé, and in poem after poem describing gratified desire, those husbands and lovers are praised who are most gentle and warm, releasing rather than repressing their own feminine qualities."

"Gratified desire" is, of course, a phrase made immortal by William Blake. Alicia Ostriker's first published work of scholarship was *Vision and Verse in William Blake*. She also edited Blake's *Complete Poems* and I always feel his hand (or wing?) on her shoulder when she writes. William Blake is certainly one of those male poets who never, never had to transcend the flesh. He made flesh itself transcendent. A confirmed nudist, his spirit was made manifest in matter. Blake lovers will remember the story his wife told when asked how Blake could keep so clean while printing and engraving with inks and dyes, etc. She replied, "Mister Blake, *he don't stain.*" Of course she is also reported to have said she had little of Mister Blake's company as he was always in paradise.

In my own experience, I find it to be true that women are more grounded in their views of the flesh. Perhaps there are fewer surprises for those who change diapers and tampons? It is ironic because women are required to behave more modestly than men, that is, to shower privately and cover their breasts — and other such western habits. Some of this has begun to change. Women are acknowledging their own sexuality, and this has come as quite a shock to both sexes.

Alicia describes role reversal in women's poetry and women taking the initiative in lovemaking. She writes of "Elizabeth Sargent, who picks up and takes home a sailor, enjoys his battle tales, and is entertained when asked if she is a virgin: 'No, I'm a poet, I said. Fuck me again.'"

It's always dangerous to demystify sex. I was told it would cause impotence in males. No one told me what caused impotence in me. I'm afraid that the masculine dread of woman which crops up everywhere, in poetry and anywhere you chance to look, is what causes impotence in me.

Leonore Kandel wrote: "I am not sure where I leave off, where you begin."
Once I quoted this line to a lover and he took off before there was time to
really begin. He didn't like to get things blurred. When I read men's poetry, I
feel their worries and hear their little asides which tell me that they bind up
Eros with Thanatos more than women like to admit. It isn't that a man
doesn't love his wife as she grows older, it is only that she has become his
mother in truth. And only a young woman can dispel his fear of death.

Finally Alicia asks the question of what becomes of eroticism when we
get beyond the bedroom door, when we get to the world at large. How does
female metaphor apply to the arms race, so to speak. "Female sexuality
exploits metaphors of safety and security. Its most joyous act is mutual
letting go." In my experience, female eroticism is not often associated with
violence. (With the usual exceptions to prove the rule.) I can remember
many times when I was scolded or laughed at by men for "letting go" too
much. Obviously it was not mutual letting go. I was told that I became
unaware of my surroundings while making love, or did not pay close
attention to where I was, etc. Men can be stuffy about female self-expression.

Alicia points out that: "To release sexual libido is to subvert social and
political order, as we learn in male western literature from Euripides'
Bacchae to Blake's *Marriage of Heaven and Hell*, from Rabelais to de Sade, and
from Freud and Reich to Orwell's *1984*, where the triumph of Big Brother
depends on the poisoning of sex. 'The personal is the political' is a key
feminist slogan, and the connection between erotic need and the need to
be 'disloyal to civilization' is central in feminist poetry. As gratified desire
emerges from beings who are equivalent rather than polarized, sexual
union becomes a figure in women's poems for every reunification needed
by a divided humanity. Relationships between friends and lovers become
paradigmatic for the conduct of political life."

For example, can you imagine a couple (male and female couple at first,
one revolution at a time) as rulers of a state? I had hoped the Soviets might
try it, but that was wishful thinking. Can private and public life become
indivisible? Can we come clean? A nun who left the church once wrote that
we are as sick as our secrets. Today's big secret is the one everyone
knows: We are not what we seem. We are starved for the erotic. Not just for
genital sex, although there can never be too much of that, but for Eros, for a
compassionate world.

Back in the '50s when I first became aware of some of these things, I
was shocked to read in Wilhelm Reich's *Psychology of Fascism* that the first
duty of a tyranny was the suppression of sexual desire, of sexual *need*. Nazis
don't *need* women. They use them of course, but they don't associate with

them. The suppression of Eros is the first business of fascism. Eros is messy. It doesn't make the trains run on time. Eros is disorderly and doesn't always finish buttoning her dress. Eros, for fascists in the 1930s, was Rosa Luxemburg, the communist whore who wanted to destroy feudal order.

Strange that on the surface it is women who are often blamed for the suppression of sex. Or perhaps it's not so strange. I believe that only unhappy or sick women reject Eros and that the reason they are sick or unhappy is because they are humiliated and not allowed to passionately pursue erotic ecstasy when they are capable of it. When women are truly released from their bonds then order goes out the window and society (patriarchy) gasps in horror.

Female Eros is subversive in ways even women are fearful of. To embrace Eros is the ultimate high, the final freedom, the best moment life has to offer. Once Eros possesses us, we have nothing to lose, and Thanatos, death, has no hold over us. To live as one already dead is to become Eros.

Alicia refers to Judy Grahn's underground classic, *A Woman Is Talking to Death*, a long poem which connects female eroticism with the need to combat racism, misogyny, and class oppression. She quotes a long passage in the poem in which there is a mock interrogation and the woman in the poem is asked over and over if she has kissed any women. No matter how much the woman describes the suffering she has seen, and speaks of the terrors and joys of all the women she has known, the question asked over and over still seems to be: "You didn't actually kiss her?"

The love of woman for woman, the love of woman for herself, whether sexual or spiritual or only sensible, is still the ultimate subversion. What Alicia's book made me understand is that the last thing a woman should do is to write poetry as men do. Is it Stein who said that the difference to be a difference must make a difference?

The woman poet does not wish to write as a man does. We do not wish to join the club. It is not that we serve a different master, although we do. It is that we are sick of service and the master has made masochists of us all. Woman's motive in writing is not mastery, either of herself or her material. Women do not wish to equal men as artists. They wish to find a new voice. Equity within the literary establishment would be nice but it will not, I think, occur. Besides, equal is not the same. What women will give us is more of themselves. For a poet, style is the only morality. If woman's style is to seek an end to separation and a trend toward intimacy, then there is hope for literature in our time.

NOTES ON THE BRONTES

"Sadism knocks down barriers between an isolate soul and others. Violence forces reaction. That unity of souls may be linked to sadism is the sad riddle of the world."

> Susan Howe
> *My Emily Dickinson*

I *am* Heathcliff!

> Emily Bronte
> *Wuthering Heights*

Impossible to synthesize my thoughts on the Brontes. A familiar essay should pare things down until they *mean* something. When I contemplate these Celtic colossi (well, Charlotte was only 4′ 9″) I can catch only a glimpse of their haunted faces at the windows of that gray parsonage with its Anglican angst, its alcoholism (and brother Branwell's addiction to opium), neurasthenia, isolationism, and what Charlotte herself called "barbarism."

Once, in a dream, I was talking to Charlotte about the hot chocolate desire in her poems and demanding to know if she was orgasmic. Suddenly Emily appeared in a fury, throwing a great tomato at my head. I was terrified at first but then she stopped and took another tomato in her hand and sliced it very fine. She threw the center slice right smack in my face and it covered me with a blood red cape and the seeds turned to jewels and shone like moonstones in the dark.

The Bronte sisters, Charlotte, Emily and Anne, are the fundamental touchstones for women like me who imagine that we can transcend our lives through art. Under the most appalling difficulties, these women strove relentlessly to create order out of chaos. What is special about them, of course, is that they pulled it off.

Who were these women and why should we care about them? They died young. They were not prolific. When I proposed to include Emily Bronte as poet (this would exclude her only novel, *Wuthering Heights*, considered to be her major work) as one of the three major authors to be studied for my orals exam for an M.A. degree I took in 1975, I was informed by the academic powers-that-be that I might use the complete works of all three sisters Bronte and that such a study would constitute *one* major author. I could not help but think of Virginia Woolf's reference (in her essay *A Room of One's Own*) to the "professor with a measuring-rod up his sleeve."

I care about the Brontes because of their visionary genius. I regret that they were exhausted by their efforts to play the role Virginia Woolf describes as "the angel in the house." In particular, this role was anathema to Emily Bronte who was more attached than all the others to the moors and to her own sacred convictions.

Emily was a Celtic seer who worshipped the chthonian gods of the earth while at the same time living the outward life of a Victorian Christian. She was a heathen in her heart. The dictionary tells me that a heathen originally meant one who lived on the heath, that is to say, in the country. On 7 December 1838, Emily Bronte wrote:

> "Come, sit down on this sunny stone:
> 'tis wintry light o'er flowerless moors —
> But sit — for we are all alone. ..."

The purple heather of Emily Bronte is the same symbol of liberty and ecstasy today that it was in her lifetime. "Leave the heart that now I bear/ And give me liberty!" she wrote in 1841, seven years before her death at age twenty-nine.

Let's go dust the graves. First there was the father, Patrick Bronte. He was born on Saint Patrick's day in 1777. A native of County Down in Ireland, he was bog-Irish, that is to say, a farmer or peasant rather than what is called lace-curtain Irish, or landed gentry. He changed his name from Brunty to Bronte and opened a school at age sixteen. He became a tutor and proceeded to St. John's College, Cambridge in 1802 where he obtained a B.A. degree and a curacy in Essex, and finally settled in Yorkshire. "Mr. Bronte has now no trace of his Irish origin remaining in his speech; he never could have shown his Celtic descent in the straight Greek lines and long oval of his face. ..." So writes Elizabeth Gaskell in her famous biography, *The Life of Charlotte Bronte*, first published in 1857.

Mrs. Gaskell met Patrick Bronte on a visit to Charlotte during the years following the deaths of all the other children. Charlotte lived alone with her father who only joined the two women at tea as an honor to his guest. "What he does with himself through the day I cannot imagine," Mrs. Gaskell writes. And, "He talked at her sometimes." She adds, "Mr. Bronte bears a great fancy for firearms of all kinds . . . this little deadly pistol sitting down to breakfast with us every morning." She notes that Mr. Bronte never goes anywhere without a loaded gun. (Remember Emily Dickinson's line: "My life had stood, a loaded gun.") She concludes: "He was very polite & agreeable to me; paying rather elaborate old-fashioned compliments, but I was sadly afraid of him in my inmost soul; for I caught a glare of his stern eyes over his spectacles at Miss Bronte once or twice which made me know my man."

Mrs. Gaskell, in letters to friends, wrote that she believed Mr. Bronte should never have married. He was apparently much in love with his wife, Maria Branwell, when he was a young red-haired Irishman flushed with ambition and a pal of Lord Palmerston at Cambridge, etc. Maria is a pale figure as a mother. She had borne six children in seven years when she died in 1821 at the age of thirty-nine. Patrick lived to be eighty-five, dying in 1861. When Mrs. Gaskell wrote her biography, she was doubtless inhibited by the fact that Mr. Bronte still lived. Here is an extract from a letter from Mary Taylor (a friend of Charlotte's) to Mrs. Gaskell from Wellington, New Zealand, 30 July 1857:

[Your] book is a perfect success, in giving a true picture of a melancholy life, and you have practically answered my puzzle as to how you would give a true description of those around. [Meaning Branwell, the self-destructive brother, as well as Patrick, the tyrannical father.] Though not so gloomy as the truth, it is perhaps as much so as people will accept without calling it exaggerated, and feeling the desire to doubt and contradict it. I have seen two reviews of it. One of them sums it up as 'a life of poverty and self-suppression,' the other has nothing to the purpose at all. Neither of them seems to think it a strange or wrong state of things that a woman of first-rate talents, industry, and integrity should live all her life in a walking nightmare of 'poverty and self-suppression.' I doubt whether any of them will.

Yet Charlotte could laughingly sign her letters, "Charles Thunder." Bronte means thunder. Certainly nobody stole Charlotte's thunder unless it was Emily and that did not happen until long after both were dead. Virginia Woolf insisted Emily was the greater artist because she left the "I" out of her work. Like Jane Austen and William Shakespeare, it's hard to find the author in the work. Charlotte, on the other hand, often slips up and delivers a sermon which has an all-too-personal ring. For my money, I do not care whether a writer hides behind her characters or speaks right through them, just so long as the writer makes me feel s/he gives a damn about what is being said. As an aside, I have to repeat that Virginia Woolf did finally grasp the notion that aesthetic distance is a patriarchal plot and that all that matters is that a writer write truly, without altering a hair on the head of her vision, as Woolf put it.

To get back to the graves. Any sketch of the Brontes must include the deaths of the first two children, Maria and Elizabeth, who died in May and June of 1825 aged twelve and eleven. The death of these two seems to have haunted the remaining four for the rest of their lives. Maria and Elizabeth had been sent to Cowan Bridge School — an institution for the genteel poor which served as the model for Lowood, the malevolent girls' school in *Jane Eyre*. Maria and Elizabeth had weak lungs and an epidemic of typhoid fever finished them off. Perhaps most remarkable of all is the fact that Mr. Bronte then sent both Charlotte and Emily to attend this school until their ill health forced him to bring them home to Haworth. It was a question of money, apparently.

Patrick Bronte treated his children as if they were miniature adults. In this he was no different from many other early Victorians. He was not in a class with the Reverend Carus Wilson, founder of the Cowan Bridge School and the living model for the fictitious character of Mr. Brocklehurst, founder of Lowood in *Jane Eyre*. Henry Daniell, the renowned Hollywood actor who played Brocklehurst, bears an astonishing resemblance to the sketches Charlotte made for the book. When her publisher suggested these sketches be used as illustrations she termed them "mere scribblings."

While the Reverend Bronte did not subscribe to the theory, so dear to the hearts of men like the Reverend Wilson, that children's clothes caught fire to teach them a lesson, he did believe in admonishing their parents for neglect. In a letter entitled "Cremation" which was published in the *Leeds Mercury*, he very sensibly points out that, "I have performed the funeral service over ninety or a hundred children, who were burnt to death in consequence of their clothes having taken fire," and he goes on to state that they were in every case clothed in cotton or linen. He recommends silk or wool.

Unfortunately, his nurturing efforts on behalf of his own children had rendered them mute by the time the youngest (Anne) was about four. The father used the device of a mask in order to persuade them to express themselves freely. Mrs. Gaskell quotes Patrick: "I began with the youngest and asked what a child like her most wanted; she answered, 'Age and experience.' I asked the next (Emily) what I had best do with her brother Branwell, who was sometimes a naughty boy; she answered, 'Reason with him, and when he won't listen to reason, whip him.' I asked Branwell what was the best way of knowing the difference between the intellects of man and woman; he answered, 'By considering the difference between them as to their bodies.' I then asked Charlotte what was the best book in the world; she answered, 'The Bible.' And what was the next best; she answered, 'The Book of Nature.' I then asked the next (Elizabeth) what was the best mode of education for a woman; she answered, 'That which would make her rule her house well.' Lastly, I asked the oldest what was the best mode of spending time; she answered, 'By laying it out in preparation for a happy eternity.'"

The oldest, Maria, is the model for the character of Helen Burns in *Jane Eyre*. Helen is a saintly child whose patience is quite maddening. She is punished ruthlessly for untidy habits and dies more from neglect than illness. By the time this same character found her way into a Hollywood film, her vice had become vanity — Hollywood seemed to assume that the Victorians hated sex — and a prepubescent Elizabeth Taylor has her long black curls cut off and stands all night in the rain to catch her death of cold. The vision of the Victorians as sexually suppressed is just as typical today as it was in that rather lurid 1943 film.

It is imperative to study the harsh realities of Victorian life and to get away from the vague romantic picture which the textbooks tend to settle for. The bills at Cowan Bridge School required pinching pennies down to the last stocking. In later years, the three Bronte sisters bought their writing paper two sheets at a time. During their infancy, their mother was nearly always bedridden. Their only escape, both physically and psychologically, was their long walks on the moors.

Mrs. Gaskell writes: "From their first going to Haworth, their walks were directed rather out toward the heathery moors sloping upwards behind the parsonage than towards the long descending village street. A good old woman who came to nurse Mrs. Bronte in the illness, an internal cancer which grew and gathered upon her not many months after her arrival at Haworth, this woman tells me that at that time the six little creatures used to walk out hand in hand toward the glorious wild moors which in afterdays they loved so passionately, the elder ones taking thoughtful care for the toddling wee things. They were grave and silent beyond their years, subdued probably by the presence of a serious illness in the house, for at the time my informant speaks of, Mrs. Bronte was confined to the bedroom from which she never came forth alive. 'You would not have known there was a child in the house, they were such still, noiseless, good little creatures. Maria would shut herself up, Maria, the eldest, but seven, in the children's study with a newspaper and be able to tell one everything when she came out. The debates in Parliament and I don't know what all. She was as good as a mother to her sisters and brother. But there never were such good children. I used to think them spiritless, they were so different to any children I had ever seen. They were good little creatures. Emily was the prettiest.'"

We know from the measurements of the coffins that Emily was the tallest. She was a thunderous thing at 5′ 3″ while Charlotte stood 4′ 9″ and the others, including Branwell, were equally diminutive.

Mrs. Gaskell goes on: "Mrs. Bronte was the same patient cheerful person as we have seen her formerly. Very ill, suffering great pain, but seldom if ever complaining. At her better times begging her nurse to raise her in bed to let her see her clean the grate because she did it as it was done in Cornwall. [Cornwall was Maria Branwell's seaside home, an altogether more comfortable and hospitable place than Haworth.] She was devotedly fond of her husband. He warmly repaid her affection and suffered no one else to take the night nursing. But, according to my informant, the mother was not very anxious to see much of her children, probably because the sight of them, knowing how soon they were to be left motherless, would have agitated her too much. And so the little things clung quietly together for their father was busy in his study and in his parish or with their mother. They took their meals alone. They sat reading or whispering low in the children's study or they wandered on the hillside, hand in hand."

In August of 1846, Charlotte went with her father to Manchester where he had a cataract operation on both his eyes. During the weeks of his convalescence, Charlotte was forced to sit with him in the dark. Leeches were put on his temples but not on his eyelids. Belladonna, prepared from the deadly nightshade, was put in his eyes to expand the pupils. Charlotte herself was agonized by toothache at this time and the pain; she wrote to a friend, had left her "stupified." It was in this atmosphere that she forced herself to write in order to escape the torment of her existence. It was perhaps not so much an escape as a transmutation. Modern critics have suggested that she wrote in a trance state. It is to this circumstance that we owe the novel *Jane Eyre*.

The trance theory is one of my favorites. See a chapter titled "The

Spectral Selves of Charlotte Bronte," in *The Madwoman in the Attic: The Woman Writer and the Nineteenth Century Literary Imagination*, written by Sandra M. Gilbert and Susan Gubar (New Haven: Yale University Press, 1979). There is much to be said for the theory that the madwoman in the attic (Bertha Rochester in *Jane Eyre* for one) is the repressed self—the unconscious self that Virginia Woolf buried so deep it only emerged during her psychotic breaks when she, too, like Bertha Rochester, attacked her husband.

In a trance or not, Charlotte seemed to be able to reach down into her unconscious and dredge up a madwoman. Of course, she's Irish. As a nineteenth-century clergyman's daughter, she was forced to suppress her darker nature or to cloak her feelings of rage in Christian thoughts.

Today, scholars still like to assume she didn't know what she was doing. Perhaps she did not have what Gertrude Stein calls conscious consciousness. Perhaps yes, perhaps no, but really it does not really make any difference. Charlotte's world view demanded justice and her Christianity translated into transcendence. It was perhaps the only choice available to her. The severe physical and financial hardships of her life made the Calvinist vision all the more appealing. Her day-to-day life was a wretched round of aches and pains, migraine headaches, toothache, failing eyesight, and general debilitation. A meager diet filled with potatoes was not much help. Trances and transcendental modes are no substitute for aspirin but they did produce masterpieces. In her novel *Villette*, Charlotte describes a drug experience with opium and her contemporaries asked her how she knew about such things. She did not speak of her addicted brother, Branwell, who may have been a source of her knowledge. She stated that she had dreamt the experience, or used her imagination if you will. This is one instance of her deliberate daydreaming, a habit condemned by her male mentor, the then poet laureate Robert Southey. Southey warned her that such dreams might cause her to neglect her domestic duties:

> The day dreams in which you habitually indulge are likely to induce a distempered state of mind; and in proportion as all the ordinary uses of the world seem to you flat and unprofitable, you will be unfitted for them without becoming fitted for anything else. Literature cannot be the business of a woman's life, and it ought not to be. The more she is engaged in her proper duties, the less leisure will she have for it, even as an accomplishment and a recreation. To those duties you have not yet been called, and when you are you will be less eager for celebrity. You will not seek in imagination for excitement. ...

Charlotte might have been able to bear up under this male condescension if she had had some measure of health and wealth. (As did her vigorous and energetic contemporary, Harriet Martineau.) However, the ignorance of her time was not only moral and intellectual, it operated in areas which affected her very survival—areas such as medicine and civil engineering.

Haworth was one of the unhealthiest villages in England during the Bronte years. It was more hazardous to human health than the slums of London during the same era. Open privies and dung heaps were the rule. Is it any wonder the children fled to the moors rather than try to go among their fellows in the village? In 1820 Haworth had no drainage system and possessed not one water closet. The parsonage was surrounded on three sides by a graveyard in which there was an average of *two burials a week*. The well which supplied the Brontes with their drinking water was sunk into this cemetary. They literally drank death every day. Reports of the health inspectors indicated that the church smelled moribund. "The exhalations from the remains of past generations inside the building have long rendered it a most undesirable place in which to worship without being too pungently reminded of the ultimate end of all things." The graves were close set and covered over with stone slabs and there were no trees at that time so decomposition was not allowed to take its course. The water supply was poor and often gave out completely in the summer heat when typhus raged. The parsonage had one double-seated privy out in the yard. Imagine what it must have been like to live in that tiny house with six children and two servants. A government inspector's report dated 1850 describes a situation in Haworth which had not altered much in thirty years: "Two of the privies used by a dozen families each are in the public street, not only within view of the houses, but exposed to the gaze of passers by, whilst a third, as though even such a situation were too private, is perched upon an eminence, commanding the whole length of the main street, The cesspit of this privy lies below it, and opens by a small door into the main street; occasionally this door is burst open by the superincumbent weight of night soil and ashes, and they overflow into the public street, and at all times a disgusting effluvium escapes . . ." No wonder that Aunt Branwell wore pattens, the raised shoes necessary for walking in the street.

The reason I give these details is to suggest that when the Brontes wrote, they were trying to escape or transmute the mordant realities of their world. They did not lie about their time, they only tried to shape it and to give it meaning and significance. Emily tried to create an order where in truth she saw only chaos. An ordered universe suggests the possibility of God. Ah, well, perhaps in that they were romantics after all. But the Christianity of the Brontes was never soft or sensual, as Charlotte and Emily both liked to describe the "Romish" (Catholic) sort of religiosity they met with in Brussels. Straight is the gait for these stern and stoic daughters of the Calvinist cloth.

And who could have been less well equipped for a life of self-denial than these oh-so-vulnerable early Victorian geniuses. With no more material wealth than the peasants and laborers among whom they lived, they were required to keep up a show of gentility and refinement. Charlotte writes to a friend that she tried a new-fangled thing—a shower-bath—and "found it most refreshing." Imagine living with no running water and the sanitary situation with, say, the rags used to absorb menstrual blood. Most of all, there was the crippling cold and damp. Candles were expensive and often the sisters would walk around and around the dining table in the evening in the dark in the hope of wearing themselves out and getting a night's sleep. After the death of the others, Charlotte continued this habit alone as her eyes gave her a good deal of trouble and it was hard to read in the evening.

The mortality rate in Haworth equaled that recorded in the London slums of the period. The average age at death was at times as low as 19.6 years with 41 out of a hundred children dying before their sixth birthday. The first public health act in England was not passed until the 1840s. The act made a connection between the burial of the dead in towns and the prevalence of disease. Apparently the notion that cadavers contaminate was new. Even in the hospitals, there was little effort to separate the living from the dead.

During these years the germ theory of disease had yet to be promulgated and physicians often went directly from examining a corpse to delivering a baby without washing their hands. Mothers were dying of septicemia or childbed fever all over Europe and England. It is hard for us to imagine the prevalence of so much death on a day-to-day basis.

For the Brontes, eternity was no metaphor. Sitting in the parsonage, Charlotte writes: "There have I sat on the low bedstead, my eyes fixed on the window, through which no other landscape than a monstrous stretch of moorland and a grey church tower rising from the centre of a churchyard so filled with graves that the rank weeds and coarse grass scarce had room to shoot up between the monuments."

For Emily, all this bleak world was a source of passion.

"There is a spot mid barren hills
Where winter howls and drives the rain …
… the house is old, the trees are bare,
Moonless above bends twilight's dome …
… the mute bird sitting on the stone,
The dark moss dripping from the wall,
The thorn trees gaunt, the walks o'ergrown
I love them, how I love them all."

Emily used her life to fuel her art. The graves of Cathy and Heathcliff in *Wuthering Heights* serve as metaphors for love beyond the grave. When the long-dead Cathy (who died in childbirth at the age of twenty-three) is to be joined by her recently deceased husband, Edgar Linton, Heathcliff opens her grave and discovers her body has scarcely decomposed. Perhaps Emily Bronte had seen such things in the graveyard that surrounded her home on three sides. Perhaps it is true that the heavy stone slabs used on the tombs did slow down decomposition. Heathcliff tells his housekeeper, Nelly, about his plans for joining Cathy in the earth:

" … yesterday I got the sexton, who was digging Linton's grave, to remove the earth off her coffin-lid, and I opened it. I thought, once, I would have stayed there, when I saw her face again — it is hers yet — he had hard work to stir me; but he said it would change, if the air blew on it, and so I struck one side of the coffin loose, and covered it up: not Linton's side, damn him! … I bribed the sexton to pull it away, when I'm laid there, and slide mine out too. I'll have it made so, and then, by the time Linton gets to us, he'll not know which is which!"

Scenes such as this were not uncommon in the literature of the early nineteenth century. I think of the description George Sand gives in her *Historie de ma vie* of her last farewell to her father as she kisses his lips ten years after his burial. During the funeral of her grandmother, her tutor discovers that her father's head has come apart from his body. His neck was broken in a fall from his horse. The tutor invites George Sand to enter the crypt and kiss her father goodbye as she never had an opportunity to do so when he was alive. Sand describes the experience as very moving.

Remember the exhumed body of Marguerite Gautier in the novel *La Dame aux Camélias* (1848) by Dumas? And of course the exhumation of Lizzie Siddal, the young wife of Dante Gabriel Rossetti. Rossetti buried his libretti in her coffin but then some seven years later he recovered from his grief and decided to dig them up. Lizzie had killed herself with an overdose of laudanum, the wine or tincture of opium. The story goes that her golden hair had kept on growing and that it filled her coffin. "Golden Lizzie" is perhaps the woman made famous as the tormented creature in Christina Rossetti's (Dante's sister) poem *Goblin Market*.

My mind always wanders to Dante Gabriel Rossetti when I think of the Brontes because he wrote my favorite review of *Wuthering Heights* in 1854. "It is a fiend of a book. The action is laid in Hell, only it seems places and people have English names there."

Seems the nineteenth century was as close to its dead as we are estranged from ours. Edgar Allen Poe was perhaps too close and mingled too intimately with the dust of the grave. Still, those who forget the taste of death often forget the flavor of life. Life in Yorkshire for the Brontes was miserable and mystic, severe and sensual, holy and horrible, all at once. The wretched world of reality drove them into subjectivity. Fantasy was a necessity.

Charlotte Bronte once wrote in a letter to a friend that expecting compassion from Papa, "was like expecting sap from firewood." The male models which the Brontes used for their novels ranged from tyrannical overbearing types like Patrick to drunkards like their brother Branwell and supercilious curates like the ones who came to serve their father in his parish. The curates were not without their charms, although for the most part they found their way into the novels as satirical characters. There was one named William Weightman who died in the cholera epidemic of 1842. The then twenty-year-old Anne may have been in love with him. The other sisters called him "Miss Celia Amelia" and Charlotte considered him a flirt.

If it is true that Anne Bronte suffered a loss when this young curate died, this may account for her later melancholy. Willy was reported to be quite cheerful and he had made a difference in their lives for several years. Anne has been described as the most "religious" of the sisters. Charlotte wrote that Anne, "Wept at the foot of some secret Sinai . . . ." She may have had a predisposition for religious morbidity. Only eight months old when her mother died, she slept in her Aunt Branwell's room as a child. Aunt Branwell was her mother's unmarried elder sister and a staunch Methodist. Perhaps her solicitude for others and her ability to bear her life as a governess with more patience than was evidenced by Emily or Charlotte stems from her early contact with her aunt.

Anne had a lisp. As the baby in the family she is described by a friend, Ellen Nussey, as: ". . . quite different in appearance from the others. She was her aunt's favorite. Her hair was a very pretty light brown and fell on her neck in graceful curls. She had lovely violet-blue eyes, fine pencilled eyebrows, and a clear, almost transparent complexion."

From a third person account, Mrs. Gaskell writes: "The first impression made on the visitor by the sisters was that Emily was a tall, long-armed girl, more fully grown than her sister Charlotte and extremely reserved in manner. I distinguish reserve from shyness because I imagine shyness would please if it knew how whereas reserve is indifferent whether it pleases or not. Anne, like her elder sister Charlotte, was shy. Emily was reserved." She adds: "They all of them thought there could be no doubt about Branwell's talent for drawing and I have seen an oil painting of his done I know not when but probably in the early 1820s . . . it was a group of the three sisters, not much better than sign painting I thought as to execution, but the likenesses were, I thought, admirable. On the deeply shadowed side was Emily with Anne's gentle face resting on her shoulder. Emily's countenance struck me as full of power, Charlotte's of solicitude, Anne's of tenderness."

Anne was certainly more charitable in her judgments than either Emily or Charlotte. Hers was a forgiving kind of love. It is perhaps for this reason that her books lack the ferocity and power of her sisters. Not enough animus perhaps? Raised by aunt more than father? The scholars always point to the element of the social tract in her novels *Agnes Grey* and *The Tenant of Wildfell Hall*. Anne was shattered by the grief of living with a brother who was both drunkard and drug addict and her books read like warnings to young women to avoid marriage with such men. I can't argue but that her descriptions of close confinement with a drunkard are morbid, although I imagine that this was moving stuff for women living in such hells as she portrays. It is only in the light of such multi-layered works as her sisters produced that hers seem perhaps simplistic. Anne died when she was twenty-nine and she was buried, not with the others, but at Scarborough by the sea.

The death of her brother and sisters was the darkest period in the life of Charlotte Bronte. Branwell died, "after twenty minutes' struggle, on Sunday morning, September 24th (1848). He was perfectly conscious till the last agony came on. His mind had undergone the peculiar change which frequently precedes death. . . . A deep conviction that he rests at last — rests well after his brief, erring, suffering, feverish life — fills and quiets my mind now. The final separation, the spectacle of his pale corpse, gave me more acute, bitter pain than I could have imagined. Till the last hour comes we never know how much we can forgive, pity, regret a near relative. All his vices were and are nothing now. We remember only his woes. Papa was acutely distressed at first, but, on the whole, has borne the event well."

Even as Charlotte wrote this letter to a friend, Emily had caught cold at Branwell's funeral and was to die on 19 December. Charlotte describes her own bilious fevers and illnesses during the following months as she determines to grant the last wish of the dying Anne who longs to visit the sea. Charlotte takes her to Scarborough on May 24th of 1849. There she and Charlotte walk on the sands of the beach and Charlotte's describes her sister's joy in a sunset. Anne had never visited the sea before and her happiness was such that Charlotte decided to bury her there when on the 28th of May, she died without a murmur, only admonishing Charlotte to "take courage."

Charlotte went on living until March of 1855 when she died at the age of thirty-nine. In the summer of 1854, Charlotte had married her father's curate, Arthur Bell Nicholls, and her subsequent pregnancy was perhaps the final drain on her consumptive constitution. Charlotte wrote to a friend that one of her reasons for marrying was to assist her father. "Papa has taken no duty since we returned (from her wedding trip to Ireland to visit relatives of Mr. Nicholls): and each time I see Mr. Nicholls put on gown or surplice, I feel comforted to think that this marriage has secured Papa good aid in his old age."

Charlotte was a dutiful "angel in the house." She did confess that marriage allowed her little time for herself but she supposed this was as it should be. She was well aware that her earlier romantic dreams were not to be fulfilled by such a man as Nicholls, whose appeal seems to have been his authoritarianism—a trait Charlotte was accustomed to. As far as his intellectual sympathies are concerned, she expresses gratitude in a letter to a woman friend when he allows her to sit alone and reflect by herself and does not intrude upon her solitude. She is aware that her husband is not her intellectual peer. She writes: "The destiny which Providence in His goodness and wisdom seems to offer me will not, I am aware, be generally regarded as brilliant, but I trust I see in it some germs of real happiness."

On Charlotte's wedding day, her father abruptly refused to give the bride away and a woman friend had to be pressed into service. Patrick's motives might not have been entirely selfish as he had seen his own wife die of marital bliss. Once in a letter, he even hints that his wife died angry, or that "the great enemy, envying her life of holiness, often disturbed her mind in the last conflict." Although the rest of the letter is platitudes about how much confidence he has that she "fell asleep in Jesus," he says finally that she died, "if not triumphantly, at least calmly." Who can doubt that this death which took place at a time when all six of his children were ill with scarlet fever had made a lasting impression on the soul of Patrick Bronte.

What does all this have to do with the work? Well, it *is* the work. *Jane Eyre* and the other novels are how-to books for women which examine the ways in which spiritual and psychological survival are possible for a Victorian woman. Of course, Jane Austen was much more sensible and she concentrated on the money which is why she is still called classical. The Brontes are romantic on the grounds that they worried most about their souls. "I cannot live without my life, I cannot die without my soul," cried Heathcliff, the animus of Emily Bronte herself.

Emily is so powerful, she pulls my thoughts away from Charlotte at every turn. That's not fair because Charlotte is a genius in her own right and if her obsession with love's fulfillment is a bit out of fashion at the moment, well, there's sure to be a revival soon. I think always of Charlotte's "Black Swan," her Brussels professor to whom she wrote such masochistic and desperate letters after she had returned from the continent. Her biographer alludes to these letters but tries to hide their overwhelmingly sexual nature. After all Charlotte's biographer, Mrs. Gaskell, was writing her book in the late 1850s when both father and husband still lived. Mr. Nicholls was said to approve of the book — that is, until he thought about it. It had to be pointed out to him that the portrait drawn of him was not altogether flattering.

Charlotte's work is often laced with hot chocolate desire. As I have stated elsewhere, D. H. Lawrence wrote that it borders on the pornographic. She herself was unconscious of this because in her sensibility, lust *was* love. Mrs. Gaskell writes: "This seems a fitting place to state how utterly unconscious she was of what was, by some, esteemed coarse in her writings . . . . I remember her grave, earnest way of saying, 'I trust God will take from me whatever power of invention or expression I may have before He lets me become blind to the sense of what is fitting or unfitting to be said!'" Charlotte was so distressed when a fellow author told her that they had both "written naughty books" that she went to her publisher's wife to ask if there was anything so wrong in *Jane Eyre*.

Of course it is Charlotte's innocence which is evident. The innuendo is lost on her when Thackeray and his cronies make jokes about cigar smoke and hint that her character, Mr. Rochester in *Jane Eyre*, is hovering somewhere nearby. Others note Miss Bronte's inability to pick up on such snide references and attribute it to her inability to imagine sex as prurient.

Charlotte's high-mindedness was lost on the wife of her "Black Swan" — Paul Heger, the headmaster of the girls' school in Brussels where Charlotte went as student and later became teacher. Charlotte adored him and found him kind at first. "Nothing refines like affection," she wrote. Once her crush became obvious, Heger became aloof and certainly this episode of unrequited passion bore fruit in Charlotte's novels.

Here are a few lines from Charlotte's letters to Paul Heger in Brussels. "When day by day I await a letter and when day by day disappointment comes to fling me back into overwhelming sorrow ... I lose appetite and sleep — I pine away." And in another letter, "All I know is, that I cannot, that I will not, resign myself to lose wholly the friendship of my master. I would rather suffer the greatest physical pain than always have my heart lacerated by smarting regrets. If my master withdraws his friendship from me entirely I shall be altogether without hope; if he gives me a little — just a little — I shall be satisfied — happy; I shall have a reason for living on, for working."

Charlotte's desperate lack of confidence in herself as a woman seems to have had its masochistic side. She had a nervous dread of strangers which Mrs. Gaskell attributes to her belief in her personal ugliness. Charlotte herself wrote: "I notice that after a stranger has once looked at my face he is careful not to let his eyes wander to that part of the room again." Charlotte's London publisher, George Smith, wrote: "I must confess that my first impression of Charlotte Bronte's personal appearance was that it was interesting rather than attractive. She was very small, had a quaint, old-fashioned look. Her head seemed too large for her body. She had fine eyes but her face was marred by the shape of the mouth and by the complexion. There was but little feminine charm about her and of this fact she herself was uneasily and perpetually conscious. It may seem strange that the possession of genius did not lift her above the weakness of an excessive anxiety about her personal appearance but I believe she would have given all her genius and her fame to have been more beautiful. Perhaps few women ever existed more anxious to be pretty than she or more angrily conscious of the circumstance that she was not pretty."

Charlotte protested that even plain women could find love. She once told her sisters that they were wrong to make their heroines beautiful. They told her it was impossible to make a heroine interesting on any other terms. Charlotte said she would prove to them that it could be done, that she would show them a heroine as plain and as small as herself. And she did. Plain Jane Eyre is the sort of adolescent fantasy that swept me away at the age of eleven. Jane is the suffering martyr/conquering hero that all adolescents become for those years when the world seems to overwhelm them. The book is a Christian fairy tale one moment, and a Victorian guide to manners the next. Rochester suffers from pride and so he is brought low. Pussy-whipped perhaps?

Most readers are familiar with Jane's odyssey from orphanage to her final embrace in the "stout arms of a lord of creation," a phrase Charlotte herself used to refer to the best of men —lords of creation she called them. Yet she blinds Rochester in a fire. He is heroic in matters of physical courage and his injuries come as a result of his attempt to *rescue his imprisoned* "mad" wife who set the fire which burned Thornfield to the ground. Charlotte's monumental symbology and Gothic splendors give this tale a mythic size. It has all sorts of flaws and can even be described as a soap opera, but as a psychodrama it has few equals.

Consider the drag scene. Rochester dresses up as a gypsy fortune teller, the better to discover Jane's real feelings toward him. Charlotte has a pagan impulse and calls him a soothsayer or Sybil. Rochester is incredibly coy in this scene and his lines could only be the invention of an author who is willing to project feminine feelings onto a male persona. Needless to say, this scene never made it into the Hollywood film in which a young Orson Welles played Rochester as a demon lover, a dark titanic force of nature. Welles roamed the black stones of the moors like a Byronic poet, cape flowing and with a voice from the nether world. Tyrannical in manner, his humor is bitter, self-deprecating, and despairing. Much as I adored Orson Welles, it has to be said that the Byronic style is not altogether true to Bronte. Of course, Charlotte did idolize Lord Byron and she wrote many tales during her childhood in which a kingdom called Angria was awash with Gothic romance. But her intention in *Jane Eyre* was also to present Edward Rochester as a stuffy, pedantic, Victorian male. Oh, not that these character-istics were altogether unattractive to her. There is a scene in which Jane Eyre shows her employer, Rochester, the watercolors which she has painted. He feels free to act as art critic, psychiatrist, boss and parent. It is this scene which makes me believe that Charlotte's basic orientation was Oedipal; that is, that her significant other was always her father and that her husband was later simply an extension of that fundamental relationship.

For the benefit of Freudians, Jungians, and other poets, I think it is important to review the watercolors which Jane Eyre, spinster and feminist, romantic and Christian, is said to have produced. Charlotte herself tried to paint until her eyes failed her. There is a large and illuminating collection of Bronte drawings and sketches. Branwell's notebooks are full of death angels and death masks. Bloodthirsty and morbid in much of his poetry, Branwell seems to have begun with a flare and then failed because of some romantic excess or grandiosity—Mrs. Gaskell refers to his "Cowper-like gloom." Charlotte and her sisters, too, painted a world the Pre-Raphaelites might envy. Here are Jane Eyre's pictures, found in Chapter 13 of the novel.

"The first (picture) represented clouds low and livid, rolling over a swollen sea: all the distance was in eclipse; so, too, was the foreground; or rather, the nearest billows, for there was no land. One gleam of light lifted into relief a half-submerged mast, on which sat a cormorant, dark and large, with wings flecked with foam; its beak held a gold bracelet, set with gems, that I had touched with as brilliant tints as my pallette could yield, and as glittering distinctness as my pencil could impart. Sinking below the bird and mast, a drowned corpse glanced through the green water; a fair arm was the only limb clearly visible, whence the bracelet had been washed or torn.

"The second picture contained for foreground only the dim peak of a hill, with grass and some leaves slanting as if by a breeze. Beyond and above spread an expanse of sky, dark blue as at twilight: rising into the sky was a woman's shape to the bust, portrayed in tints as dusk and as soft as I could combine. The dim forehead was crowned with a star; the lineaments below were seen as through the suffusion of vapour; the eyes shone dark and wild; the hair streamed shadowy, like a beamless cloud torn by storm or by electric travail. On the neck lay a pale reflection like moonlight; the same faint lustre touched the train of thin clouds from which rose and bowed this vision of the Evening Star.

"The third showed the pinnacle of an iceberg piercing a polar winter sky: a muster of northern lights reared their dim lances, close serried, along the horizon. Throwing these into distance, rose, in the foreground, a head,—a colossal head, inclined towards the iceberg, and resting against it. Two thin hands, joined under the forehead, and supporting it, drew up before the lower features a sable veil; a brow quite bloodless, white as bone, and an eye hollow and fixed, blank of meaning but for the glassiness of despair, alone were visible. Above the temples, amidst wreathed turban folds of black drapery, vague in its character and consistency as cloud, gleamed a ring of white flame, gemmed with sparkles of a more lurid tinge. This pale crescent was 'The likeness of a kingly Crown'; what it diademed was 'the shape which shape had none.'"

I call the first picture Death and the Maiden, the second And the Name of the Star is Called Wormwood, and the third, The Snow Queen. These images are all open to interpretation. I think they express Charlotte's sense of having been usurped, of having been raped by forces and powers beyond her control. These are images of the betrayed feminine. Also there are images or dreams of an ancient goddess, of a Queen of Heaven whose crown has been stolen. In the light of what we now know about the suppression of the old religions, this material grows even more exciting. Charlotte has lost and is seeking her mother light. Her own mother died when Charlotte was an infant. Her aunt is withdrawn. All her nurture came from overbearing males who doubtless had their own repressions and confusions to deal with. (Evidently Patrick Bronte had tried to remarry without success and Paul Heger lived a sensual life within his family circle.)

It is often true that modern critics blame Charlotte for the masochistic denials that led her to her death. They are less quick to note that these same characteristics also fueled her art. Charlotte is at once pitied for her need to be loved and then blamed for her solitude and inability to achieve health and happiness in a man's world.

In the light of what we know today, Emily looms a bit larger than Charlotte because we see she preferred power to love. "Love I laugh to scorn," she wrote. Emily is a mythopoet. Her archetypal lovers in *Wuthering Heights* are a celibate pair. Brother and sister of sorts. Remember Emily died only three months after her beloved brother Branwell. It's true she advised he be whipped if he couldn't behave. She felt that way about all the wild animals. But it was wildness which recommended animals to Emily. For Charlotte it was their weakness which recommended them. Charlotte loved what she could pity. Emily loved power, that is, capacity.

Emily's animus, her masculine creation, is the orphan Heathcliff. Heathcliff is a dark, gypsy-like vagabond brought home to Yorkshire by Cathy's father who found the little beggar in the backstreets of Liverpool. Heathcliff makes anarchy in the household because he is an adopted son—taken in by the father in the pagan fashion of lineage without the mother's authority. Heathcliff has no mother. He is his father's son. He is, of course, a bastard.

When Emily was a child, she and Anne wrote of an imaginary kingdom of Gondal. While Charlotte and brother "Brany" wrote of their kingdom of Angria in which there was a lot of aristocratic sex and violence, Emily and Anne wrote of a Gondal in which there were heros, sons of a special race, *ubermensches* of the sort Nietzsche was to immortalize, beings who recognized no law but that of nature—that is to say of their own nature. Such a one must be stoic, courageous, and somehow above the common destiny of ordinary men. Muriel Sparks writes that such beings are "absurd" but Emily seems to have been attracted to them. After all, if you have to bake the family bread every morning and take care of children for a living, demi-gods might offer the kind of lives worth daydreaming about.

Gondal's queen was mystically united with nature; amoral and ruthless. Such a being partakes of the extremes of passion. She is primitive in action, mystic and remote in her contemplation. Just the way any suppressed genius would feel if she had to spend her life in a closet? Emily has been described as inflexible, unsociable, contemptuous and scornful of her own creative efforts. Muriel Sparks writes that at the end of her life, Emily "had gone sullen." Such a thought brings tears to my eyes when I imagine what it must have been like to write *Wuthering Heights* and be told it was a failure. One of the more obvious signs of a broken heart is a sullen exterior. Think of all the Emilys we know, even today.

When Emily writes of nature, she reads like Werner Herzog when he describes the violence of life in the rain forest. (See Les Blank's documentary film, *Burden of Dreams* in which Herzog describes primal existence as unending murder.) During Emily's stay in Brussels, she wrote a student essay titled *The Butterfly*.

She describes a forest scene and writes about what was then called "natural order." She finds in nature not order but insanity. "Life exists on a principle of destruction; every creature must be the relentless instrument of death to others, or himself cease to live ... the universe appeared to me a vast machine constructed only to bring forth evil. ..." She goes on to write that transmutation is possible, that ugly caterpillars turn into splendid butterflies and that suffering is seed for a divine harvest and harmony can and must be created out of chaos. It is from the genesis of these ideas that she creates the libidinous creatures, Cathy and Heathcliff—explosions of the human id—and then sets out to try to civilize them in the next generation. That is, they self-destruct but their children mellow out.

Naturally, when Hollywood got around to making the movie, once again only the primal stuff got on the screen. The civilized and androgenous second generation is left out of the film. The sexy stuff is the demi-gods, the masculine and feminine archetypes found in Cathy and Heathcliff. This is epic drama and the drives of these characters are like the passions of Greek tragedy—fatal. There is Catherine Earnshaw Linton, the self-centered girl who becomes a suicidal invalid. Heathcliff is homicidal in his selfishness. Catherine says of him: "He's not a rough diamond, a pearl-containing oyster of a rustic; he's a fierce, pitiless, wolfish man."

As Elizabeth Hardwick has stated, these two have a schizophrenic indifference to the claims of others. She calls them lost natures. Emily was all too familiar with ferocious natures. She loved them. Yet she knew that we must reach beyond darkness. Cathy does not mate with Heathcliff. She marries civilized refinement. Of course it doesn't take. The scene during which she is torn by the dogs at Thrushcross Grange (the refined house of patriarchal privilege) symbolizes her menarche or coming of age sexually. She attempts to hide from her own nature by marrying a man who represents safety. But she has denied herself and lost her authenticity.

Pouring out her heart to the housekeeper, Nelly, Cathy says: "... heaven did not seem to be my home; and I broke my heart with weeping to come back to earth ... because he's (Heathcliff) more myself than I am. Whatever our souls are made of, his and mine are the same; and Linton's is as different as a moonbeam from lightning, or frost from fire."

Emily knows the uses of darkness, the secrets of sadism, and the wisdom of barbarism. Such was the reaction to the book that Charlotte felt the need to apologize. In a preface to a later edition she writes: "Whether it is right or advisable to create things like Heathcliff, I do not know: I scarcely think it is. But this I know; the writer who possesses the creative gift owns something of which he is not always master — something that at times strangely wills and works for itself."

This something (genius) has been called everything from an iron whim to a sacred conviction. Charlotte writes of Emily: "Her spirit was altogether unbending ... on herself she had no pity.... Had she but lived her mind would of itself have grown like a strong tree, loftier, straighter, wider-spreading, and its matured fruits would have attained a mellower ripeness and sunnier bloom; but on that mind time and experience alone could work: to the influence of other intellects, it was not amenable."

The will to power is a curious thing to find in an impoverished girl in a Yorkshire parsonage. Emily, of course, had no power of any kind, except the power of the poet. There is no greater.

If it is not too Jungian, I think it must be said that doubtless one source of Emily's (and Charlotte's) animus was the Reverend Patrick Bronte. He too, walked the moors alone. He carried a gun. Emily took her pen. Patrick published several pedantic tracts and was certainly a frustrated author. Even when the children were young he was a recluse and took his meals alone. Emily was a recluse who made the meals. Patrick's thwarted ambitions came to fruition through the pagan prism of Emily's passions. That may be excessive. Perhaps it is enough to say they had the same red-gold curly hair, and even some of the same rigidity. In Patrick, resignation became a vice. In a letter written in 1859 when he was eighty-two years old and Charlotte had been dead for four years, he admonishes the mother of a dead child expressing the popular sentiment that death is a merciful dispensation. I find the letter suggests that we are better off dead. Curiously, I came across this letter in a sort of picture book from England first published in 1975 and written by Brian Wilks, a gentleman from Leeds who is just as stuffy and phallocentric in his view of the Brontes as Patrick might have been. His heart goes out to Patrick as a husband and father, and he emphasizes again and again Patrick's compassion. Still, it is hard to forget Charlotte's remark that trying to get compassion from Papa was like trying to get sap from firewood.

Some of his Calvinist flint seems to have stuck to Emily, although Emily was a poet not a parson. In *Memoir of Emily Jane Bronte*, Charlotte writes: "My sister Emily loved the moors. Flowers brighter than the rose bloomed in the blackest of the heath for her; out of a sullen hollow in a livid hill-side her mind could make an Eden. She found in the bleak solitude many and dear delights; and not the least and best loved was—liberty."

Her mind could make an Eden. For Emily, life was the search for Eros. Patrick shriveled down to Thanatos, at least in his literary output which is pedantic, didactic, and generally insufferable. If he did possess a Promethean heat (and he must have, to have produced such a coven of Celtic celebrants) then it is Emily who best expressed his passions. Like him, she was ruthlessly individual. She preferred animals to men. She once told her students at Roe Head school that she much preferred her dog to them. Keeper, her great dog, was only one of her many wild creatures. Her hawk, Hero, is seen in many of the drawings done by the Brontes. There was a dog called Flossy, canaries, cats, pheasants, and a goose named Victoria. In my pantheon, Emily is a Druid priest, an earth goddess, a barbaric mythopoet who looks like Rousseau's Noble Savage one moment and writes like a late twentieth-century psychiatrist the next.

Some years ago I wrote a short play in which the long dead Emily visits Carl Jung in his study and helps him formulate his theories of the anima and the animus. In order to draw her wandering ghost to him, he leaves little bird nests about the room—the sort of things she always brought home from the moors. Of course, the difficulty is that Emily has been in the other world so long she has become cosmopolitan. She has taken up with Bohemians like Isadora Duncan and dry wits like Berny Shaw. She's even hung out with Oscar Wilde, although she gave him the brush after thinking about it. Her particular favorite is Voltaire—he cultivates gardens while she lets them grow wild, but they have a lot of fun argufying. She has grown a bit tired of her early philosophical work on sado-masochism but still, she is willing to turn Carl on to the theory of anima and animus; that is, the inner or repressed self which tends to be feminine in males and masculine in females—the self we put on the shelf during our adolescent crisis.

This is the piece of ourself we need if we are to make it as artists. Without some depth, some layers to the psyche, an artist is simply boring. Now Emily has to explain to Carl that the psyche is split when we are young and it is the work of a lifetime to make it whole again, the way it was in childhood. What Emily describes to Carl is the path to enlightenment. Carl calls it individuation but the names don't matter. It's just the Tao of consciousness.

Wuthering Heights is not a love story. It is Charlotte who wrote love stories. *Wuthering Heights* is a psychodrama. It is a poem about the unconscious. It is about neurotic love, the love which cannot transcend childhood. The primal passions of the youthful pair cannot withstand the assault of society, of the civilized world of Victorian patriarchy so gently symbolized by the Lintons at Trushcross Grange. This local ruling class family is the essence of refinement and their household is guarded by the male bulldogs who symbolically rape Cathy when she tries to peek in at a window to watch the gentry at play. "The devil had seized her ankle. . . . I heard his abominable snorting. She did not yell out—no! She would have scorned to do it." Heathcliff goes on to describe his efforts to shove a stone down the throat of the bulldog, but his efforts are in vain and the barefoot Cathy is carried off into the seductive comforts of soft living and privilege.

The book is a poem about the lives of women and men who are crushed by a society which demands they live a lie. Cathy is the victim of the Victorian feminine mystique. Like the Brontes themselves, she is almost an invalid. She sinks into suicidal depression and dies, literally, of womanhood—that is to say, in childbirth. Heathcliff sinks into aggression, into violence. With her masculine hand, Emily wrote of this volanic and powerful part of herself. Charlotte describes Emily's capacity to create Titans in her work, ". . . refusing absolutely to make ropes out of sea-sand any longer, (she) sets to work on statue-hewing."

The central characters in *Wuthering Heights* are the beginning of a new mythology for women. They incorporate the ancient archetypes—like Greek gods they represent Hubris, the overweaning arrogance and pride which bring down the tragic hero. In these adolescent souls we see the unleashed libido and the will to power which has its source in the id, in the grasping infant within all of us. Yet Emily insists that after their deaths, their children *grow up*. It is instructive to realize that even today no one is much interested in the second half of the book in which the succeeding pair behave in what Virginia Woolf would call man-womanly and woman-manly fashion. This is the new mythology which we are still trying to act out more than a century and a half later.

Emily herself died a hero. In the preface to the 1850 edition of *Wuthering Heights*, Charlotte wrote: "Never in all her life had she lingered over any task that lay before her, and she did not linger now. She sank rapidly. She made haste to leave us. I have seen nothing like it; but indeed, I have never seen her parallel in anything. Stronger than a man, simpler than a child, her nature stood alone."

I read over the curious reports of Paul Heger, the headmaster who presumed to judge the relative talents of Emily and Charlotte when they went to Brussels to study in the hope (vain) of opening a school of their own and escaping the degradation of life as governesses. He, of course, writes of Emily: "She should have been a man." Biographer Gaskell notes: "He seems to have rated Emily's genius as something even higher than Charlotte's; and her (Charlotte's) estimation of their relative powers was the same." She goes on to observe that Heger felt that Emily's gifts were impaired by a stubborn tenacity of will which rendered her obtuse to all reasoning. She appeared egotistical and exacting compared to Charlotte.

On the day she died, Emily refused to see a doctor. In a letter to a friend Charlotte wrote: "The morning grew on to noon. Emily was worse: she could only whisper in gasps. Now, when it was too late, she said to Charlotte, 'If you will send for a doctor, I will see him now.' About two o'clock she died."

Emily Bronte's sacred conviction was that her soul was her own. She believed that the chaos that is our life on earth could be sculpted, could be formed into order. Emily Bronte is in no sense masculine or feminine. She knew that the soul is in the stone, in the earth itself. She is a manifestation of mother light, of Maya-Shakti, the All-Mother, *mater-genetrix, mater omnium,* call it what you will.

In Charlotte's book *Jane Eyre*, there is a vision of the Great Mother during a scene in which Jane is torn between her desire to submit to a man and her desire to save herself. The Goddess of the Moon appears to her and says, "Daughter, flee temptation!" Charlotte too, knew in her bones that there was an ancient religion which, even in a Christian costume, guided her choices.

For Emily, these divine substances were not only available for emergencies, they were the stuff of daily life. Maya-Shakti is the source of all energy, male and female. The phallic pillar itself has been described as maya. The maya of the gods is their power to assume diverse shapes. So the maya of the artist is the generative power to create Heathcliff, to create a thing which was not there before. A work of art is never an opinion. It is a thing which once made, goes its way in the world independent of parent/creator. Just as the creations of Homer still stalk the earth, so too the monumental figures of those lost lovers on the heath.

Emily's work is still far too unique to be grasped on all its levels. Her novel is read as a romance. Forties film director Willy Wyler ended his Hollywood version of *Wuthering Heights* with a silly shot of Cathy and Heathcliff walking away together into ethereal heavenly clouds. For the popular mind, things need to be wrapped up in happy-ever-after? Always we are sold the reductive lie which supports the illusion that we will not die. What Emily Bronte tells us is that we will, and *that* is the wonder of it. Our comfort must be to embrace loneliness. And perhaps as a consequence of that embrace, to study what we might do with existence, such as it is. Emily found something worth doing.

Charlotte writes: "One day in the autumn of 1845 I accidently lighted on a MS. volume of verse in my sister Emily's handwriting. Of course I was not surprised, knowing that she could and did write verse: I looked it over, and something more than surprise seized me—a deep conviction that these were not common effusions, nor at all like the poetry women generally write. I thought them condensed and terse, vigorous and genuine. To my ear they had also a peculiar music, wild, melancholy, and elevating. ..."

THE REVISIONIST IMPERATIVE:

OR, DON'T ROCK THE BOAT — SINK IT!

> I don't accept that equality is a moral principle.
> Former Federal Budget
> Director David Stockman

During the early '80s, I became a publicist for the revolution. Any revolution would do. The Revolution of Touch was my favorite. I began with plays and fiction which I hoped would illustrate the need for radical chic, just when it was going out of style. I wanted people to understand how important it is to be out of step with the times. I wrote about being an advocate and practitioner of "free love" in the '50s and a disciplined celibate in the '60s and a community activist in the "me decade" of the '70s. Whatever's in is out, I proclaimed. One parody is worth a thousand polemics, I thought.

Almost at once, I discovered there isn't time to be subtle. I switched to journalism. I wanted to make the world safe for satire again. I learned

---

This essay is a compilation of material gathered from twenty-eight familiar essays written for the Berkeley newspaper *Grassroots* in 1981, 82, and 83. I had hoped for a synthesis, but there is just too much material. The essays appeared in a column titled "Bread and Roses" and much of what survives here is elliptical and feels a bit like a stone skipping across the waters of time. Still, it is good to sit by the water and gaze into the deeps and wonder what is down there under all the detritus that floats on the surface of our age.

quickly that no one will hire an anarchist. The free press is free to those who own it, not to the rest of us.

"The more they pay, the less you say," said my son Peter. I set out my articles on the kitchen table and marked each with the amount paid for my writing and the number of words cut by the editors. At one end was a review of Rosalynn Carter's book, *First Lady From Plains*, for which the *San Francisco Chronicle* paid me $100. They cut the part about Rosalynn's prophecy of the coming revolutions in Central and South America. It's the best part of her book and describes her journeys through many Latin nations where she finds that our example during the '60s is one of the inspirations for the revolutionary fervor in Latin America. (See the uncut review on page 25.)

Much further down the table is an article I wrote for the women's newspaper *Plexus*. It reviews a television play about J. Robert Oppenheimer, the father of the atom bomb. (See page 93.) The editors did not change the text in any significant way, but my pithy title was, "Oppenheimer: Faust or Fraud?" and they retitled the piece, "The Oppenheimer Legacy." Well, I sighed, they pay you a salary, I guess they own you. The fee for that article was $16.

At the far end, the bottom of the table, are my articles written for papers not able to pay writers for their contributions. In my experience, it is only here that a writer can be almost certain that no editor will mess around with her work.

Which brings me to Berkeley's most honest publication, *Grassroots*. I will not argue its merits, only its freedom from the ills of exploitation. A paper which pays no member of its staff, except of course the typesetter, cannot be said to have vested interests. *Grassroots* kept the community honest. Well, it tried. I came to *Grassroots* in the fall of 1981. It died in the mid '80s, a victim of the kingdom of take-the-cash-and-let-the-credit-go. It wasn't just the yuppies. It was the inability of the community to produce a new crop of old lefties. The young will doubtless thrash through the same old straw and become new lefties, and historical imperatives will probably be seen next on underground videos.

My first piece in *Grassroots* dealt with the imprisonment of Dr. Nawal El Saadawi, an Egyptian Marxist feminist radical and the author of *The Hidden Face of Eve*, a study of the practice of female genital excision in the Arab world. Dr. Saadawi's work as a physician gives her the kind of grounding in female oppression which is inspirational to my western sensibility. In later years, I heard her speak; she cautions western women against condescension. In the East they only cut off genital nerve tissue. In the West, we excise brain tissue. Dr. Saadawi doesn't put it quite like that, but she suggests we look at Freud's work, at our billboards, and exploitation of women as commodities, and then ask ourselves if mind control is not as powerful as sexual mutilation when it comes to suppressing the existence of women.

Dr. Saadawi was interrogated on September 28, 1981, regarding her participation in the U.N. Mid Decade Conference for Women held in Copenhagen during the summer of 1980. In July of 1980, at that conference, a reporter for the Peoples' Translation Service in Oakland, CA, interviewed Dr. Saadawi and published her statements in *Newsfront International* in October 1980. I took Dr. Saadawi's creed for my own. She declares:

"To be revolutionary means that one examines the problems of women from all aspects: the historical, the sociological, the economic, and the psychological. And if you carry out this analysis, you should be against the establishment, the patriarchal class system. As a radical feminist, I think you should oppose imperialism, Zionism, feudalism, and inequality between nations, sexes, and between classes.

"Feminism means you have to read a lot, to understand a lot, to feel a lot and to be honest. And to say what you believe. In spite of the establishment, the government, or the institutions where you work. You may have to sacrifice a lot. That's feminism.

"We should come together, be politically organized. We need a political party of women, not social organizations.... They have to be afraid of us. We have to challenge governments, to make them fall if necessary. But to just talk and write, that won't get us anywhere.

"Because women have no collective power, male authority will tell women to go back home once the revolution is successful. Women must come together and become politically powerful as a preventive measure against relapses in the revolution.

"We are still begging, because we are powerless. Throughout history, no group of people has ever obtained their rights by begging peacefully; they have snatched it from the hands of the authorities. Women shall win no other way."

I continued to write about Dr. Saadawi's stay in Kanatir women's prison outside Cairo. I went on KPFA Public Radio and pleaded for letters to the consulate. It was, in fact, at that time that I began to broadcast regularly at KPFA in Berkeley. I read parts of her book on the air and received complaints that it was unsuitable for children to hear. This is true. She writes:

"My profession (as a physician) led me, at one stage, to examine patients coming from various Arab countries. Among them were Sudanese women. I was horrified to observe that the Sudanese girl undergoes an operation for circumcision which is ten times more cruel than that to which Egyptian girls are subjected. In Egypt it is only the clitoris which is amputated, and usually not completely. But in the Sudan, the operation consists in the complete removal of all the external genital organs. They cut off the clitoris, the two major outer lips (*labia majora*) and the two minor inner lips (*labia minora*). Then the wound is repaired. The outer opening of the vagina is the only portion left intact, not however without having ensured that, during the process of repairing, some narrowing of the opening is carried out with a few extra stitches. The result is that on the marriage night it is necessary to widen the external opening by slitting one or both ends with a sharp scalpel or razor so that the male organ can be introduced. When a Sudanese woman is divorced, the external opening is narrowed once more to ensure that she cannot have sexual relations. If she remarries, widening is done again."

Dr. Saadawi writes that the need of the state to control and subjugate women's bodies demands that Arab women be made into "blind pussy cats." She believes that the savage practices which suppress women are the direct result of the economic interests that govern society. The father must know that his children are his own flesh in order to hand down his property. If women were to seize the means of reproduction, patriarchy would perish. The sexual mutilation of females is a practice which dates from antiquity. Herodotus mentions female excision seven hundred years before Christ.

The Hidden Face of Eve is a catalyst book for me, just as James Baldwin's work was in the '60s. Racism and sexism are world views and they will not give way until the world turns around. Dr. Saadawi writes that in the late '70s, for example, the number of Egyptian women who went to the polls did not exceed 0.53 percent of the total votes cast in the general election. For Dr. Saadawi, feminism is synonymous with revolution. She believes that class structure and exploitation must cease before woman can regain her "natural and reasonable right to name her children and decide their descent."

The "violation" which sent Dr. Saadawi to jail was of an Egyptian law "for the protection of values from shame." I asked Dr. Saadawi about this law when she came to Berkeley after her release from prison. She talked to an audience at Wheeler Auditorium on the U.C. campus about religious fundamentalism and the suffering of women under patriarchal religions, both East and West. Concepts of "shame" were discussed and a large group of veiled women who were in attendance, left the auditorium *en masse* in order to protest the event. Dr. Saadawi explained to us that the veil dates from the advent of slavery which is far more ancient than Islam. It is not the Koran that oppresses women, she told us. It is patriarchy.

As the evening wore on, lines of students and disparate others stood in the aisles to question the doctor. Everyone seemed to exist in his or her own movie, asking bizarre and unrelated questions. One male put an official curse on the scholar who had come to enlighten us. She was gracious throughout. And I remember best her bright red sweater, and how young and healthy she looked, with her wiry frame and gray hair. The kind of Eastern Wisdom that gets things done.

My next assignment at *Grassroots* was to cover a *People's World* lunch honoring Michael O'Riordan, the General Secretary of the Communist Party of Ireland. O'Riordan's Celtic charisma was almost as exciting as Vladimir Posner's Russian romanticism at the latest (1987) *People's World* luncheon. O'Riordan held forth at Goodman's restaurant in Oakland's Jack London Square, on November 14, 1981. Born in County Cork in 1917 of Gaelic speaking parents, his book *The Connolly Column*, is about the life and times of James Connolly, an Irish socialist who died in the Easter Rising of 1916. O'Riordan also fought Franco in Spain, went to jail in Dublin, and became an Irish Transport and General Union man.

Recognized as a great internationalist, O'Riordan spoke of liberation movements all over the world. Ireland has been under the yoke of England since 1169 A.D. when Henry II attacked the people with weapons blessed by the Pope. O'Riordan expressed hope for the Irish clergy which he says is being educated through contact with liberation struggles in countries like El Salvador. He spoke of the struggles of the Irish working class, forty-five percent of which is now organized into trade unions. The unions brought about the closure of the low-paying McDonald's food chain throughout Ireland.

Another Irishman, George Bernard Shaw, wrote in *The Intelligent Woman's Guide to Socialism and Capitalism* (1928): "The notion that our present system distributes wealth according to merit, even roughly, may be dismissed at once as ridiculous." Certainly this is still true today. Ireland is a Third World country, a result almost entirely of its exploitation. O'Riordan says: "We are politically and historically the Africans of Europe." Ireland, he points out, is not a member of NATO. England fears the strategic loss of this little island because many British believe that if they get out of Ireland, why it just may turn into another Cuba. Now there's an idea!

Over the years I have come to love going to the *People's World* Banquet.It gives me a sense of *belonging*. Of course as an anarchist and existentialist, I have never belonged to anything or anyone. I'm afraid it might inhibit my love—the way marriage inhibits romance.

On this occasion in 1981, things weren't particularly romantic. The people seated at my table were glum. There were no movies about Jack Reed to banter about (Warren Beatty and Diane Keaton in *Reds* hadn't been released) and so my small talk was limited. The local media did not rush to greet our Irish communist and my only companion at first was a dour reporter from the Soviet News Agency, TASS. At last the table filled and we ate our chicken surprise and sang labor songs and waved our red napkins as we listened to the songs of the Belfast Folk. We handed around the wine to comrades and fellow travelers who found their way to our table. *People's World* reporter Ann Washington co-chaired the event with trade unionist Stephanie Allan. The Young Workers' Liberation Party was nearly as boisterous as the Lincoln Brigade and speeches were given with much panache. Harry Bridges was there, Angela Davis sent regrets and well wishes.

I give these details to indicate the general atmosphere of solidarity and good faith in which I found myself on November 14, 1981. It was on this date that I decided to begin writing a "Bread and Roses" column for *Grassroots*. The reason is this: during that warm and hopeful luncheon, I was standing in the hall waiting in line for a drink when a personable young man began to talk with me about my articles on Dr. Saadawi. He expressed some incredulity. I referred him to Fran Hosken's work: *The Hosken Report: Genital and Sexual Mutilation of Females*. I told him where to obtain copies of this book as well as Dr. Saadawi's *The Hidden Face of Eve*. He was irritated that I presumed to instruct him and seriously informed me that Islamic culture was none of my business. We had no right to interfere in the religions and traditions of other nations. Then he smirked a bit and said that yes, he had heard of those excisions practiced on women in forty African and Arab countries. He said he had been told it is done with some sort of metal tac. Yes, he grinned, it's what they call an excise tax!

I looked around at the group. None of the gray heads in the room would have spoken in such a way. The new wave of anti-feminism is coming from the young. It feels like Red-baiting. I remember once in the late '60s, right here at Jack London Square, a soldier in uniform hurled my leaflets in my face and shook his fist in fury. At least he expressed honest indignation. He called me a commie because he'd been hurt by commies. That makes some sense.

I looked at the young man and wondered if he despised women because he'd been hurt by them. His reaction was one of contempt, not one of pain. Yes, this was backlash. I asked him if he could not empathize with these women. He told me that there was not necessarily much pain associated with the practice of genital excision, that various herbs are used as anesthesia and for asepsis. I requested documentation but he only shrugged.

For my "Bread and Roses" column, I forced myself to sit through a documentary film showing the genital mutilation of a seven year old girl. It was done in *real* time. There were no edits to give the audience a break. I saw this documentary at a private screening at Berkeley's Pacific Film Archive in the University of California Museum of Art. Visiting Egyptian filmmaker Laila Abou-Saif allowed me a long interview after the screening. I have seen her again over the years and she has had to leave Egypt permanently, primarily because of her writings. Ms. Abou-Saif is the only woman in Egypt to teach acting and stage direction at a University level. She was at Cairo University in 1981 and when she came to the U.S. with her film, *Enaba, Aziza, Wa Abeer*, she was aware that her documentary would face a difficult reception and indeed it received almost no distribution. However, she told me that the BBC bought it and so this film document is in an archive for anyone who wants to study it.

The film records the lives of three women in a rural village outside Cairo. The midwife explains that excision is a purification needed to qualify girls for marriage. She says if the clitoris is not cut off, it will grow into a penis. Virginity before marriage and chastity after are the desired outcome of the destruction of woman's sexuality.

We see a thirty-year-old mother, Aziza, living a feudal life. She cannot read or write, she says, and so her life is no more than the life of one of the village cows. (The slaughter of a cow to feed the village is juxtaposed with the footage of the little girl's excision later in the film.)

Enaba is a fourteen-year-old woman with great awareness. She wishes to change her life. Abeer is the seven year old. An older woman appearing in the film explains that excision is done to make the surface smooth — I think she said smooth like a pomegranate or like a melon — so that the male organ will not be impeded. Female excision has been illegal in Egypt since 1956, yet one source indicates that as many as fifty percent of urban educated Egyptian women are still excised.

A curious thought came to me after the film. Why do these women seem wiser than western women? They are not pitiable. They are survivors and they are joyous and they are realists. Enaba seemed to me much more self-aware than most American adolescent females. She knows what hit her.

My worst reaction was toward the older women in the film, the ones who carry out the oppression and mutilation of younger females. For the midwife in Egypt, it is her livelihood. For the older woman in the Western world, it is her psychological well-being which is at stake when she forces young women to be subservient, teaches them to be slavish, etc.

I have a permanent memory of the screams of the helpless little girl in this film, her despair as she later bangs her arms repeatedly against the back of her bed, refusing the belated comfort and arms of those who have betrayed her . . . this is the primal scene for every little girl or boy who has been assaulted by "grown-ups" and who suffers a deep division from the self as a result. This terrible division which many of us suffer in childhood leaves us incomplete forever. It alters our capacity to love ourselves and others. Trust is shattered.

After the film, I sat over a cup of herb tea in the museum's Swallow Cafe while I talked with Laila Abou-Saif. She inhaled her brown cigarette deeply. She received her Ph.D. in Theater from the University of Illinois and has spent many years teaching in the U.S. as well as in Cairo. Her appearance was glamorous even though she was coming down with a cold. I asked her about Dr. Saadawi. She replied that Mrs. Sadat has done more for Egyptian women than ten Dr. Saadawi's. She implied that Dr. Saadawi is working in a vacuum. She offered the opinion that Dr. Saadawi has been heavily influenced by her radical husband, Dr. Sherif Hetata.

So it goes. I thought of the sadness in Dr. Saadawi's voice when she spoke at the Copenhagen Conference (a tape of which aired on KPFA Public Radio on November 5, 1981). I remembered the first section of *The Hidden Face of Eve* in which she describes her own "circumcision" — excision/mutilation are the correct terms — at the age of six on the cold tiles of the bathroom floor, and her deep shock when she found her mother's face, smiling and laughing, among the faces she imagined to be robbers or murderers trying to kill her. Later in the book she writes: "Women in Europe and America may not be exposed to surgical removal of the clitoris, nevertheless, they are victims of cultural and psychological clitoridectomy."

And we let it happen. Feminism is out of fashion. Feminism is perceived, in the mass media at any rate, as limiting rather than liberating. Progressives do not often list feminism as part of the forward march. The defeat of the ERA depressed too many people. Women turn their backs on rhetorical speeches. They want real change. The inflated economy has driven them up against a wall. Most American women are still employed by males, either as wives or workers. For middle-of-the-roaders, feminism has failed to deliver. The majority of women simply can't afford it.

When I graduated from college in 1955, women got 62 cents on the male dollar. Today, in the late '80s, it's hovering around 57 cents. So much for progress. Of course, money isn't everything. Today we respect ourselves. In the '50s we respected men. So much for progress. Was there ever a time when human beings were in harmony? What is harmonious?

My column needed a logo, something to illustrate a world in balance. Imagery can change thought! I told myself. I rummaged through my art books. I studied the illustrations from Judy Chicago's *The Dinner Party*, that much maligned work of woman's art. (See "Strictly From Hunger," the hysterical vilification of Chicago's work writted by J. Richardson in the April 30, 1981, *New York Review of Books*.) When I first saw Judy Chicago's *Dinner Party*, I thought I had found my church. Sensually, I felt like a kid at Christmas, when sensations were new, when texture, color, and light were magical. It's what's called the stained glass experience. Written on the flowing tapestries hung in the symbolic entrance hall was my prayer:

> "And She gathered
> All before Her
> And She made for them
> A Sign to see
> And lo they saw a vision:
> From this day forth
> Like to like in all things
> And then all that divided them merged
> And then Everywhere
> Was Eden
> Once again ..."

I put this prayer over my typewriter and began. Pessimism of the intellect and optimism of the will, I told myself. We do not live in Eden, we long for it. After considering this carefully, I chose for my logo the ceramic plate from Judy Chicago's *Dinner* which symbolizes the British warrior queen, Boadaceia, who lived in the first century A.D. Chicago's symbolic table is a triangle with thirty-nine guests in all, beginning with the ancient goddesses and legendary figures. Boadaceia's plate is twelfth at table; it contains an image of Stonehenge, a monument central to my personal mythology. I took my name from Stonehenge.

Boadaceia's history was tragic. Celtic queens didn't go over with the Romans and her estates were seized; she was bound, beaten, and forced to watch brutal Roman soldiers rape her daughters. She gathered an army and won several battles against the Romans who later revenged themselves by killing more than 80,000 of Boadaceia's people. She took poison rather than surrender.

It's an old tale, of course, but the message is still true: if you mean business, get yourself an army. These days I'd settle for a political party. Boadaceia dates from the pre-Christian era when the Celts still worshipped women. Not that it's *wise* to worship, it just seems to be a human instinct, and if people are going to do kinky things like worship gods or heroes, it's just as well they start with the childbearers. The Romans, on the other hand, worshipped the male principle, the gods of war, guys like Mars. They had to. They were a military state. They were advanced.

In an effort to shape my mood, I put Bellini's opera *Norma* on the tape player. I listened to "Casta Diva", the aria to Diana, the chaste goddess of the moon. That's the one in which Norma tells her Gothic clan not to fight the Romans, that Rome will fall of its own weight. Patriarchy contains within itself the seeds of its own destruction. Which is all very well and good I thought, but what if it takes the rest of us with it. In the opera, Norma is in love with a Roman soldier. Aren't we all. It is his betrayal that symbolizes the betrayal of the feminine principle. Maria Callas sings this aria with all the anguish of a woman who lost her "Roman" — that guy Onassis — to a younger woman — Jackie O. In the opera the younger woman will have none of the Roman commander's love if it means destroying her mistress, Norma.

Are these tensions and wars between masculine and feminine inevitable? Art would certainly be barren without them. Or would it? We have always made art, even before the world became male dominated. A friend reading my work asked me if I would chuck out books like *The Illiad* and *The Odyssey*. I asked him if he thought there was any chance I could succeed! He got stuffy, so I tried to explain the revisionist imperative.

Helen of Troy was not a toy. If she, or any other woman in the ancient world had left us a scrap of writing, we might have another tale. Helen knew what it was to be married to Menelaus. Paris was a young man, an Adonis or Romeo type. Perhaps he was worth a kingdom. There are only two truths about men and women: hers and his. Most of us must choose.

What we choose will depend on what we are taught. If language *is* thought, then we think women are a sub-species. Once, while lecturing, I wrote on the chalkboard a quotation from G. K. Chesterton (1874-1936): "Men are men, but Man is a woman." A middle-aged male failed to penetrate this thought and looked at me clinically, asking if I wanted to be a man. I told him I was one.

As most of us know well enough, our society uses language to keep women in their place. Any pre-school child of either gender knows quite well that a *man* is male. Why then, do we still come across a research-report titled: "Development of the Uterus in Rats, Guniea Pigs, and Men."

When I was a sophomore in college in 1953, I asked an elderly science professor why these incongruities exist. He grinned and put his arm around me, hugging me paternally, saying: "Don't worry my dear, *man* embraces *woman*."

Most of us get no historical background on language as a tool used by the ruling class to define our roles in society. In *The Handbook of Nonsexist Writing*, by Casey Miller and Kate Swift, the authors write:

"Ercongota, the daughter of a seventh-century English king, is described in *The Anglo-Saxon Chronicle* as 'a wonderful man.' In Old English the word *man* meant 'person' or 'human being,' and when used of an individual was equally applicable to either sex. It was parallel to the Latin *homo*, 'a member of the human species,' not *vir*, 'an adult male of the species.' English at the time of Ercongota had separate words to distinguish the sexes: *wer*, equivalent to the Latin *vir*, meant 'adult male' and *wif*, meant 'adult female.' The combined forms *waepman* and *wifman* meant, respectively, 'adult male person' and 'adult female person.'

"In the course of time *wifman* evolved into the modern word *woman*, and *wif* narrowed in meaning to become *wife* as we use that word today. *Man* eventually ceased to be used of individual women and replaced *wer* and *waepman* as a specific term distinguishing an adult male from an adult female. But *man* continued to be used in generalizations about both sexes. As long as most generalizations about people were made by men about men, the ambiguity nestling in this dual usage was either not noticed or thought not to matter. By the eighteenth century the modern, narrow sense of *man* was firmly established as the predominant one."

As the textbooks came to be written for boys, the girls not finding their way into educational institutions until very recent years, the universal pronoun *he* became the rule. Indeed, the use of *he* as the universal pronoun was established by act of Parliament in England. Once I experimented with high school students. I used the pronoun *she* exclusively on all their worksheets. They were outraged at my sexism.

The most common response to all this fuss about language is just to declare that it's a trivial issue. When I protest, the professors give me a certain look. I know they suspect me of pronoun envy. These are the establishment linguists who wish to keep the language "pure." It is in their best interests to do so. As Miller and Swift write in *Words and Women*:

"What standard English usage says about males is that they are the species. What it says about females is that they are a subspecies. ...

"Our sex-differentiated cultural categories are in the main male-positive-important on the one hand, female-negative-trivial on the other."

Words and Women is my favorite handbook on sex-mantics. There is a very funny parody about MALE, a group calling itself Men Against Linguistic Equality, which meets in Johannesburg as often as not and does whatever it must to "keep the language working for us." The males are required to attend meetings in the buff to insure against infiltration. The authors Miller and Swift are trying to laugh at the notion that there is a conspiracy going on. Of course there *is*. Conscious and unconscious. From William Safire at the *New York Times* to Dick Cavett on TV, the establishment malestream winces at any change in their language habits. Cavett begged Bella Abzug please not to say "chairperson," and she said she used the word "chair," so he relaxed and got through the interview.

All this moaning about changes in language is simply the discomfort that goes with the alteration of any preconscious conditioning. It's like being asked to learn to walk again. Language is learned in infancy. It's curious that speech, the thing which most distinguishes the species, is our most *instinctive* behavior as well. Most of us do not use speech to express thought. We use it to express feelings. My boss in 1972 felt bad about using the term Ms. He said it felt *southern*. Did I want to be *Miz*, he asked. I told him he'd get used to it. The *London Times* has called Ms. a lonely, fatherless word. The East coast U.S. papers take a dim view of the term. As Miller and Swift point out in their chapter on the power of naming, selfhood is the ultimate defection. If a woman names herself, casting off her father's name and her husband's name, and yes, even her mother's name, then she is a pariah in a patriarchal world. She belongs to no one. She is no man's property. This blows up the store. It's what Malcolm X did when he cast off his slave name, his connection to his owners.

In the future, the meaning will select the word. Language must express precise conscious thought, not fear and rationalization. Words must evolve along with awareness. Miller and Swift write;

"Margaret Mead believes masculine and feminine labels are even more destructive for a male who wants to depart from the cultural norm than they are for a female. Her point is that since men's activities are universally considered more prestigious than women's, the man or boy who is attuned by temperament to activities assigned to women loses more than the woman or girl who seeks fulfillment in fields considered proper only for males. Yet our insistence on drawing up mental lists contrasting what is 'masculine' with what is 'feminine' diminishes not only individual women, but women as a class. It does so because male prestige is maintained by limiting female prestige — at the expense, ultimately, of the human wholeness of every individual."

Or, as that ghastly grammarian, Shakespeare, dared to put it, "God send everyone their heart's desire." My own father used to go through the roof if I said something like, "Will everyone please take *their* seat." When I pointed out to him that "everyone" included both males and females, he was not soothed. He did not live to hear President Kennedy make this oh so sensible grammatical adjustment. Clearly, if we are talking about a male man we say *he* and if we are talking about a female man we say *she*. But what happens when we don't know who we are talking about? The future President, for example. Will s/he be qualified? I used *s/he* in an article once, and the editor wrote back protesting that it looked funny, that it appeared to indicate that the *he* was contained in the *she*. Yes, I told him, that had happened to me twice.

Well, after several articles on linguistics, my male friends told me I was getting boring. I felt like Andrea Dworkin (*What's Left of the Left* on PBS television, 1-10-82) when she was asked about the battering and oppression of women. She shrugged and said: "We have to face the fact that a hell of a lot of people just don't care."

Most males won't touch feminism with a fork. Even those who profess sympathy (I've met *two* who profess empathy) are seldom activists. They tell me they have other fish to fry. They keep their priorities straight.

One of the reasons for this is that women have shut them out. It's analogous to what happened to blacks and whites during the Civil Rights Movement in the '60s. Some whites were shut out, told it wasn't their cause. When I tried to teach W.E.B. DuBois and Richard Wright and James

Baldwin in my English classes in an urban Oakland high school, one of my students asked me if I wanted to be black. I asked if that was wrong, to want to identify with someone else, to feel what it was like to be someone I wasn't He said yes, it was wrong. He said I should identify with "my own people." Who are they, I wonder. I'm still looking.

When I taught black kids, one of the hardest things I had to explain to them was that the white community didn't necessarily hate them. For the most part white people were/are indifferent to their oppression. So, too, most men do not concern themselves with the socio-cultural underprivilege of women. So, too, when the Jews rode by in the boxcars, the people in the countryside did not identify with them. Racism and sexism are primarily crimes of omission. All of us have other fish to fry.

Back in 1910, Emma Goldman had her own press, Mother Earth Publishing Association. In a piece called *The Traffic in Women*, she wrote: "Only when human sorrows are turned into a toy with glaring colors will baby people become interested — for a while at least. The people are a very fickle baby that must have new toys every day."

Watching TV today, this very moment, as I write this — October 5, 1987 — a young woman is going to jail for the contract murder of her father. She is eighteen and an incest victim. She says she feared her father was going to victimize her younger sister and so she paid a classmate to kill her father. Well, the young man did as she asked. Is this not empathy? Did he not identify with the young woman? Did he not act out male mythology by coming to her aid and destroying her persecutor?

Albert Einstein once said that two things are infinite, the universe and human stupidity and he wasn't sure about the former. In the case mentioned above, the young woman got six months. The young man got up to twenty years. The father figures who sentenced them feel that an example must be set.

The most interesting detail in this story is the fact that a friend (female) of the young woman had gone to a school counselor with the story of incest (bruises and other evidence), but she had been turned away and told that the victim would have to make the complaint. Is it not clear that the young cannot trust adults to have their best interests at heart? Is it not becoming clear that grown-ups do not often *identify* or *empathize* with children? The root of the problem is the lack of human love.

Like Martin Luther King, I have a dream that one day parents and children and females and males will take each other by the hand and cry, "Free at last, thank God or Goddess Almighty, free at last!" The truth is we still live in a sado-masochistic culture. We still believe that punishment will control behavior. We have our flashes of sentiment and then it's back to fear and loathing. Carl Jung's shadow or concept of "otherness" haunts our daily lives. Some call it paranoid ideation, or the need to project our inner fears onto others. Our need to take the dark spot in our own soul and attribute it to another. And what is more fundamentally *other* than woman?

In her book, *Lies, Secrets, and Silence*, Adrienne Rich writes: "In Bangladesh during the revolution, it has been estimated that 200,000 women were raped by Pakistani soldiers. Many were victims, according to Joyce Goldman in the August 1972 issue of *MS.*, of highly organized, almost mechanized gang rape. Some were children as young as eight. The husbands, fathers, brothers, fiancés of these women immediately disowned them, made them outcasts of that allegedly revolutionary new society. Many of these women committed suicide, others gave birth to children whom they later murdered. Every one of these women was raped twice: first physically by the enemy soldier, then psychically by the enemy in her own household."

Most of us here in the Western world seem to believe that this sort of barbarism is a thing of the past. That is an error. The war on women is as violent today as it has ever been. A few women have made extraordinary gains and their images pervade the malestream media, giving a false impression of how things are going for the masses. In most quarters feminism is considered passé, either because it is believed women have already achieved equality or because the subject is simply too tiresome. Back in the nineteenth century it was still a romantic cause and men could feel good about espousing rights for women. John Stuart Mill, Henrik Ibsen, August Bebel, Thorstein Veblen, Friedrich Engels, and even Frederick Douglas all made serious contributions to the literature and philosophy of feminism. In 1853 William Lloyd Garrison spoke about the "Intelligent wickedness," of men: "I believe in sin, therefore in a sinner; in theft, therefore in a thief; in slavery, therefore in a slaveholder; in wrong, therefore in a wrongdoer; and unless the men of this nation are made by woman to see that they have been guilty of usurpation, and cruel usurpation, I believe very little progress will be made."

In the September/October 1983 issue of *The Black Scholar* we read: "It was no easy thing for a male to espouse women's rights in the nineteenth century. Those who did risked being labeled 'Aunt Nancy Men' or worse. The *New York Herald* described one convention of the Equal Rights Association as composed of, 'Long-haired men, apostles of some inexplicable emotion or sensation. ... Negro-worshippers, sinners, and short-haired women. ... Women in Bloomer dresses to show their ankles and their independence; women who hate their husbands and fathers, and hateful women wanting husbands ... altogether the most long-necked, grim-faced, dyspeptic, Puritanical, nasal-twinged agglomeration of isms ever assembled.'"

Today we have men like Bill Moyers, the television journalist whose show on abortion was far and away the best media plea for woman's right to reproductive freedom that has aired on the tube. The irony is that today, any male with brains is a feminist. The tragedy is that any male with brains is too smart to say so.

Today, women must depend on themselves. At the end of the radical renaissance of the '60s, women saw that freedom was something that might be in the cards for them as well as for leftist males. Just as the abolitionists made nineteenth-century women conscious of the aspects of slavery in their own lives, so the leftist women who made coffee for the campus radicals in the '60s came to realize that they too had been had.

The Bitch Manifesto, written by Joreen in 1970 and republished in the anthology *Radical Feminism* (Quadrangle Press, edited by Koedt, Levine, and Rapone) defined bitches as those women who live outside the social order, women who can take care of themselves. The bitch/witch is a pariah. She is isolated whenever possible. Bitches do not believe in their inferiority. They are arrogant and egotistical. They do not wait, as ladies do, to be taken care of. There are more of them every day.

Why do women act like ladies or bitches? Like angels or vixens? Like whores or madonnas? Why does a slave shuffle? Why does a wounded person strike back? The answer of course is to get what she wants.

Sigmund Freud wrote: "The great question that has never been answered, and which I have not yet been able to answer despite my thirty years of research into the feminine soul, is: what does a woman want?" What a poet old Sigmund was. Always the metaphor, always the idea of a thing rather than the thing herself. Finding out what "a woman" wants is much like finding out what "a man" wants. Have to ask them one at a time. Get to know them. You know, Joe Stalin, Al Schweitzer.

Freud wanted to pin women down. Like bugs. Like a number of phallocentric nineteenth-century Jewish patriarchs (yes, he was the kind of guy who slept with his wife's kid sister), he had hardening of the categories when it came to women. In an age when male man was the measure of all things, woman was a disabled or castrated male. Freud felt that if he could say for certain that what woman wants is a penis, then it would all make sense somehow.

Freud's psychology is a psychology of males. When he learned that his women patients were disturbed as a result of childhood sexual trauma, he told them it was all in their heads. While treating hysteria in women, he discovered that great numbers of them had repressed frightening episodes of incest and sexual abuse. At first he believed in the reality of these stories. Then he examined his own childhood memories and something snapped. (See his published letters to his friend Fliess.) Unable to handle the implications, he adapted his knowledge to fit his theories. Women became guilty Eves once more.

Freud compounded his patients' illnesses by making them responsible for and even guilty of the Oedipal "fantasies" in which woman imagined —because Freud believed she desired—rape or incest. (Judith Lewis Herman's book *Father-Daughter Incest* from Harvard Press sheds some light into this darkling closet.)

Most of us now recognize the fact that childhood sexual trauma is common in our society, and that it crosses all lines of race and class. Children themselves will often deny its reality, in the same way Freud did, in order to protect their self-esteem, the self-regard necessary for mental health. I was one of these children myself and it was only through the act of writing fiction that I was able to dredge up memories buried for more than twenty years. We now know that children have strong survival instincts and that they often alter their perceptions of reality in ways which will help them maintain the illusion of control, or they simply refuse to acknowledge that certain things have happened. In Freud's case he was convinced that his own Oedipal desires were so strong that he could have/even did imagine seduction. He transferred his view of reality to the population at large and the result, for women anyway, was a catastrophe.

At the risk of going Freud one better, I will attempt to speak for women in general. It's my guess that one of the first things women *want* is the sure knowledge that they are safe. They want some sign that they are not going to have their throats cut or their food stolen or their persons violated. Primal fear is no joke and it dates from the stone age.

Women were perhaps the first "class." Sexual politics is as old as property. It is an illusion to imagine that females are in a socio-political position to make free choices. Their sexual behavior is based on things like who pays their bills. Freud's female patients didn't pay his bill. Their fathers and husbands paid him to "cure" their women, to restore them to the status quo, to feminize them if you will. Men require mirrors and many nineteenth-century women reflected what no man would wish to be, an image of a maimed male.

We have not come very far from Freud's phallocentrism. On the cover of the January 1982 issue of *Reader's Digest* we read: "What Women Really Want From Sex." I kept this article in my files because in some ways it is so comic. Male authorities on female sexuality tell us: "Orgasm is not inevitably a part of sex for women; indeed for some women it is not even terribly important." And, "Male orgasm is necessary for reproduction, while female orgasm is not". This is the sort of stuff D. H. Lawrence used to hand out in novels. James Lincoln Collier is the author of this retrograde study. He writes that the meaning, if not the sensation, of orgasm is different for women. He is right on that one! For one thing, an orgasm is what many women unashamedly call a spiritual experience.

But even without the subtleties, there is the question of economic, social, political, and biological relativity. We are all of us in a marketplace and the male buyers have the edge. It's the old problem of those men who don't think, they measure. Equality does not mean "the same." If it's true, as the thoughtless Mr. Collier states, that women are less "promiscuous" than men, could it be because they cannot yet afford to be? If men could get pregnant, would their behavior change?

It is always arrogant to generalize, even about women. The gender gap, or the genital gap, is still a schism. The women's movement has made some progress and brought about some understanding, and it is, by the way, the greatest spiritual revolution the world has ever known. But it still spreads as much heat as light.

The funniest and most uplifting effort to update sexual anthropology is a book by Elaine Morgan, *The Descent of Woman*. It exposes the nonsense in Desmond Morris's book, *The Naked Ape*. Morris tells us that women developed great white round breasts in order to inspire males to come around to the missionary position, the males being earlier intrigued by great round buttocks and needing something to replace them visually. Elaine Morgan takes the radical position that breast development may have had something to do with babies. I like her theories about the evolution of female sexual response. She understands the physiology better than any doctor I've ever read. Best of all, she understands the psychology of sex. Her chapter on male bonding was a revelation to me. She is careful to point out that women seldom fear men individually. The postman is so cheerful, etc. It's bonding that makes the male a killer. And males, *as a group*, have a strange pathology with regard to women. Whether it's at Bohemian Grove or the Vatican, woman is the perceived threat.

> I applied mine heart to know, and to search, and to seek out wisdom, and the reason of things, and to know the wickedness of folly, even of foolishness and madness: And I find more bitter than death the Woman, whose heart is snares and nets, and her hands as bands; whoso pleaseth God shall escape from her; but the sinner shall be taken by her.
>
> Ecclesiastes 7 — 25/26

"Sinners" often love women. For the misogynist, however, woman represents the dangerous other, the shadow self, the part of his soul he has lost or repressed, his mom, his anima, even his own sexuality. Driving out the demon woman is a way of repressing and controlling his sexual urges. This is always evident when it is expressed violently in the murder or rape of women. It is not always so easily recognizable in its more subtle manifestations which often take the form of rendering women invisible. Not allowed in the club, in the anthology, in the locker room, in the driver's seat, in the halls of Congress, etc.

The gender gap is not a simple political division. Equal pay is a red herring. This is a *religious* war. It has its origins in pre-history. Religious fundamentalism in the old old days took the form of female worship. Before what Joseph Campbell calls The Great Reversal (the rise of patriarchal mythology and religion), Woman was sacred and embodied the Great Goddess, that is, life and death.

> The earth that's nature's mother is her tomb;
> What is her burying grave that is her womb.
>
> *Romeo and Juliet*
> Act II, Scene 3

Now I think that death part depresses males. I know it depresses the hell out of me. This dread of death and going back into the pot of creation, Kali's cauldron, this is the mythos which portrays woman as darkness, as a devouring monster. Christianity was very advanced in its efforts to simply obliterate woman and all she symbolized. Women became ribs or anyway scapegoats or best of all *invisible*. Oh, there was always the Virgin Mary, the emasculated Great Mother; not even the Christians could create a motherless god.

After The Great Reversal, the alienation in male mythology created a divorce from the earth. This has led to first Western man's and now even Eastern man's rejection of the creative principles which ancient men lived by. Modern man does not see himself as part of a circle of life. He has an edifice complex. He is hierarchical. He climbs the ladder of life. He sits at the top of a pyramid.

In 1968, Anais Nin wrote in her book *The Novel of the Future*:

"There is a curious contradiction between those who complain that we have too many novels obsessed with the incapacity to achieve relationships and those who constantly upbraid the writers who deal exclusively with personal relationships. Feminine writing is often attacked as small, subjective, personal. The impotence to relate to another is the impotence to love others, and from this impotence to crime is a natural step. ...

The man who has made the definitive conquest of nature, the American man, is the one most afraid of *woman as nature*, of the feminine in himself. The American created a monolithic image of maleness which is a caricature of maleness, an exaggeration of maleness (no sensitivity, only toughness, logic, factualness). The European did not achieve such a domination of nature but did not feel totally estranged from it and thus he lives more comfortably in a state of friendship with woman and feminine nature."

Well, even in Europe, the gender gap is anything but a tender trap. Sexism changes styles faster than Paris couturiers. Our friendship with nature simply does not go as deep as our alienation from it. The same goes for women. Man's friendship with woman does not go as deep as his alienation from her. As the comedian Mort Sahl put it, "A woman's place is in the stove."

Males aren't nearly as stupid as they look. The guys who engineer ideologies to fit the current level of economic exploitation are as sharp as the slavers who preached racial inferiority to justify the practice of chattel slavery. It's all malestream propaganda.

Take Wilhelm II of Germany (please). He defined woman's responsibility within the state as *Kinder, Küche, und Kirch* (children, church, and kitchen). Like the Ku Klux Klan, these three K's can terrorize and torment, even today.

Hitler played this game in the formation of Nazi Germany before World War II. He had to wipe out the gains made by feminists after World War I. In Gloria Steinem's notes on "The Nazi Connection," (*MS.* October,

1980) she writes that women had "achieved the vote in 1918 as part of the Weimar Constitution that followed World War I. By 1926, moderate feminists had elected 32 women deputies to the Reichstag, the national parliamentary body that symbolized this brief flowering of democracy, just as the great German novelists and the Bauhaus came to symbolize the between-the-wars flowering of literature and art. (In the same era, there were only 15 women members of the British Parliament, and *women in the United States Congress had reached the total of three*.)"

Women in the United States aren't much better off today. The defeat of the Equal Rights Amendment, and the continued efforts to pass anti-abortion legislation and "family protections" all threaten to make the world safe for male supremacy. In her notes, Steinem goes on to state: "Radical German feminists had also begun to organize against the protective legislation that kept women out of many jobs, and to work toward such international goals as Pacifism. German families had become much smaller, and married women had gained the right to their own salaries.

"Precisely because such changes were both obvious in daily lifestyles and profound, they were often resented by those who longed for the hierarchical, 'undefeated' days before the war. As unemployment and inflation grew worse, women in the work force were scapegoated along with Marxists and Jews. ... The Weimar Republic began to ban married women from competing with men for government jobs, and to restrict access to contraception. ...

"'The right of personal freedom,' Hitler explained in *Mein Kampf*, 'recedes before the duty to preserve the race.' The Nazi leaders would not deprive women of the vote, they said, but they ridiculed feminists, liberals and socialists who were 'masculinizing' women by treating them *the same as men*. Their own answer to women was '*gleichwertig aber nicht gleichartig*': equivalent but not the same."

Remember "separate but equal" accommodations? The female proletariat knows how this game is played, especially if she has been "protected" right out of a job. Today's system of corporate feudalism demands that women function in the labor force. The question is how to render them impotent in the marketplace in the same way that they were powerless in the home. History has played us a neat trick. The liberated woman is expected to have a home and leave it too. It's called the superwoman bind. Working class women are often too tired to organize and the women who continue to work for affluent males (as wives or mistresses) tend to identify with the class interests of the males upon whom they are dependent.

As American fascism escalates, so does the attack on the feminine. Steinem describes Nazi rule: "Antifeminism was not a minor or opportunistic component of National Socialism, but a central part of it ... and once Hitler came to power, popularly elected in part by the patriarchal backlash against feminist successes, he delivered on his promise to restore male supremacy.... In 1933, feminists were removed from teaching and other public posts by the same law that removed 'non-Aryans' from such jobs. All women were banned from the Reichstag. ... Propaganda portrayed the ideal woman as healthy, blond, no makeup; a chaste and energetic worker while single, a devoted wife and mother as soon as possible. The magazine advertisements for contraception that had been commonplace were outlawed as pornographic. Birth control clinics were padlocked—much as some anti-abortion groups are demanding today."

Steinem goes on to describe the arguments used by Heinrich Himmler who demanded that all Aryan women complete their pregnancies. He wrote: "Supposing Bach's mother, after her fifth or sixth or even twelfth child, had said 'that'll do, enough is enough'—the works of Bach would never have been written."

When women decide to seize the means of reproduction, there is hell to pay. Consider the 1980 Convention of the National Right to Life Committee. Henry Hyde described himself as a "653-month-old fetus." Some males wish to slap the hand that rocks the cradle and rule the world themselves. If they lose the baby, they've dropped the ball. Their abuse of power is a violence against women. As sobering as the choice to have an abortion may be, it cannot compete with the prospect of forced pregnancy. After all, *if Bach had been a woman*, her works might never have been written if she had been forced to bear more than a dozen children.

Which brings us to the subject of the gender of genius. As the German philosopher, Arty Schopenhauer once wrote: "Women have great talent, but no genius, for they always remain subjective." Schopenhauer's essay, "Of Women," is so subjective his burnt-child, hurt-male reflexes scorch the page. Scratch a misogynist and find an abandoned, unloved child. Many men have been so hurt by the women in their lives, they "objectify" the whole gender into gorgons. (A gorgon may have talent, but never genius?) Women too, have done the same to the opposite sex, although few can compete with Schopenhauer's nonsense:

"You need only look at the way in which she is formed, to see that woman is not meant to undergo great labor, whether of the mind or of the body. ... The keenest sorrows and joys are not for her, nor is she called upon to display a great deal of strength. ... Women are directly fitted for acting as the nurses and teachers of our early childhood by the fact that they are themselves childish, frivolous and short-sighted; in a word, they are big children all their life long—a kind of intermediate stage between the child and the full-grown man, who is *man* in the strict sense of the word. See how a girl will fondle a child for days together, dance with it and sing to it; and then think what a man, with the best will in the world, could do if he were put in her place."

Schopenhauer is equally hilarious when he tries to explain the capacity women seem to have for outsmarting him:

"It will be found that the fundamental fault of the female character is that it has *no sense of justice*. This is mainly due to the fact that women are defective in the powers of reasoning and deliberation; but it is also traceable to the position which Nature has assigned to them as the weaker sex. They are dependent, not upon strength, but upon craft; and hence their instinctive capacity for cunning, and their irradicable tendency to say what is not true. For as lions are provided with claws and teeth, and elephants and boars with tusks, bulls with horns, and cuttle fish with its clouds of inky fluid, so Nature has equipped woman, for her defense and protection, with the arts of dissimulation; and all the power which Nature has conferred upon man in the shape of physical strength and reason, has been bestowed upon women in this form. Hence, dissimulation is innate in woman, and almost as much a quality of the stupid as of the clever. It is as natural for them to make use of it on every occasion as it is for those animals to employ their means of defense when they are attacked; they have a feeling that in so doing they are only within their rights. Therefore a woman who is perfectly truthful and not given to dissimulation is perhaps an impossibility, and for this very reason they are so quick at seeing through dissimulation in others that it is not a wise thing to attempt it with them."

Schopenhauer's essay, *Of Women*, from which the above paragraphs are taken, is the sort of misogyny that tells us more about Arty himself than about women. His descriptions of woman's slave mentality are cruel indeed, but it is easy to read between the lines and discover his own humiliation and guilt as he is forced to rationalize his relationship with the feminine. For example, he needs to believe that males mature later than females because "the nobler and more perfect a thing is, the later and slower it is in arriving at maturity." Women live in the present only, and see only that which is under their noses. This is much the same argument used by slavers to dehumanize captives. And of course, wise women know the

violence which this attitude embodies. In Emily Bronte's poem, "No
Coward Soul Is Mine," she wrote:

> "Vain are the thousand creeds
> that move men's hearts: unutterably vain;
> Worthless as withered weeds,
> or idlest froth amid the boundless main."

When Emily wrote that in 1846 she was fully aware that all the
nonsense written about male objectivity and female subjectivity (in art as
well as in life) was just gender benders. Gender gaps are in the mind of the
beholder. Filmmaker Michelle Citron writes in "Women and Film: A
Discussion of Feminist Aesthetics," in *New German Critique*, No. 13, winter
1978, p. 104:

"The culture assumes in general, that male films (read art, journalism,
scholarship, etc.) are objective and female films are subjective; male subjectivity is still perceived as *the objective point of view* on all things, in particular
women."

Genius has no gender, nor can it be labeled subjective or objective.
James Lowell once said, "Talent is that which is in a man's power. Genius is
that in whose power a man is." Genius is possession. When the power of
genius possesses a woman, we get into trouble. In the past, genius in
woman was often aborted or it led to madness. Most were fettered failures.
Sylvia Plath turned suicide into success but the price was a little high. Most
women tried to compromise, to accommodate the moods of their time. As
Virginia Woolf writes in her 1928 essay, *A Room of One's Own*:

"I thought of all the women's novels that lie scattered, like small
pock-marked apples in an orchard, about the secondhand book shops of
London. It was the flaw in the centre that had rotted them. She (the woman
writer) had altered her values in deference to the opinion of others."

Even the acknowledged woman of genius of the past is known for
distortion, for writing in code. Her "subjectivity" (read sublimation, translation, or sleight-of-hand) was a result of the necessity to produce works
acceptable to the consciousness of her time. At the same time, the genius of
the past invented ways to write on many levels at once. Today we recognize
Charlotte Bronte's *Jane Eyre* as a psychiatric poem. Even today, the scholars
bicker about whether or not the Brontes knew what they were doing when
they wrote works which revealed so much of the unconscious. *Jane Eyre* can
be read as the tale of a Victorian true-heart. A Christian how-to book on
marriage and a career. It is also a thundering revenge story in which male

arrogance and pride are brought low. Best of all, it gives us the madwoman in the attic, the repressed sexual and psychotic self which Victorian womanhood kept in the closet and which Victorian manhood still fears.

Emily Bronte had an even tougher time than Charlotte when it came to her struggle with Victorian forms and sentiments. She was an epic dramatist and Promethean poet stifled by the confines of the novel. In her poetry, we see her feminist fury: In a poem called "The Prisoner," she wrote:

> "My master's voice is low, his aspect bland and kind,
> But hard as hardest flint the soul that lurks behind. ... "

Form follows function and it is not until we come to Emily Dickinson that we find a woman who can follow a form suited to her own needs. And even today, the malestream literary establishment keeps making "corrections" in her work. Gertrude Stein wrote: "Patriarchal poetry makes no mistake." Together Gertrude Stein and Emily Dickinson blew up the store.

Women are out on a limb. They must go to each other for help, or to the Irish faery Queen Mab, that midwife of dreams. Genius is a gift of the gods, or the faeries, or the serpent of knowledge — genius visualized as a familiar spirit and meaning Genesis, to beget or bring forth. And the truth is, both genders beget, whether their nether regions have seeds or pods. And both men and women desire immortality and a seat among the gods — the gods being Sappho and Shakespeare, Stein and Yeats, all those who found voice and sang.

> Whether or not we find what we are
> Seeking, is idle, biologically speaking.
> Edna St. Vincent Millay

But what about the real world? Poets are one thing, but what about babies? What about biology and men and women and money and marriage? When I was still into biology, I divided my life into eras. B.C. = Before Children. A.D. = After Divorce. Emerson tells us all life is a preface until one has children. Perhaps.

It's a curious state of affairs, this begetting and rearing of other human beings. Here we have half the race required to gestate another generation and into the bargain they are required to persuade or coerce the other half of the race to help them along with the chore. (One of their techniques might be to persuade men that child-rearing is far too significant a task to be left entirely in the hands of women. Thus far this ploy has been unsuccessful and the mass of males "with the best will in the world" have no idea what to do with children.)

Consider, if you will, that children are our number one gross national product and they are produced and distributed *free*. They are the labor force which maintains the oligarchy which is the western capitalist world. The workers who produce them are charged for their support, taxed for their education, and seldom receive any return on this huge investment once the children become workers themselves. It was Hitler himself who wrote in *Mein Kampf*, "It must be considered as reprehensible conduct to refrain from giving healthy children to the nation."

If women were to seize the means of reproduction and pay themselves for their child-producing labor, then we would have, at long last, a social revolution worthy of the name. In her book, *The Second Sex*, published in 1949, Simone de Beauvoir wrote:

"A world where men and women would be equal is easy to visualize, for that precisely is what the Soviet Revolution *promised*: women raised and trained exactly like men were to work under the same conditions and for the same wages. Erotic liberty was to be recognized by custom, but the sexual act was not to be considered a "service" to be paid for; woman was to be *obligated* to provide herself with other ways of earning a living; marriage was to be based on a free agreement that the spouses could break at will; maternity was to be voluntary, which meant that contraception and abortion were to be authorized and that, on the other hand, all mothers and their children were to have exactly the same rights, in or out of marriage; pregnanacy leaves were to be paid for by the State, which would assume charge of the children, signifying not that they would be taken away from their parents, but that they would not be *abandoned* to them."

As we see by the horrendous statistics on battered and abused children in our country today, our children have indeed been *abandoned to their parents*. Life within today's nuclear family is grim indeed. With the usual exceptions to prove the rule, most children appear to be the victims of their parents and often manage to grow up and victimize their parents in return. One reason for this state of unhealth is the role of the woman as family flunky. When mothers are fired from the patriarchy (much as slaves were once fired from the plantations) they lose the doubtful comfort of their jobs as wives and their children must share their loss of fortune, their lives as dropouts outside a paterfamilias.

Any male who's ever had to support a family will tell you it's no picnic. Any mother who's had to raise small children will tell you it's the hardest work anyone can do. Why any single adult would attempt both jobs is beyond my imagination. In today's selfish world, family life is a prescription for disaster. Is there a way to create a place we can call *home*? Is there a definition of family that really means a place where people give a damn about each other; a place where economic democracy is practiced so children may learn there's enough to go around; a place where intimacy nourishes the spirit and laughter informs the intellect?

The political Right would have us believe that family is a microcosm of the State. Since the Right also believes that it is the duty of the State to make people good, it is obvious that they see the role of the family in a similarly oppressive way. Good fascists keep their kids in line?

The concept of family is a false ideal. The Right wing is crying because they feel mother will never come home again. The Left wing imagines child-care centers will save us. (They might.) But the real question is always who will love the children until they are old enough to find lovers of their own. And make no mistake about it, children are the neediest creatures on earth and they must have deep attachments, the kind of attachments that can survive even today's "quality time" fashion in childcare.

No one I know thinks Robert Young or even Bill Cosby knows best anymore, but neither do they have any very creative ideas about who does. I think this is progressive. If nothing else, I think children can do a better job of raising themselves than the average parent has done in the past.

In *The Politics of the Solar Age*, Hazel Henderson writes: "The Latin root of family, *familia*, meant originally all the slaves belonging to one man, over whom he had the power of life and death."

Women are second only to children in health risks found in family life. According to a 1978 nationwide study sponsored by the National Institute for Mental Health, 1.8 million women are beaten by their mates each year. National insurance statistics tell us that the healthiest Americans are married men and single women. This is a historical trend which won't go away. Long ago Anna Garlin Spencer (1851–1931) wrote in her essay, "Woman's Share in Social Culture":

"It is not alone the fact that women have generally had to spend most of their strength in caring for others that has handicapped them in individual effort; but also that they have almost universally had to care wholly for themselves. When we read of Charles Darwin's wife not only relieving him from financial cares but seeing that he had his breakfast in his room, with 'nothing to disturb the freshness of his morning,' we do not find the explanation of Darwin's genius, but we do see how he was helped to express it. . . . No book has yet been written in praise of a woman who let her husband and children starve or suffer while she invented even the most useful things, or wrote books, or expressed herself in art, or evolved philosophic systems. ..."

In thinking about this passage, I realized recently that I had indeed from time to time arranged my life in such a way that there would be "nothing to disturb the freshness of my morning." But of course it never happened two days in a row, nor could I imagine in my wildest dreams, someone arranging such a thing *for* me!

In Ibsen's famous play, *A Doll's House* (1879), the central character, Nora, announces when she leaves her home and family to find out who she really is: "I have a *higher* responsibility (than husband and children), I have a responsibility to *myself*." More than a hundred years after the first performance of this play it is interesting to speculate how many women and men truly believe that. George Bernard Shaw wrote that it's always a mistake to sacrifice yourself to others; that those to whom you sacrifice yourself will end up loathing you for it. He mentions guilt, but more than that a resentment, an anger at obligation and irritation at the masochism of the sacrificer. Virginia Woolf bemoaned her mother-in-law's endless insistence that her sons affirm her existence as matriarch, all the while having nothing to bring to them except her own emptiness.

Modern woman must be practical. In a study reported by Michael Minton in *Plain Speaking*, February 1–15, 1982, he estimates that women's unwaged labor in the home in 1980 was worth $793.79 per week or $41,277.08 per annum. I think he must have been studying suburban housewives. Most of the women I know find housework so entropic and oppressive as well as ecologically corrupt, they either eliminate all but the bottom-line chores or they do as I do, they post Dorothy Parker's epigraph where it may be easily seen by all visitors: "Excuse my dust."

Once I too was a suburban housewife and I must confess that before enlightenment, I too probably earned $793.79 per week while I single-handedly kept Proctor & Gamble in business and doubtless destroyed at least one river all by myself with the chemicals I poured down every drain in a desperate effort to drive out the devil—that is, the dreadful thought that what I was doing was irrelevant and immaterial. I begin to know now, just why my mother hated germs so much. My childhood was soaked in sani-flush. In recent years, I have an image of Americans washing their hands compulsively, like Lady Macbeth, in an obsessive attempt to cleanse themselves of a guilt which all the perfumes of Arabia can neither sweeten nor disguise.

It is obvious that things must change, are changing. The originator of Modern Dance, the immortal Isadora Duncan (1878-1927), once remarked that any woman who reads the marriage contract and then goes through with it, deserves everything she gets. Germaine Greer says that if marriage and family depend upon the castration of women then let them change or disappear. Margaret Sanger (1883-1966) thought birth control was the answer. She believed it would free women sexually. In a 1920 essay called "Woman and the New Race" she wrote:

"The most important force in the remaking of the world is a free motherhood. . . . woman has, through her reproductive ability, founded and perpetuated the tyrannies of the Earth. Whether it was the tyranny of a monarchy, an oligarchy or a republic, the one indispensable factor of its existence was, as it is now, hordes of human beings — human beings so plentiful as to be cheap, and so cheap that ignorance was their natural lot. Upon the rock of an unenlightened, submissive maternity have these been founded; upon the product of such a maternity have they flourished. . . . Today, however, woman is rising in fundamental revolt."

And today things are more revolting than ever. What Emma Goldman called the universal ignorant motherhood still makes 'em so the men can break 'em in love and war. If I were a man, I'd say to hell with it. But even that privilege is denied me. In *The Dialectic of Sex*, Shulamith Firestone writes: "A man is allowed to blaspheme the world because it belongs to him to damn." In Lois Gould's *Final Analysis* (1974) she writes:

> "'Why the hell don't women ever make a scene? Men are *always* making scenes, yelling in the halls. Why can't *you* yell in the halls?'
>
> 'Because,' she sighed, 'women don't get away with yelling in the halls. They call you a hysterical bitch if you yell in the halls.'
>
> 'Also,' Sophy noted wryly, 'they fire you. It's *their* halls.'"

In 1980, at the United Nations World Conference on Women, held in Copenhagen, the program notes included these statistics: "Women represent 50 percent of the world adult population, and one third of the official labor force; they perform nearly two-thirds of all working hours, and receive only one-tenth of the world income, and own less than one percent of all world property."

But what difference does it make in the end, so long as the mass of the

world's women prefer love to power? Dr. Helen Caldicott has gone into this
subject at length and she is responsible for calling women to task for their
complicity in male domination of the planet. Curiously Caldicott is often
criticized for her "hostility" toward men, when her main point is usually to
explain how she has been seduced and coopted by them. She answers
such criticism by telling men to try to think, not just to react emotionally.
Where's your systematic perspective? she asks the typical male crank.
Women's covert complicity in male power structures has long been a
subject avoided by feminists. Feminists may be afraid to further alienate
those women who cower behind the illusion of economic safety within
middle-class families. Or perhaps we just can't face our own cowardice. No
one likes to admit to self-deception. Most of us spend our days inventing
new ways to think well of ourselves. For women, this is an all-consuming
task, as there are so many detractors waiting for any false move. Let a
woman express even a shadow of self-doubt and both women and men will
rush from the wings to reveal her to the audience as the fraud she must
surely be.

One of the most depressing detractors to come along in a long time
was Jay Cocks, whose cover story for *Time* on July 12, 1982, "American
Women, the Climb to Equality," seemed to me to be the death knell for the
women's movement. I have filed this article under epitaphs, and since its
publication more and more women shy away from using the "f" word
(feminism). Cocks (!) has read his Virginia Woolf. He understands women,
he just can't stand them.

"After the batterings of Selma and Viet Nam, several assassinations and
summers of psychedelic overload, the country needed a warm bath and a
bit of soothing. What it got instead was a fresh, hard needlepoint shower
from the ranks—indeed, from the home. It was a little too much. Doors
slammed, windows rattled shut. The national circuits had temporarily
shorted out, and, in the prevailing gloom, the feminist torches looked less
like beacons than sputtering pilot lights from the stoves the women were
threatening to abandon.

"Women's lib it was called then, short for liberation, of course, but
unconsciously, closer to women's lip. ... "

Cocks goes on to make the word libber sound like nigger. He does not
deny facts. Denying the historical oppression of women is like denying the
holocaust (there's a gang of neo-fascists in southern California working on
that one). What Cocks emphasizes is how *unattractive* the whole thing is.
(Goddess knows, I still hear men telling women they won't get anywhere if

they take "that tone.") Cocks writes:

"'A lot of the failures of the movement are built into the people who are speaking for women.' says novelist Anne Tyler. 'Basically I agree with everything they say, but I find myself wanting to disagree because of the way they say it. If people like me, who are pro-women, are put off by it, imagine other people.' Or imagine a sympathetic parent, particularly a father, leafing through the beginning of a feminist guide to child rearing and banging a shin on the following parenthesis: '(See Chapter 24 for a full discussion of language as an exclusionary tool of male supremacy.)' Imagine getting to Chapter 24; imagine turning the page.

"It does not do, though, to be so easily put off. Movements all have their excesses. They come with the territory, even if they sometimes seem to cover it, like drifting snow over new paths. Indeed, should the father have persevered, he might have found some first-rate advice about children in that very same book. He would also have found a kind of zip-lock naiveté that insulates author Letty Cottin Pogrebin inside a cocoon of ideology. How else could a writer suggest, never mind believe, that children might be encouraged to forsake the music of the Rolling Stones (sexist, of course) for the uplifting ballads of Gay Feminist Holly Near. Ideology infringes on reality; one suspects it can also skew the sense of rhythm."

For Jay Cocks, reality is the Rolling Stones. Music is, by definition, male. Turn on the radio and see. "Zip-lock naiveté" may be another phrase for terrorized mind set. As I go around the house tonight locking doors and checking windows I consider that it's years now since I have been assaulted in my home. I shouldn't still be naive enough to worry about my status as victim, or my role as prey. I picture Jay Cocks watching me check to see if my neighbor's dogs are in the yard, in hopes they will bark at intruders. I remember the men who joked and laughed about the sort of old ladies who look under their beds at night. All the innuendo and contempt implied in their laughter still echoes in my psyche, prevents me from calling the police late at night, even once after a rape. On another occasion, again a rape, I *did* call them, only to discover I was right the first time. I have since learned that to mention personal trauma is very often to loose ground in arguing for women's issues. My position is then seen as subjective. Always women must be cool, objective, clinical, and what I call terminally adult. Cocks writes:

"On the occasion of a Miss America pageant, a marginal faction of young women threw their underwear into an Atlantic City, N.J., garbage can, attempting some clumsy metaphorical gesture, and grabbed headlines, air time, and a disproportionate share of posterity. If 'libbers' were the dreary drones of the movement, 'bra burners' were the lacy lunatic fringe."

Think of the media response to male "panty raids" some years ago. Exactly why was that "fun" and female antics "lunatic fringe" behavior? I suppose if the women had staged panty raids (I think there were a few) in retaliation, that would have been viewed as a healthy turn-on. It's the turn-off, the rejection of sex role stereotypes, that galls males like Cocks.

That *Time* would have assigned a male journalist to evaluate the success or failure of the women's movement in America is all we need to know. He manages a degree of condescension so acidic and depressing it is sure to charm the malestream. He is honest. He reports on the feminization of poverty. He notes that the five hundred million set aside for childcare in the federal budget has been cut. He reports on the "curious blend of naiveté and arrogance" evidenced by advocates of the ERA. In short his examination of woman is scarcely more civilized and enlightened than that of Arty Schopenhauer back in the nineteenth century.

Putting the Cocks' article back in my epigraphs file, I stop to stare at the photo of Phyllis Schlafly in a frilly white blouse with a string of pearls; she is holding three balloons in her hand. She's the one who symbolically baked the bread for the breadwinners. She's the gal on the wedding cake, the complicitous cutie who knows which side her bread is buttered on. Perhaps she's got the right idea after all. It's four in the morning and I'm alone in a house in a crime-ridden neighborhood. Should I get a big dog? Keep a gun? Marry a cop? Lone women are pariahs, citizens without a country. When my depression really hits hard, I ask myself, what would Ernest Hemingway do? Hum. No, even I'm not man enough for that.

What Jay Cocks fails to address is the effect of economics on the condition of women. He states it. He does not analyze it. Remember back when freed slaves were promised forty acres and a mule? (Not that they ever got them.) Today's woman is starting out on the road to freedom without any reparations for past inequities. The lurch to the political Right in the 1980s is clearly a backlash response to the ideological gains made by women in the 1970s. In "The Nouveau Poor," an article written for the August 1982 issue of *MS.* by Barbara Ehrenreich and Karin Stallard, we read:

"George Gilder, President Reagan's favorite social theorist, believes that female wages undermine men's ability to control their destructive impulses: 'If they cannot be providers, they have to resort to muscle and phallus.' In his one known departure from a pure free-market economic philosophy, Gilder advocates *enforcing* wage differentials between women and men—because unemployed men are potentially dangerous, while 'unemployed women can perform valuable work in creating and maintaining families.'"

Who was it said hard times is when the only work is woman's work? Truth is, most of the jobs men seek today are to some degree dehumanizing, or at least enable them to avoid their responsibilities to other human beings who might need them. "The job" has always seemed to me the ultimate male excuse for ignoring his family and neglecting his friends.

Because he has to do what a man's gotta do. That is, kill. Whether he makes a killing in the marketplace or the military or whether he just steals, it's the prestige function in our society to bring home the bacon. Remember the golden rule? The one who has the gold makes the rules. Women are sick of being broke, and so they are trying to do what the men do. God helps the bimbo with the bucks. In the article quoted above the authors also state:

"Two out of three adults who fall into the federal definition of poverty are women, and more than half the families defined as poor are maintained by single women. In the mid-sixties until the mid-seventies, the number of poor adult males declined, while the number of poor women heading households swelled by 100,000 a year, prompting the National Advisory Council on Economic Opportunity to predict: 'All other things being equal, if the proportion of the poor in female- householder families were to continue to increase at the same rate as it did from 1967 to 1978, the poverty population would be composed solely of women and their children before the year 2000.'"

Women *as a class* are losing economic ground rapidly. Never mind that the *image* of women has changed. That's just malestream propaganda. The same thing happened to blacks at the end of the Civil Rights Movement. Women and blacks got jobs as TV journalists and the nation imagined both groups had arrived.

Divorced women are thrown out of the middle class. Poverty begins with single parenthood. Forty percent of departed fathers contribute nothing to the support of their children. The average payment provided by the other sixty percent is less than two thousand dollars a year. Ehrenreich and Stallard write: "Also contrary to the myth, the latest census figures show that the number of men raising children on their own declined between 1970 and 1980."

In the black community, more than forty-five percent of families are now headed by women, compared to 31 percent in 1970. Black women stand only a twenty-nine percent chance of being awarded any child support by the courts, compared to a seventy-one percent chance for white women. In spite of these brutal statistics, half of all the young black people who go to college come from female-headed households.

Federal cuts in childcare are a hideous threat to our future. Ehrenreich and Stallard: "Women, if they can get to jobs and arrange for childcare, earn, on the average, just over $10,000 a year, compared to an average of $21,000 for men. According to the Bureau of Labor Statistics, it takes $25,407 a year to maintain a family of four at an 'intermediate' standard of living—$15,000 more than the average woman's earnings."

In 1980, the average AFDC monthly payment for a family of four was $398. (That's *before* Reagan's budget cuts.) Only a handful of women can meet the needs of a family by working. Jobs aren't enough. Women must *earn a living*. Gender job segregation is increasing. Ehrenreich and Stallard conclude that "gender inequality has begun to blur into class inequality."

Why then, in the face of the facts, do so many women continue to tackle single parenting? Why, in fact, are the brighter women doing so? Could it be that there are worse things than being broke? Ehrenreich and Stallard observe: "Perhaps surprisingly, college-educated women of both races are more likely than others to become single mothers. In his study, 'Economic Policies and Black Progress,' issued by the National Urban League, Robert B. Hill found that female-headed households are increasing ten times faster among college-educated black women than among black women who have not completed high school. Among white women, households headed by college educated women are increasing five times faster than those headed by women who did not complete high school. By 1980, college-educated women were heading more than one fifth of all female-headed families. Thus the female-headed household can no longer be regarded as a telltale feature of the culture of poverty."

Well, perhaps there is more to life than money. Perhaps the women who are the authors of their own existence have more authority. Of course, on another level it's the money that validates. Authentic being takes cash. Often it's the lack of male income that "breaks" the home. Broken homes can only be put back together again when Humpty-Dumpty falls off the wall of patriarchal prejudice, a notion which bricks the brains of those who cannot grasp that a family is not a biological unit but a group of kindred souls. This is what the Irish describe as the kith as well as the kin, the clusters of people who live together because they like the sound of one another's voices and the gist of one another's talk. Better the financial poverty of many matrifocal homes in which women and men too come together freely and make a creative life for children. Far better than the emotional poverty found in many patriarchal households in which the pecking order torments all the members of the group and leads to a society which is damn near psychotic in its interpersonal relationships.

A central question today, is whether women alone can effect change in the society at large. The mass of women will not separate themselves from men, and so it is clear that if feminism is to flourish, males must join the fight. In a letter to her biographer, Elizabeth Gaskell, on August 27, 1850, Charlotte Bronte wrote:

"Men begin to regard the position of woman in another light than they used to do, and a few men, whose sympathies are fine and whose sense of justice is strong, think and speak of it with a candour that commands my admiration. They say, however — and, to an extent, truly — that the amelioration of our condition depends on ourselves. Certainly there are evils which our own efforts will best reach; but as certainly there are other evils — deep-rooted in the foundations of the social system — which no efforts of ours can touch; of which we cannot complain, of which it is advisable not too often to think."

When I began to write feminist "Bread and Roses" columns, the response I got from males was often very thoughtful. Yet there were always doubts, reservations, hints that I might not be altogether objective in my views, especially on one occasion when I wrote of the rape of a young woman in Berkeley. My account was eventually dismissed as biased by my own deep emotional involvement. I was taken to task for my failure to keep a journalist's perspective.

In *Media File*, October 1981, Jessica Mitford writes: "All journalism is subjective and slanted because it is written by flesh-and-blood human beings with built-in political and philosophical biases."

Objectivity is a fallacy. Male resistance to female rage is not only subjective, it's probably clinically paranoid. Take Norman Mailer (please). His sexual politics are certainly his civil right, but his fantasy life is fucking up the lives of women everywhere. Do his rights end where our noses (prurient joke may be substituted) begin? Can male "reality" be altered in any way so as to take in a larger concept of what females call reality? Women and men use the same vocabulary to mean utterly different things. I pick up the newspaper and read a male journalist who describes what he calls a "forcible rape" — surely a redundancy. I think males would take sexual assaults more seriously if we simply labeled them felony assault with intent to do grave bodily harm. For the male, there is still an element of romance in rape.

In Susan Brownmiller's 1975 book, *Against Our Will: Men, Women and Rape*, she writes:

"A female definition of rape can be contained in a single sentence. If a woman chooses not to have intercourse with a specific man and the man chooses to proceed against her will, that is a criminal act of rape. Through no fault of woman, this is not and never has been the legal definition. The ancient patriarchs who came together to write their early covenants had used the rape of women to forge their own male power—how then could they see rape as a crime of man against woman. Women were wholly owned subsidiaries and not independent beings. Rape could not be envisioned as a matter of female consent or refusal; nor could a definition acceptable to males be based on a male-female understanding of a female's right to her bodily integrity. Rape entered the law through the back door, as it were, as a property crime of man against man. Woman, of course, was viewed as the property."

Brownmiller goes on to write of bride price (more than what Judas got for Christ!), theft of virginity (a crime against the father's property), and Moses' careful neglect of "Thou shalt not rape," as an essential Commandment. In law, a raped married woman was an "adultress," and therefore had to be stoned to death at the gates of the city.

Now it is true that all this was four thousand years ago and there have been a few changes. Why only two thousand years ago Christ said, "He that is without sin among you, let him first cast a stone at her," hinting that well none of us is perfect after all, and women have feelings too. (Throughout history a few male poets and saints have believed that women have souls. We don't know what women believed.)

Since the beginnings of "civilization" rape has been a metaphor for male oppression. It symbolizes man's assault on nature and his rejection of his own source, the mother who gave him birth, the part of himself he rejects in the neurotic desire to divorce himself from the earth which he knows will claim him again in the end.

Rape is symbolic murder. It is a tool of war. It keeps women in an underclass. It is used to degrade the men to whom women "belong." It is an effective weapon against female mobility in modern society. One rapist can keep thousands of women at home in a given city. The rape of Helen of Troy was an excuse for a ten years' war. The rape of chattel slaves in America little more than a century ago was merely a property right. (No white male has ever been executed for the rape of a black woman in the U.S. Of the 455 men executed for rape between 1930–68, 405 were black. For every white man convicted of rape, at least four black men are convicted.)

Many days I feel as Charlotte Bronte did, that these are crimes about which it is perhaps better not to think. Denial is, after all, a survival mechanism. In our own dark age, we see rapists chatting on TV talk shows, wallowing in tales of atrophied feeling and child abuse. In an age in which greed and lust stalk the land like some Biblical plague, it is easy to view sex as just one more thing *to be had*. It is the mythos of moderns.

What is most often ignored or neglected when we address the war on women, is the fact that it is part of a larger historical breakdown, a descent into decadence that makes the Fall of Rome look like a pink tea. In our country, it is nothing less than neo-fascism. The costumes have changed and the clever authors call it "friendly fascism." But the result is the same. We are eating our own tail.

For me, the discovery of the direct connection between the misogyny of our age and the self-destructive national imperialism which followed World War II (and which may presage our historical nemesis) came when I read some passages in Quentin Bell's biography of his aunt, Virginia Woolf.

In her suicide note one of the reasons Woolf gave for her final despair was the terrible times in which she lived. (She drowned herself in the River Ouse on Friday, 28 March 1941.) Her beloved nephew, Julian Bell, died fighting Franco in Spain in 1937. In his biography, Julian's younger brother Quentin Bell writes:

"Virginia asked me why, in my opinion, things had gone so very wrong with the world during the past few years. I replied with what I suppose was the stock answer of any young socialist: the world economic crisis, of which the American stock-market crash was the grand symptom, was the prime cause; it has bred unemployment, revolution, counter-revolution, economic and political nationalism, hence Communism, Fascism and war . . . all these things were but the effects of an economic cause. She was frankly amazed, neither agreed nor disagreed, but thought it a very strange explanation. To her, I think, it appeared that the horrible side of the universe, the forces of madness, which were never far from her consciousness, had got the upper hand again. This to her was something largely independent of the political mechanics of the world. The true answer to all this horror and violence lay in an improvement of one's own moral state; somehow one had to banish anger and the unreason that is bred of anger. Thus she tended, unlike Leonard (her husband), to be an out-and-out pacifist; she never made this clear in terms of policy, but it was her instinctive reaction, the feminine as opposed to the masculine — 'the beastly masculine' reaction."

Quentin Bell's affection and regard for his aunt are evident throughout his biography, however he shows the limitations of his understanding in oblique ways. He condemns Virginia for her aversion to certain masculine principles. "Virginia hated violence — she associated it with masculine assertiveness. But were we then to scuttle like frightened spinsters before the Fascist thugs? She belonged, inescapably, to the Victorian world of Empire, Class and Privilege. Her gift was for the pursuit of shadows, for the ghostly whispers of the mind and for Pythian incomprehensibility, when what was needed was the swift and lucid phrase that could reach the ears of unemployed working men or Trades Union officials."

Virginia's shadows were not the ephemeral kind. There is nothing more substantial than the presence of evil in the human mind. Woolf suffered from sexual abuse as a child and in her essay, "Three Guineas," she makes a direct connection between Fascism as it had arisen in Europe and the treatment of women "in the private house." Neither the critics nor her friends would sit still for this. Virginia was too far ahead of her time. Today we all know fascism begins at home but for some reason that hasn't changed things.

I have a great affection for Virginia Woolf's approach to politics. Quentin says her attempts to deal with what he calls political reality were bewildering and at times exasperating. His account of her tenure as Secretary of the Rodmell Labour Party is ironic. He describes his despair when trying to get the party to pass resolutions urging the formation of a United Front — or something equally vital to his masculine sensibility — "and Virginia managed to turn the debate in such a way that it developed into an exchange of Rodmell gossip. In this, of course, she was much nearer to the feelings of the masses, if one may thus describe the six or seven members of the Rodmell Labour Party, than I was. I wanted to talk politics, the masses wanted to talk about the Vicar's wife."

Virginia was trying to humanize what her nephew calls politics. She was trying to live in what she believed was the sane world. She, more than those around her, was acutely aware of the madness which lurks in the human soul. She had suffered acutely from the masculine oppression of her father and the overt sexual abuse inflicted upon her by her half-brother.

When Virginia suffered bouts of madness, she met the shadow within herself. She knew that there is darkness within *all of us*. Unlike the Fascists, unlike Hitler, she was unwilling to project her shadow unto others and so suffered its wrath. Hitler slaughtered millions to alleviate his own fears, to drive out the devils within his paranoid soul. A poet like Virginia Woolf could only suffer tragic enlightenment, knowing that the only way to destroy the shadow in the soul is to destroy the self.

Finally, any honest look at sexism in modern society must conclude that most of us live a lie. As Virginia Woolf herself wrote: "We all know—the *Times* knows—but we pretend we don't." There is the economic lie, the social lie, the romantic lie. W. H. Auden calls it a folded lie. For me it is simply a damned lie. The lie that I am free in a world which oppresses me. Oh, I know that if I am very quiet and don't put up any resistance, they will probably let me live. But I must be careful. I must not make waves.

Once, in the early 1970s, in the aftermath of a rape, I spoke with a lover who suggested I might have met the rapist at a local bar, might have given him my name or in some way led him to believe I was available. It is strange at this great distance of time, but I still date my final disillusion from that moment. Oh, there have been thousands of other moments. Great crimes and small. But it was then that I understood that it was not the lone criminal I am up against. It is male supremacy, the attitude that my position on earth is not that of a fellow man.

When I imagine utopian worlds I visualize a world of skinless folk. What color is the soul? Red, perhaps. Can you imagine a world in which rape no longer exists? A world in which such an idea is incomprehensible? I can hardly make the leap.

First of all, I'd open my windows. I'd open my doors to the gossamer mist that I see outside this very morning. I would not have to live locked up in rooms. I could take the nails off the windows on the first floor, the windows that have been broken so often. If there were no rape, would the concept of theft be thrown out as well? If property is theft, then no one would need to grasp *things*, to covet, to cling to goods or girls or anything else.

Second, I'd quit wearing a shirt. Who would care if a middle-aged woman watered her yard and her ferns without a bra, without anything to cover her breasts. Clothes are a torment, and civilized peoples act accordingly. What difference does it make what a woman wears as she wanders the streets in the dark, or treks the woods at night alone. Imagine going grunion hunting in the moonlight down in Southern California without watching out for cops and bathing nude anywhere there's sun (and even where there isn't) without checking everywhere for trouble. Imagine sleeping naked in the woods in the heat of summer or near a great fire. Imagine being free to talk to men anywhere anytime, without being wary, without being careful not to be "too friendly." Imagine setting out on an earth walk, even a van trip, all alone and with no weapon. Imagine walking the world without fear.

As things are, women still live the lie. We live as hypocrites and/or in a state of defensive mental adjustment. It is called seige mentality. All women, East and West, live behind a veil. In the West, our purdah is pretense. From puberty onward, we play our roles. Lady or tramp, we are still at the mercy of terrorism. And the terrorist is not just the physically violent male, although he is real enough. The terrorist is the sexist in the soul of every human being alive.

HOMAGE TO JAMES BALDWIN
(1924-1987)

> Raging waves of the sea, foaming out their own shame; wander-
> ing stars, to whom is reserved the blackness of darkness forever.
> Jude 13

James Baldwin died in Paris on the first day of December, 1987. Born in Harlem in 1924, he is the link between Richard Wright and the black women writers of today. These are the writers who go to the heart of things. When I was young, I imagined that black writers were better Christians than white writers. Of course, when I was young, they *were*.

Times change. For a vitriolic view of black writers and their literary legacy, see an article written by Stanley Crouch for the October 19, 1987 issue of *The New Republic*. Crouch writes: "Much of the Afro-American fiction written over the last 25 years derives from a vision set down by James Baldwin, who described the downtrodden as saintly." Crouch goes on to state that as a result of Baldwin's writing, "Race became an industry." His article is titled "Aunt Medea," and it is a frontal attack on Toni Morrison's novel, *Beloved*, as well as an assault on black women writers in general.

As I read Crouch's article, I found myself scribbling in the margin the observation that for black women writers, the leap from being ignored to being hated seems to spell success. The attacks on Alice Walker have been the most petulant, but Crouch's article on Morrison is a veritable temper tantrum in which he stamps his feet like some cranky Rumpelstiltskin because a woman has spun gold from straw and he's jealous. He writes: "*(Beloved)* is designed to placate sentimental feminist ideology, and to make sure that the vision of black women as the most scorned and rebuked of the victims doesn't weaken. . . . *Beloved*, above all else, is a blackface holocaust novel. It seems to have been written in order to enter American slavery into the big-time martyr ratings contest."

Well there are those who believe that chattel slavery on this continent might just *be* the winner of the big-time martyr contest, if that's what we're calling it this season. (For a definitive study of the Atlantic slave trade, see *Black Cargoes*, by Daniel Pratt Mannix, published by Viking in 1962.) Crouch adds that Morrison, "lacks a true sense of the tragic . . . she perpetually interrupts her narrative with maudlin ideological commercials."

I can't help thinking of the ideological commercials in Richard Wright's 1940 novel of social realism, *Native Son.* I'm afraid that critics such as Stanley Crouch are simply unhappy men descended from Virginia Woolf's hypothetical figure of Professor von X, the guy in her essay *A Room of One's Own* who was engaged in writing his monumental work entitled, *The Mental, Moral, and Physical Inferiority of the Female Sex.* Woolf opines that such angry misogynists were perhaps laughed at in their cradles by a pretty girl. Whatever the reason, their reactions are subjective. They do not wish to have their existence (*their* suffering?) described, defined or rendered into poetry by a woman. They wish to keep their pain to themselves.

James Baldwin did not keep his pain to himself. He was capable of that intimacy which women are said to crave — he shared his feelings. He poured forth his deepest convictions and they became literature. Baldwin did not deny his pain, nor did he detest women. Some say this is because he was a homosexual and perhaps that is so, but just the same he did not detest women. What is more, he did not detest black people, nor did he detest himself. He says he did so in the beginning, when he was a child. It is called internalized oppression. He believed some of what the white world said about him. Then he thought about it. (He once said he had to live in Paris for nine years in order to be convinced someone could hate him for himself, not for his color.)

Baldwin *was* a kind of literary saint and one of the sources of his sainthood was the downtrodden condition in which he lived as a child in Harlem. Now we all know that suffering does not necessarily ennoble people. Richard Wright illustrated that in *Native Son*, a story in which racism turns a man into a brute. Just as, perhaps, it has desensitized Stanley Crouch. In fact, Crouch may be a grouch for neo-racist reasons. He quotes

Baldwin:

"I do not mean to be sentimental about suffering — enough is certainly as good as a feast — but people who cannot suffer can never grow up, can never discover who they are. That man who is forced each day to snatch his manhood, his identity out of the fire of human cruelty that rages to destroy it knows, if he survives his effort, and even if he does not survive it, something about himself and human life that no school on earth — and, indeed, no church — can teach. He achieves his own authority, and that is unshakable. This is because, in order to save his life, he is forced to look beneath appearances, to take nothing for granted, to hear the meaning behind the words. If one is continually surviving the worst that life can bring, one eventually ceases to be controlled by a fear of what life can bring; whatever it brings must be borne. And at this level of experience one's bitterness begins to be palatable, and hatred becomes too heavy a sack to carry."

So Baldwin threw down the sack. (Remember Malcolm X writing that a similar thing happened to him after he visited Mecca?) He embraced the world and what love there is in it. He never denied the hatred. He studied it and wrote about it, but he was essentially a religious, a man whose presence gave off light — what the Zen prophets call the light of infinite compassion.

The week that Baldwin died I was surprised to find myself suffering from an acute sense of loss. I'm sure it was in part selfish. I mean that it was a sense of personal loss for a time gone by, for an era as well as a man. In the '60s we called him Jimmy; "we" being, I suppose, a rather naive handful of black and white liberals who believed that everything was going to work out after the Revolution. I suppose we thought we would all become tea-colored, at least psychologically.

James Baldwin was responsible, certainly more than any other writer in the '60s, for my own awakening — consciousness-raising, if you like. When I heard about Baldwin's death, I was sitting in the Caffe Mediterraneum in Berkeley. There was live music coming from The Print Mint across the street. I had an acute attack of *deja vu*. Twenty years slipped away and I was back in 1967. We were so sure of ourselves then. I saw myself full of hope. How we lived on hope back then. Hope was the rope we hung ourselves from.

I thought of my years as a suburban housewife from 1960 until 1966 — my exile into marriage out in Lafayette, not far from Berkeley in miles but ideologically on another planet. Baldwin came into that world. I can even say that he had something to do with my divorce in 1966, although I didn't know him personally.

Baldwin left America in 1948 and commuted back from France to be with Martin Luther King. He was at the intellectual center of a monumental movement which changed American consciousness forever, which gave us the radical awareness that led to both the Civil Rights Movement and the Women's Movement.

I'll never forget his first appearances on television, his vivacity, his electric intelligence, his passionate Christianity. Some whites looked on in shock, some even said he looked like a monkey. (His great eyes and gnomic poetics were like nothing we had seen before.) Baldwin himself once said his father had told him he was the ugliest child, the ugliest nigger he'd ever seen. He thought about that and came to the conclusion that nobody knows what a writer looks like and so he decided he would be a writer. A lot of us know that feeling—the feeling that we will not be loved for ourselves and so we must express our love at one remove: between the pages of a book or behind a microphone.

The soul of James Baldwin was easy to see, even on TV. The diverse reactions to him when he appeared on mass media were exactly what I needed to separate the wise observers from those mired in fear and prejudice—those Americans who, as Baldwin himself wrote, fear blacks because they fear death itself, because they are afraid of dark places, afraid of their own shadows in fact.

Baldwin blew our minds when he wrote that racism has something to do with our fear of death. Today we know that applies to sexism as well. Deep down in our reptilian brain stem there is an antipathy to that which is different from ourselves—the black, the Jew, the woman, anyone who is alien, who is *other*. In the psychotic individual, this paranoid ideation is acted out and we get Hitler. The poetic view is that this rejected other is very often a lost part of ourselves, a lost part of our own souls.

When I first read the work of James Baldwin, I felt an instant recognition. I found a piece of my own soul that I'd been looking for. Oh, I know that like Richard Wright before him, some of his work is didactic. Sort of like Tolstoy's. He wrote about suffering, and in particular about humiliation. The humiliations inherent in the human condition are perhaps the most serious subject for any novelist. He was a moralist in the true sense of one who wishes to lessen suffering in the world.

Baldwin began in the church. He preached in a Harlem storefront during his teens. He was into redemption early on. He also has observed that the church was safer than the streets, that the streets would have made him a junkie or a pimp. I remember when, at just the same age, I found a home, a sanctuary, in the theater after I realized what was expected of nice white girls in the 1940s and '50s. Baldwin's theater was a pulpit and he stayed in it for several years. Preaching and acting are both skills which shape writers. Of course disillusion sets in when there is time to think.

Baldwin's autobiographical novel *Go Tell It On the Mountain* examines his early life in Harlem. It's the only one of his novels which has come to the screen. The production is faithful and Alfre Woodard has a smoldering role as an early lover of Baldwin's father. (There is also a hilarious scene of Baldwin as an adolescent boy sitting in a movie house watching Bette Davis shrieking at Leslie Howard in *Of Human Bondage*.)

At the heart of the novel is Baldwin's profound love/hate relationship with his father. Actually, it was his stepfather, but who can doubt that it is the ones who raise us who imprint our psyches. Baldwin wrote that his father hated the white man and was powerless against him so he went into the church to ask God to kill the white man. His father's rage is what killed him and Baldwin's aching love for his father, his overwhelming sadness over his father's wasted life, are what remain in the reader's mind. Some of this material was successfully televised in the '60s, not in the film which was not made until thirty years after Baldwin wrote the book, but in a documentary which juxtaposed the childhoods of James Baldwin and Hubert Humphrey!

This was one of the first times I have seen a television production succeed in combining sociology with poetry. Still photos of Humphrey as a soda jerk and children looking out the windows of Harlem tenements are the backdrop for the contrasting lives of the midwestern white boy whose life is all affirmation and mashed potatoes and the urban black boy whose humiliation at the hands of a white policeman when he's ten leaves scars that never heal. Baldwin once said his birthright was to live in the world as a man, but his inheritance in America was to be a despised nigger. Humphrey's confidence in himself comes not from being a rich kid — his father was a pharmacist — but from being a loved kid. Baldwin's concluding lines at the end of this astonishing docudrama, as he stands over his father's grave, speak of a father who never knew who he was, never knew what hit him. Baldwin believed that his father's life was not only empty, but unresolved and full of hate. The only way to prepare for death is to live fully, to make the journey into darkness, into the nether world.

The writer's journey, like that of the mythic figures of the ancient world (the legendary Inanna, the Sumerian goddess who sought her sister in the

underworld in order to find the wisdom to rule her kingdom back on earth)
involves exile and descent into the dangerous labyrinth of one's own time. I
believe that if anyone ever made the trip to hell and came back home to tell
us about it, it was James Baldwin. He used both his mind and heart to seize
the pomegranate, the apple of knowledge as well as the snakes of sensuality
and wisdom. It is the hero's journey; it is, as well, the path of saints.

Baldwin is a transcendent figure. He came out of Harlem an artist in
spite of his experiences there, as well as because of them. Will he prove to
be one of the last great men in American letters? I define a literary giant as a
great lover, as one so passionate his/her love overflows and embraces the
many. Today the great men of literature are Toni Morrison and Alice Walker;
their books too, are about loss, redemption, and the uses of suffering. They
too work in the hope of a better day. (Hope! that damn thing with feathers
which many of us today are sick and tired of—we want to awaken into the
present moment.) Hope is a dream deferred. Still, it is poetry in the hands
of those who write for the future, for the next generation, for what we are
becoming. The prophet must write as one who is already dead.

And when he did die the media shrugged. He got about as much air
time as a forgotten film star. During a prime time obituary we saw film of
Baldwin at his country home in France speaking with an interviewer but
we couldn't hear what he was saying. What we heard was what the
"voice-over" thought we should know. A comment about his lonely life as an
expatriate followed by a mention of *Giovanni's Room*, saying it dealt with
homosexuality. Actually it's an early work and it deals with the anatomy of
passion. When I read it in my twenties it helped me understand the
process of passion, how the obsession with another can be a disease. I saw
through a glass darkly, the face in the glass bottom boat.

Jimmy did what Gertrude Stein had not been able to do. Stein writes
about the bottom nature of things, but always for her the human mind wins
out over human nature. Baldwin got a little closer to the bone, to the marrow
of men. I wonder now, if they have gotten together on the other side. Stein,
too, went to live in Paris because she was gay. Jimmy would insist it was
because he was black, but I imagine gay had a lot to do with it. I wonder
what he might say to Richard Wright. Would they understand each other
now? Would Wright be any wiser, or do you stop becoming when you die?

Always it takes a generation or two for things to settle, for the blood to
dry. Who was it said, only the dead tell the truth, and then not for some
years. Just as Richard Wright's *Native Son* has only come to the screen in the
late 1980s, so Baldwin's work will only slowly emerge when it's old enough

to keep at arm's length, when it's history and can't hurt anymore.

Back in the mid '60s I tried to get Baldwin's play, *Blues For Mister Charlie*, produced in the suburbs. The all-white play-reading committee dismissed it, saying it was old hat and they'd done all that Civil Rights stuff last season!

In his introduction to *Blues For Mister Charlie* Baldwin writes: "(The play) is based, very distantly indeed, on the case of Emmett Till—the Negro youth who was murdered in Mississippi in 1955.... I absolutely dreaded committing myself to writing a play—there were enough people around already telling me that I couldn't write novels—but I began to see that my fear of the form masked a much deeper fear. That fear was that I would never be able to draw a valid portrait of the murderer. In life, obviously, such people baffle and terrify me and, with one part of my mind at least, I hate them and would be willing to kill them. Yet, with another part of my mind, I am aware that no man is a villain in his own eyes. Something in the man knows—*must* know—that what he is doing is evil; but in order to accept the knowledge the man would have to change. What is ghastly and really almost hopeless in our racial situation now is that the crimes we have committed are so great and so unspeakable that the acceptance of this knowledge would lead, literally, to madness. The human being, then, in order to protect himself, closes his eyes, compulsively repeats his crimes, and enters a spiritual darkness which no one can describe."

Of course the play *is* didactic, kind of like the plays of Ibsen and Shaw. Mister Charlie, the one with the blues, is a white man. Baldwin says all white men are Mister Charlie—caught in the middle, damned if they do and damned if they don't

Baldwin writes dialogues between black town and white town, between the individual and the state. My favorite passage in the play is the sermon delivered by an archetypal character, an omnipotent figure called Meridian. His sermon deals with the strange land in which we all live and with the denial practiced by these strangers with whom we are surrounded. Meridian asks what he should tell the children. Should the next generation sustain the cruelty that has been visited on their parents? And if they do resist oppression, will they not one day find themselves in the same darkness where oppression lives.

Baldwin did not believe that the battle could be won by becoming a master. He did not wish to join his oppressors. As Toni Morrison said at Baldwin's memorial service, his was a vulnerability that asked everything. She went on to describe his tenderness, saying it resembled the first turning in the womb and felt like a whisper in a crowded place. "I suppose that is why I was always a little bit better behaved when I was around you ... wanting to deserve your love ... how I loved your love."

Today there is a good deal of confusion about what liberation leads to. If what we want is a piece of the pie, then that is just what we will get. If what we want is pie for everyone — and that means *everyone*, then our work in the world will be like Baldwin's, fit for the ages.

Index

Abou-Saif, Laila, 141-142
About Men (1978), 45, 47
Abraham, 6
Abzug, Bella, 27, 146
Adonia, Festival of, 20
Adonis, 17, 20, 145
adultress, 170
AFDC, 168
Affirmative Action, 31
Against Our Will: Men, Women and Rape, 170
Age of Pericles, (480-415 B.C.), 19 - 24
Age of Reason, 7
Agnes Grey, 122
Alamos, Los, 94 - 95
Alcibiades, 20
Alexander, the Macedonian Madman (the "Great") 23
Allan, Stephanie, 140
All-Mother, 133
Alta, 49 - 58, 98, 103
Alta Bates Hospital, 58
Amazon, 22
American Dream, 93, 96
American Playhouse, 93
American stock-market crash, 171
An Actor Prepares, 61
Anderson, Sherwood, 69
Andromache, 24
"angel in the house," 87, 112, 123
Anglican angst, 111
Anglo-Saxon Chronicle, 145
Angria, 126, 128
anima, 131 - 132
animus, 130 - 132
Anthony, Susan B., 73
Antigone, 24
Anti-feminism, 140, 156
Apollo, 13 - 18
Appeal to Reason, 29
Appreciation, 79
Archeanassa, 23
Arden's, Elizabeth, 37
Aristophanes, 19 -24, 36
Aristotle, 21, 23
L'Art pour l'Art (1834), 68
Aspasia, 21
Até, 24

Athens, 19 - 24
Atlantic slave trade, 176
Attic angst, 21
Attila the Hun, 15
Auden, W.H., vii, 173
"Aunt Medea," 175
"Aunt Nancy Men," 149
Austen, Jane, 88, 113, 124
Autobiography of Alice B. Toklas, 69, 80
Autumn of the Patriarch, (1975), 45
Auzias, Nina, 79

Bacchae, 108
Bach, 72, 156
Bad Faith, 40
Baez, Joan, 14
Baldwin, James ix, 138, 147-148, 175-182
Bangladesh, 149
Barnes, Djuna, 7, 36
Barrett, Michele, 90
BBC, 141
Beatty, Warren, 140
de Beauvoir, Simone, 17, 39,-40, 76, 102, 106, 160
Bebel, August, 149
Belfast Folk, 140
Bell, Clive, 85
Bell, Julian, 171
Bell, Quentin, 84, 86, 171-172
Bell, Vanessa, 84, 85, 87
belladonna, 116
Bellini, 144
Beloved, 175-176
Ben Hur, 2
Bender, Sue, 53
Bergé, Carol, 107
Bergman, Ingmar, 42, 63
Berkeley Monthly, 13
Berkeley Poets Workshop, 98
Berkeley Repertoire Company, 59
Bhagavad-Gita, 96
Biafra, Jello, 17
Biblical plaque, 171
Big Brother, 108
Big Sleep, 44
Bitch Manifesto, 38, 150
Bitch is Beautiful, 29
Black Cargoes, 176
Black Macho and the Myth of the Superwoman, 31
Black Panthers, 43

Black Power, 33
Black Scholar, 31-32, 34, 149
"Black Sexism Debate," 31
"Black Swan," 124, 125
"Black Woman, The"34
Blake, William, 107, 108
Blank, Les, 129
Blood on the Dining Room Floor, 69
Bloomer, Amelia Jenks (1818-1894), 36
Bloomer Girls, 36
Bloomsbury, 85
Blues for Mister Charlie, 181
Bly, Robert, 1-8, 16
Boadaceia, 143, 144
Boat People, 17
Bohemian Grove, 2, 153
Bolinas Hearsay News, 9
Bombeck, Erma, 13, 27
Book of Nature, 115
Boston Common, 100
bra burners, 166
Brando, Marlon, 63
Branwell, Aunt, 121, 128
"Bread and Roses," 29, 135, 140, 141, 169
Briar Rose (Sleeping Beauty), poem by Anne
  Sexton, 3
bride price, 170
Bridges, Harry, 140
Brinnin, John Malcolm, 69
Brocklehurst, 114
Bronte, Anne, 111, 114, 116, 121-123
Bronte, Branwell, 111, 113, 115-117, 121-
  123, 126-128
Bronte, Charlotte, 84, 88, 91, 98, 106, 111-
  134, 158-159, 169, 171
Bronte, Elizabeth, 114-116
Bronte, Emily Jane, 2, 3, 24, 87, 88, 111-134,
  158-159
Bronte, Maria, 114-116
Bronte, Maria Branwell, 113, 115-116, 123-124
Bronte, Reverend Patrick, 112-116, 121,
  123-124, 128, 130-131
Brontes ix, 111-134, 158
Brothers Karamazov, 41
Brownmiller, Susan, 170
Bruce, Lenny, 63
Bryan, John, 29
Building a Character, 61
Burden of Dreams, 129
Bureau of Labor Statistics, 168
Burns, Helen, 115

Butterfly, 87, 129
Byron, Lord, 126

Caffe Mediterraneum, 42, 177,
Cairo University, 141
Calamity Jane, 55
Caldicott, Dr. Helen, 163-164
California School for the Blind, 53
Callas, Maria, 144
Cambodian refugee camps, 26
Campbell, Joseph, 153
Carter, Jimmy, 25-28
Carter, Lillian, 26-27
Carter, Rosalynn, 25-28, 136
Carter, Ruth, 27
Casta Diva, 144
castration caper, 19
Cato the Elder, 37
Cavett, Dick, 42, 146
Celts, 9-11
Central America, 27, 87, 136
Cezanne, 75
chattel slaves, 170
Chaucer, 67
Chesler M.D., Phyllis, 16, 45, 47-48
Chesterton, G.K., 145
Chevalier, Haakon, 93, 94
Chicago, Judy, 143
Chicago, University of, 67
childbed fever, 119
Cholera Epidemic of 1842, 121
Christ, Jesus, 10, 15, 95, 106, 138, 170
Chthonian gods, 112
Cinema Guild, 42
Citron, Michelle, 158
City Miner, 49, 56
Civilization and its Discontents, 100, 102
Civil Rights, 181
Civil Rights Movement, 46, 147, 167, 178
Clarissa, 90
Clytemnestra, 24
Cocks, Jay, 164-167
Colette, 15
Collier, James Lincoln, 152
Color Purple, 34, 89
Communism, 171
Communist Party of Ireland, 139
Complete Poems of William Blake, 107
Composition as Explanation, 71
Congress, 25
Connolly Column, 139

Connolly, James, 139
Convention of the National Right to Life Committee, 156
Copenhagen Conference, 142
Cordelia, 90-91
Cornwall, 116
Cosby, Bill, 161
cosmic cauldron, 104
County Cork, 139
County Kerry, 9
Cowan Bridge School, 114-115
Cremation, 114
Crone: Woman of Age, Wisdom and Power, 104
Crouch, Stanley, 175-176
Cuba, 140

La Dame aux Camélias, 120
Daniell, Henry, 114
Darrow, Clarence, 61
Darwin, Charles, 161
Davis, Angela, 140
Davis, Bette, 179
Day After Trinity, 94
Dead Kennedys, 17
Death of a Salesman, 95
Deirdre of the Sorrows, 10
De Plessis, Rachel Blau, 102
Derechos Humanos!, 27
Descent of Woman, 152
Dialectic of Sex, 163
Diana, 90
Dickens, Charles, 95
Dickinson, Emily, 113, 159
Dinner Party, 143
Dionysus, 13-18
Di Prima, Diane, 104-106
Dodge, Mabel, 78
Doll's House, 162
Dora, 90
Douglas, Frederick, 149
Drummond M.D., Hugh, 17, 95
Dublin, 139
DuBois, W.E.B., 147
Duckworth, George, 83-84
Duckworth, Stella, 85, 87
Duncan, Isadora, 70, 131, 163
Dumas, 120
Dworkin, Andrea, 147
Dylan, Bob, 14, 63

Easter Rising, 139

Eccesiastes, 153
ecofeminist, 86
Economic Policies and Black Progress, 168
Eden, 104, 143
Ehrenreich, Barbara, 166-168
Einstein, Albert, 72, 95, 148
Electra complex, 17
Eliot, T.S., 79, 101
Emerson, 159
Enaba, Aziza, Wa Abeer, 141, 142
Engels, Friedrich, 149
Equal Rights Amendment, 27, 36-37, 143 155, 166
Equal Rights Association, 149
Ercongota, 145
Eros, 97-109, 131
Ethical Culture School, 96
Euripides, 19-24, 108
Eve, 151
Everybody's Autobiography, 71

Fall of Rome, 171
Family Protection Act, 37
Fascism, 87, 94, 161, 171-172
Father-Daughter Incest, 151
"Father of the Atom Bomb," 94
Faust, 93, 136
Feminism and Black Liberation: The Great American Disease, 32
Ferlinghetti, Lawrence, 56
Final Analysis, 163
Firestone, Shulamith, 163
First Ladies, 25
First Lady from Plains: Eleanor Rosalynn Smith Carter: Her Story, 25-28, 136
Fitzgerald, F. Scott, 5, 7, 75, 77
Fitzgerald, Zelda, 5
Flaubert, 75
Fliess, 151
Flossy, 131
For Colored Girls Who Have Considered Suicide When the Rainbow is Enuf, 32
forcible rape, 169
Forum, 42
Four in America, 67
Four Saints in Three Acts, 70, 73
Franco, 139, 171
Fraser, Kathleen, 104, 105
Freud, Sigmund, 16-17, 21, 36, 79, 85, 99-100, 102-103, 108, 137, 150-152
friendly fascism, 171

Fuller, Edmund, 79

Galbraith, John Kenneth, 14
Gans, Howard, 79
Garrison, William Lloyd, 149
Garvey, Mrs. Amy Jacques (widow of Marcus
  Garvey), 31
Gaskell, Elizabeth, 112-116, 122, 124-125,
  127, 133, 169
Gass, William, 75
Gautier, Marguerite, 120
Gautier, Theopile, 68
"The Gaze," 37
Geographical History of America, 75
gender-bender, 7, 98
Genesis, 159
Gertrude Stein: A Biography of Her Work, 72
Gilbert, Sandra M, 117
Gilder, George, 166
Giovanni, Nikki, 105
Giovanni's Room, 180
Gish, Lillian, 55
gnomic poetics, 178
Goblin Market, 121
Goddess of the Moon, 133
"Golden Lizzie," 121
Goldman, Emma, 148, 163
Goldman, Joyce, 149
Gondal, 128-129
Go Tell It on the Mountain, 179
Gould, Lois, 163
Grahn, Judy, 109
Grant, Cary, 42
Grassroots, 9, 29, 135-136, 139-140
Great Goddess, 10, 153
Great Mother, 10, 133, 153
Great Peace March, 14
Great Reversal, 153, 154
Greek Drama, 23
Greeks, 19-24
Greer, Germaine, 163
Griffin, Susan, 53, 55
Gubar, Susan, 117
Gynophobia, 21

Hamlet, 5, 80
Handbook of Nonsexist Writing, 145
Hardwick, Elizabeth, 130
Harlem, 175-176, 178-179, 180
Hawks, Howard, 42, 43
Haworth, 115, 118-119

Headmasters, 89
Heathcliff, 2, 3, 24, 120, 124, 128-130, 132,
  134
heathen, 112
Heger, Paul, 124, 125, 128, 133
Helen of Troy, 90, 144, 170
Helm, Mike, 49
Hemingway, Ernest, 55, 70, 166
Henderson, Hazel, 161
Henry II, 139
Heracles, 20
Herman, Judith Lewis, 151
Hermes, 19-24
Hero, 131
Herodotus, 138
Herzog, Werner, 129
Heston, Charleton, 2
hetaerai, 21
Hetata, Dr. Sherif, 142
Hidden Face of Eve, 136, 138, 140, 142
Hill, Robert B., 168
Himmler, Heinrich, 156
Hiroshima, 52, 96
Historie de ma Vie, 4, 120
Hitler, 86, 154-156, 160, 172, 178
Hollywood, 42, 115, 129
Holy Grail, 106
Homer, 67, 134
Horney, Karen, 102
Hosken, Fran, 140
*Hosken Report: Genital and Sexual Mutilation
  of Females,* 140
Howard, Leslie, 179
Howard, Maxine, 102
Howe, Susan, 111
Hubris, 2, 24, 96, 132
Human Life Amendment, 37
Human Rights Policies, 27
Humphrey, Hubert, 179
Humpty-Dumpty, 168
Hustler, 23
Hyde, Henry, 156

Ibsen, Henrik, 3, 63, 149, 162, 181
iconography of weaponry, 23
Illiad, 144
*Imperative of Intimacy: Female Erotics, Female
  Poetics,* 98
Inanna, 179
India, 7, 26
Intelligent Woman's Guide to Socialism and

Capitalism, (1928), 139
Ireland, 9-11, 112, 123, 139-140
Irish, 9-11, 168
iron whim, 47
Isaac, 6
Islamic Culture, 140
Isle of Ire, 9
I Was a Male War Bride, (1949), 42

James, William, 69
Jane Eyre, 88, 91, 98-99, 114-117, 124, 126, 127-128, 133, 158
Japan, 52
Jason, 23
Jean Shelton's Acting School, 49, 59-64
jockocrats, 20
Johannesburg, 146
Jordan, June, 104
Joreen, 38
Journey into the Self, Letters of Leo Stein, published in 1950, 79
Judas, 170
Jude 13, 175
Jung, Carl, 131-132, 149

Kael, Pauline, 42
Kali, 104, 153
Kanatir Women's Prison, 137
Kandel, Leonore, 98, 108
Keaton, Diane, 140
Keeper, 131
Kennedy, Flo, 37
Kennedy, President John F, 147
Keynes, Maynard, 87
Kinder, Küche, und Kirch, 154
King Lear, 89-91
King, Martin Luther, 148, 178
Koran, 139
KPFA Pacifica Public Radio FM 94, page 1, 97, 137, 142

Ku Klux Klan, 154
Ladies Against Women, 44
Latin America, 27, 136,
laudanum, 121
Lauterer, Arch, 94
Lawrence, D.H., 98-99, 106, 124, 152
leeches, 116
Leeds, 131
Leeds Mercury, 114
Lesbian erotica, 22

Letters to Women, 51
Levertov, Denise, 38
Loman, Willie, 95
London Times, 146
(A) Long Gay Book, 70
Loos, Anita, 55
Lorde, Audre, 32
Lowell, James, 158
Lowood, 114
libbers, 165
Lies, Secrets, and Silence, 149
Life of Charlotte Bronte, 112-116, 122, 124-125, 127, 133
Lincoln Brigade, 140
Lily, (1848), 36
Linton, Catherine Earnshaw, 2, 3, 120, 129, 130, 132, 134
Linton, Edgar, 120, 130,
Lintons, 132
Luxemburg, Rosa, 109
Lysistrata, 19

Macbeth, Lady, 90, 162
Machiavelli, 33
machismo, 18
madonna/whore schism, 3
madonna/whore syndrome, 105,
Madwoman in the Attic: The Woman Writer and the Nineteenth Century Literary Imagination, 117
Mahatma, 18
Mailer, Norman, 58, 169
Major, Farrah Fawcett, 61
Making of Americans, 71
MALE (Men Against Linguistic Equality), 146
Mama Bears News and Notes, 9, 97
Man Who Died, 106
Man Who Would Be God (1959), 93
Mannix, Daniel Pratt, 176
Mariah, Paul, 55
Marquez, Gabriel Garcia, 45
Marriage of Heaven and Hell, 108
Martineau, Harriet, 118
mater-genetrix, 133
mater omnium, 133
matrifocal, 168
Maya-Shakti, 133, 134
McCarthy, Joe, 95
McDonalds, 139
Mead, Margaret, 147

Mecca, 177
Medea, 23
Media File, 169
Meditation in my Favorite Position, 105
megabomb, 94
Mein Kampf, 155, 160
Melanctha, or Each One as She May, (1902), 71, 72, 74
Melos, 20
Memoir of Emily Jane Bronte, 131
menarche, 2, 130
Menelaus, 145
Mental, Moral and Physical Inferiority of the Female Sex, 176
Meridian, 181
Method, the, 61-62
Middle East, 16
Middle Way, 24
Mill, John Stuart, 149
Millay, Edna St. Vincent, 51, 97, 159
Miller, Arthur, 95
Miller, Casey, 145-147,
Miller, Henry, 7, 98
Millett, Kate, 45
Mills College, 94
mind/body cross, 68
mind/body split, 22
Minton, Michael, 162
Miss America pageant, 165
Mitford, Jessica, 169
Modern Dance, 163
Montmartre, 76
Moore, Mathilde, 95
Moreau, Jeanne, 59
Morgan, Elaine, 152
Morgan, The, 10
Morris, Desmond, 152
Morrison, Toni, ix, 74, 175-176, 180-182
Moses, 170
Mother Earth Publishing Association, 148
Mother Goddess, 23
Mother Jones, 17, 95
Mother Machree, 4, 5
Mother Nature, 15
Mother of Us All, 73
Mother Right, 10
Moyers, Bill, 150
Mozart, 72
MS. 149, 154-155, 166
"Mutilation of the Herms", 19
My Emily Dickinson, 111

My Life in Art, 61
Myth of Black Macho: A Response to Angry Black Feminists, 31

Nagaskai, 96
Naked Ape, 152
Narcissus, 85
Native Son, 176, 180
National Advisory Council on Economic Opportunity, 167
National Institute for Mental Health, 161
National Socialism, 156
National Urban League, 168
NATO, 140
"Nazi Connection," 154
Nazi Germany, 154
Nazis, 108
Near, Holly, 165
Negro World, (October 21, 1925), 31
Nemesis, 24, 171
New German Critique, 158
New Republic, 79, 175-177
New Woman, 41
New York Herald, 149
New York Review of Books, 143
New York Times, 146
Newsfront International, 137
Newsweek, 79
Nicholls, Arthur Bell, 123, 124,
Nietzsche, 21, 128
Nightwood, 36
Nin, Anais, 56, 106, 154
Niven, David, 55
"No Coward Soul Is Mine," 158
No Visible Means of Support, 51
Nora, 162
Norma, 144
"Nouveau Poor", 166
Novel of the Future, 154
Nussey, Ellen, 121

Oakland Induction Center, 14
Odyssey, 144
Oedipal "fantasties," 151
Oedipal identity, 16
Oedipus Rex, 94
Of Human Bondage, 179
"Of Women," 156, 157
Old Testament, 96
Onassis, Jackie, 144
Onassis, Aristotle, 144

O'Neill, Eugene, 63
Ophelia, 5, 90
opium, 117, 121
Oppenheimer, J. Robert, 93-96, 136
Oppenheimer: Story of a Friendship (1966), 93
O'Riordan, Michael, 139-140
Orwell, 108
Ostriker, Alicia Suskin, 97-109
Ouse, River, 86, 171

Pacific Film Archive, 141
"panty raids", 166
Paris, 145
Parker, Dorothy, 37, 55, 162
Parthenon, 19
Party, The 104
patriarchal prejudice, 168
Pauline and the Mysterious Pervert, 57
Peace Corps, 26
pecking order, 169
Peloponnesian War, 20
penis envy, 100
People's Translation Service, 137
People's World, 139, 140
Pericles, 21
Petronius, 101
phallic residuals, 23
"phallic state", 45
phallocracy, 19-24
Picasso, 51, 79
Piercy, Marge, 105
Plain Speaking, 162
Plath, Sylvia, 158
Plato, 21-23
Platonic love, 22
Plexus, 93
Plutonium Players, 44
Poe, Edgar Allen, 121
Poetry Flash, 1
Poetry and Grammar, 77
Pogrebin, Letty Cottin, 165
Politics of the Solar Age, 161
Pope, 139
Porgy and Bess, 75
Posner, Vladimir, 139
Pound, Ezra, 73, 79
Pre-Raphaelites, 127
Print Mint, 177
"Prisoner, The", 159
Proctor & Gamble, 162
Professor von X, 176

Prohibition, 26
pronoun envy, 146
Psyche, 102
Psychology of Fascism, 108
Pythian, 172

Queen Mab, 159

Rabelais, 108
Radcliffe, 69
Radical Feminism, 150
Rambo, 95
Ratch, Jerry, 55
Reader's Digest, 152
Reagan, Nancy, 26, 37
Reagan, Ronald, 27, 37, 166, 168
Reagans, 26
Red-baiting, 140
Reds, 140
Reed, Jack, 140
Reich, Wilhelm, 108
Reichstag, 155
Reign of the Phallus: Sexual Politics in Ancient Athens, by Eva C. Keuls, 19-24
reptilian brain stem, 178
Republic, 22
Revolution of Touch, 7, 135
Rich, Adrienne, 1, 107, 149
Richardson, J. 143
Rochester, Bertha Mason, 117, 126
Rochester, Edward, 91, 124, 126
Rodmell Labour Party, 172
Roe Head School, 131
Rolland, Romain, 102
Rolling Stones, 165
Romans, 144
"romantic thraldom", 102
Romanticism, 14
Romeo, 20, 145
Romeo and Juliet, 153
"Romish", 119
(A) Room of One's Own, 42, 83, 85-86, 88, 112, 158, 176
Roosevelt, Eleanor, 25-26
Rosenshine, Annette, 42
Rossetti, Christina, 51, 121
Rossetti, Dante Gabriel, 120, 121
Rousseau, 131
Rumpelstiltskin, 175
Russell, Bertrand, 21

Saadawi, Dr. Nawal El, 136-140, 142
Sacramento legislature, 43
Sadat, Mrs., 142
de Sade, 108
Safire, William, 146
Sahl, Mort, 154
Saint Patrick, 9-11
Saint Paul, 105
St. John's College, Cambridge, 112
(El) Salvador, 27, 139
San Francisco Intersection Coffeehouse, 101
Sanctuary, 107
Sand, George, 4, 55, 120
Sanger, Margaret, 163
Sappho, 51, 159
Sarah, 6
Sargent, Elizabeth, 107
Sartre, Jean Paul, 40
Sather Gate, 20
Satie, 72
Satyricon, 101
Scarborough, 122, 123
Scarlatti, 72
Schlafly, Phyllis, 44, 166
Schopenhauer, Arthur, 156-157, 166
Schweitzer, Albert, 150
SCUM (Society for Cutting up Men), 44
"Search for the Father," 1
Second Sex, 39, 160
segregation, 53
Selma, 164
September 1, 1939, vii
septicemia, 119
Sexton, Anne, 3, 6, 105
Sexual Politics, 45
Shah of Iran, 27
Shakespeare, Judith, 88, 91
Shakespeare, William, 3, 13, 78, 88-90, 113, 147, 159
Shameless Hussy Press, 49-58
shaman, 95
Shange, Ntozake, 32, 34, 55
Shaw, George Bernard, 3, 131, 139, 162, 181
Sheldon, Jana, 93
Shelton, Jean, 59-64
Siddal, Lizzie, 120
Simon, John Oliver, 54
Simon, Linda, 42
Sleepwell, Sally, 9-11
Smith, George, 125

Smith, Eleanor Rosalynn, 25
Smyth, Ethel, 83
Socrates, 21, 22
Song of the Wife, Song of the Mistress, 51
Sophists, 23
South America, 27, 136
Southey, Robert, 117
Soviet Revolution, 160
Soviets, 108
Sparta, 20-21
Sparks, Muriel, 129
"Spectral Selves of Charlotte Bronte", 116, 117
Spencer, Anna Garlin, 161
Stalin, Joseph, 150
Stallard, Karin, 166-168
Stanislavski, Constantin, 61, 62, 64
Staples, Robert, 31-32, 34-35
Stealing the Language: The Emergence of Women's Poetry in America, 97-109
Stein, Amelia and Daniel, 78
Stein, Gertrude, 9, 17, 42, 51, 56, 58, 65-81, 98, 109, 117, 159, 180
Stein, Leo, 78, 79
Steinem, Gloria, 32, 154-156
Stephen, Aunt Caroline Emelia, 88
Stephen, Julia, 83, 85, 87
Stephen, Leslie, 83, 86-87, 89
Stockman, David, 135
Stonehenge, 144
Strachey, Lytton, 85
"Strictly From Hunger", 143
studlets, 13
Styx River, 8
Sudan, 138
Sula, 74
Sutherland, Donald, 72
Swallow Cafe, 142
Swift, Kate, 145-147
symposia, 21

Tao, 132
TASS, Soviet News Agency, 140
Taylor, Elizabeth, 115
Taylor, Mary, 113
Tehran, 27
Tenant of Wildfell Hall, 122
Tender Buttons, 70
Thackeray, 124
Thanatos, 97-109, 131
Theseus, 20

Things As They Are, 69, 77
Third Rose: Gertrude Stein and Her World, 69
Third World, 139
Theater Metamorphose
Thomson, Virgil, 73
"Thou shalt not rape," 170
Three Guineas, 86-88, 172
Three Lives (1902), 71, 74, 75
Three Press Secretaries on the President: Jody Powell, George Reedy, and Jerry Horst (published in 1984), 27
Thrushcross Grange, 130, 132
Till, Emmett, 181
Time, 26, 164, 166
Times, 173
Titans, 17, 132
To the Lighthouse, 87,90
Toklas, Alice B., 42, 68-81, 98
Tolstoy, 178
Tora-Ya restaurant, 51, 52
Traffic in Women, 148
Transformations, 3
Trinity test, 96
Trojan Women, 19, 24,
Trojans, 20
Truman, Harry, 52
"two-fer," 31
Tyler, Anne, 165
Tyler, Robin, 44

ubermensches, 128
University of Illinois, 142
U.N. Mid Decade Conference for Women, 137
U.N. World Conference on Women, 163
utopian, 173
Uzi submachine gun

Valentine, Jean, 107
Valhalla, 16
Van Vechten, Carl, 72
Vatican, 153
Veblen, Thorstein, 149
Voltaire, 60, 132
Victoria, 131
Victorian, 119
Victorian heritage, 22
Victorians, 115
Vietnam, 4, 164
Vietnam War, 14
Villette, 117

Virgin Mary, 10, 153
Vision and Verse in William Blake, 107

waepman, 145
Waite, Sarita, 53
Wakoski, Diane, 106
Walker, Alice, 33-34, 89, 175, 180
Walker, Barbara, 104
Walker's Pie Shop, 59
Wallace, Michele, 31-32
warrior/wimp syndrome, 3
Washington, Ann, 140
Wasteland, 98, 101
Watergate, 26
Waterston, Sam, 93
Wayne, John, 95
Weeks, Mabel, 79
Weightman, William, 121
Weimar Constitution, 155
Weimar Republic, 155
Welles, Orson, 126
West, Vita Sackville, 85-87
"What Are Masterpieces and Why Are There So Few of Them," 80
What's Left of the Left, 147
Whitehead, Alfred North, 80
White House, 25, 37
wifman, 145
Wilde, Oscar, 13, 39, 78, 131
Wilder, Thornton, 67
Wilhelm II, 154
Wilks, Brian, 131
Williams, Tennessee, 63
Wilson, Reverend Carus, 114
WITCH (Women's International Terrorist Conspiracy from Hell), 44
Wolfgang's, 101
"Woman and the New Race", 163
(A) Woman is Talking to Death, 109
Woman's Property Act, 88
"Woman's Share in Social Culture", 161
"Women and Film: A Discussion of Feminist Aesthetics", 158
Women and Madness, (1972), 47
Women and Writing, 90
Women Who Love Too Much, 102
Women's Encyclopedia of Myths and Secrets, 104
Women's lib, 164
Women's Movement, 178
Woodard, Alfre, 179

Woolf, Leonard, 84-86, 88, 171
Woolf, Virginia, 2, 29, 42, 70, 83-91, 99,
    112-114, 117, 133, 158, 162, 164, 171-
    173, 176
Words and Women, 146
World War I, 154, 155
World War II, 154, 171
Wright, Richard, 33, 75, 147, 175-176, 178,
    180
Wuthering Heights, 2, 41, 88, 111, 120-121,
    128-129, 132-134
Wyler, William, 134
Wylie, Phillip, 3

X, Malcolm, 146, 177

Yahweh, 6, 96, 104
Yamada, Mitzuye, 55
Yeats, 159
Yorkshire, 112, 121, 128, 130
Young Workers' Liberation Party, 140
Young, Robert, 161

Zen end, 97
Zen prophets, 177
Zen slap, 5
Zeus, 20

Jennifer Stone was born in Tucson, Arizona in 1933. She got her B.A. from Mills College and her M.A. from San Francisco State University. She has lived in the Bay Area since 1951 and her sons were born there in 1960 and 1962. Her other books are *Over by the Caves* from the Berkeley Poets Workshop and *Mind Over Media: Essays on Film and Television* from Cayuse Press. Her radio shows can be heard on KPFA Pacifica Public Radio 94 FM, Berkeley, California.